cer

J

erson
Al Switzler

Mc
Graw
Hill
Education

New York   Chicago   San Francisco   Lisbon   London   Madrid
Mexico City   Milan   New Delhi   San Juan   Seoul
Singapore   Sydney   Toronto

3  4  5  6  7  8  9  0   DOC/DOC   1  9  8  7  6  5  4  3

ISBN    978-0-07-180886-6 (paperback)
MHID  0-07-180886-8 (paperback)

ISBN    978-0-07-180979-5 (hardcover)
MHID  0-07-180979-1 (hardcover)

e-ISBN    978-0-07-180887-3
e-MHID  0-07-180887-6


McGraw-Hill Education books are available at special quantity discounts to
use as premiums and sales promotions or for use in corporate training programs.
To contact a representative, please e-mail us at bulksales@mcgraw-hill.com.
This book is printed on acid-free paper.

We dedicate this book to influencers everywhere—
to the tenacious leaders who have not only added to an
ever-growing knowledge of how people change but have
also restored hope, inspired action, and made it possible
for each of us to amplify our influence to change
the world for good.

# Contents

# Acknowledgments

We are deeply grateful to many who have helped us throughout the years in our research, teaching, testing, and learning.

First, our appreciation to our families for your influence on us. Thanks for the love and support that has changed us, inspired us, and enabled us. Thank you particularly for your sacrifice and patience when we were far from home—or at home, but overly focused, head down over a keyboard.

Second, thanks to our colleagues, associates, and team members at VitalSmarts who help in hundreds of ways—working to achieve our mission, serving customers, training the skills to help change lives, and supporting one another with care, loyalty, and competence. To all (all is now a large number) we say thanks. Highlighting just a few is tough, but necessary. So an additional thanks to James Allred, Terry Brown, Mike Carter, Jeff Gibbs, Jeff Johnson, Lance Garvin, Justin Hale, Emily Hoffman, Todd King, Brittney Maxfield, Mary McChesney, John Minert, David Nelson, Stacy Nelson, Rich Rusick, Andy Shimberg, Joanne Staheli, Yan Wang, Steve Willis, Mike Wilson, Paul Yoachum, and Rob Youngberg.

Third, a special thanks to Bob Foote, Chase McMillan, and Mindy Waite, who continuously provided us with extraordinary logistical support, attention to detail, and insight.

And fourth, we're overwhelmingly grateful to our friends and partners across the planet who have turned these ideas from an interesting read into a global force for positive change. We are inspired by the soul and skill they bring to our cooperative effort.

Thanks to our U.S. associates who are gifted teachers and powerful influencers:

Doug Finton
Ilayne Geller
Tamara Kerr
Jim Mahan
Jim Munoa
Kurt Southam
Larry Peters
Margie Mauldin
Mike Quinlan
Murray Low
Neil Staker
Paul McMurray
Richard Lee
Shirley Poertner
Simon Lia

And finally we express gratitude to the partners and friends who have supported our work around the globe:

Australia—Geoff Flemming and Grant Donovan
Brazil—Josmar Arrais

China—Jenny Xu

Egypt—Hisham El Bakry

France—Cathia Birac and Dagmar Doring

India—Yogesh Sood

Indonesia—Nugroho Supangat

Italy—Giovanni Verrecchia

Malaysia—V. Sitham

Netherlands—Sander van Eijnsbergen and Willeke
    Kremer

Poland—Marek Choim

Singapore—James Chan

South Africa—Helene Vermaak and Jay Owens

South Korea—Ken Gimm

Switzerland—Arturo Nicora

Thailand—TP Lim

U.K.—Grahame Robb and Richard Pound

# Part

# 1

# The New Science
# of Leading Change

# 1
# Leadership Is Influence

*I haven't got the slightest idea how to change people, but still I keep a long list of prospective candidates just in case I should ever figure it out.*

—David Sedaris

I t wasn't the most harrowing research junket we had ever taken. Nothing like earlier adventures in our influencer research to some of the more dangerous parts of the world. No threat of deadly parasites, no confrontation with aggressive panhandlers, no fear of being kidnapped, no wrangling with corrupt politicians.

This time, our research had taken us to New York City to one of the Big Apple's finest restaurants where, as part of our demanding research regime, we'd be tossing back scrumptious appetizers while chatting with a brilliant restaurateur. (It was a tough job, but someone had to do it.) All of this was being done as part of an ongoing project aimed at discovering how some rather remarkable people routinely influence human behavior in a manner that is the envy of all who know them.

The person we were visiting on this particular day was Danny Meyer. Danny had earned the title of "influencer" by fostering a unique culture of customer service. Every one of his restaurants had been in the top 40 of Zagat's ratings of customer preference—practically since the day they first opened. We soon discovered that the reason behind his unparalleled success was his capacity to influence 1,500 ordinary employees to consistently create extraordinary experiences for their 100,000 daily guests. Actually, *extraordinary* is too small a word.

For example, a woman frantically rushes through the entrance of Gramercy Tavern, one of Danny's exquisite establishments located in the Flatiron District of Manhattan. The potential diner is distraught because she has just left her purse in the taxi that dropped her off for lunch and then sped away into a sea of yellow. The blood drains from the woman's face as she realizes that not only will she never see her purse again but she also has no way to pay for her meal. Or get back to work.

At this moment, Danny's culture of hospitality kicks into action. An employee (let's call him Carlo) notices the stranger's look of panic, learns of her problem, and invites her to join her party—who are already seated and waiting for her.

"Don't worry about paying," Carlo comforts the worried guest. "We'll settle up some other time. For now, please enjoy yourself. In the meantime, what is your mobile number?"

Surmising that the frantic customer likely left her cell phone in her purse, Carlo asks a colleague to repeatedly call the number. Thirty minutes later when the taxi driver finally hears the ring and answers the call, he's many miles north in the Bronx. Carlo then flashes the Batman signal onto the side of a building to summon the Caped Crusader . . .

Okay, the Batman thing isn't true, . . . but what Carlo does do is quite heroic. He arranges to meet the taxi halfway between the two points, and he pays the driver for his trouble, retrieves the purse, and presents it to the woman just as she finishes her lunch. We're guessing she responded by promising to name her firstborn child after the caring man who has been the very essence of hospitality.

What makes this incident remarkable is not just that it took place at all but that similar actions routinely occur in each of Danny's restaurants. Although Danny draws from the same labor pool, works in the same industry, buys the same ingredients, and builds in the same neighborhoods as 20,000 other New York restaurateurs, he has found a way to differentiate himself from all of his competitors—through *influence*. Members of Danny's staff behave markedly differently from your average restaurant employee, and this has not been the result of some lucky accident. It's been the result of Danny's systematic and intentional actions aimed at influencing very specific behavior.

That's why we traveled to New York. We went to see what made Danny an influencer.

## A COMMON THREAD

Now, let's be clear. This isn't a book about customer service. Likewise, when we later visit a woman in San Francisco who has helped tens of thousands of felons turn their lives around, we won't be studying criminal psychology. And when we look at successful change efforts aimed at implementing Six Sigma, overcoming addiction, eradicating a pandemic, improving patient safety, reducing violence against women, improving employee engagement, and turning failing schools around, our interest won't be in exploring these topics either.

What we *will* be doing is looking for the common thread that connects all successful leaders—no matter the objective or the setting. We'll be exploring a common set of principles and skills that help create quick, profound, and lasting change. We call this ability to create changes in human behavior *influence* and the people who do it *influencers*. At the end of the day, what qualifies people to be called "leaders" is their capacity to influence others to change their behavior in order to achieve important results.

Now, as you hear the word "influence," you might think that we're referring to the less impressive and more suspicious tool called "persuasion." We're not. This book is not about solving problems or hitting new targets by applying the right combination of verbal tricks. If you're looking to reach rather modest goals by stealthily exerting your will over others, this book is not for you.

This book has much loftier and more enduring goals, requiring much stronger tools. It explores how to achieve profoundly better results in everything from the nuclear family to nuclear power plants by changing human habits that can be extraordinarily difficult to alter. We'll examine in detail why people do what they do and what it takes to help them act differently. Our analysis will reveal that irrespective of whether you're stopping AIDS or starting a safety program, the key to success has little to do with pep talks, bribes, or sermons. Instead, success relies on the capacity to systematically create rapid, profound, and sustainable changes in a handful of key behaviors.

For example, let's say you work as a manager in a software development firm where dozens of software engineers write mountains of code every week. The products are so complex that the overall design is divided among several teams. After years of your employees' bringing in projects late or riddled with bugs, you discover that the key to consistent high-quality performance is getting them to practice two *vital behaviors*:

(1) admit when they have problems, and (2) immediately speak up when they won't meet a deadline. When your software designers do these two things consistently, products get completed correctly and on time. When they don't, they don't. This flash of leadership insight gives you hope that if only you can influence your people to practice these two behaviors, you'll turn the corner on achieving results.

The problem is, your people (being the normal humans that they are) are more willing to donate a kidney than follow these two requests. Only fools admit to having problems. It is a naïve person, indeed, who willingly says, "Hey, everyone, I'm in trouble!" You've posted signs, provided training, and even offered a special parking space to those who admit they're behind. No takers.

But there is an influencer out there who has found a way to help software designers to routinely speak up when they run into problems or call for aid when a deadline is at risk. This time we'll travel to Ann Arbor, Michigan, to meet with Rich Sheridan, the co-owner of Menlo Innovations. His software designers meet every single deadline—and they thoroughly love their work. How has Rich created this culture of both joy and accountability? By following precisely the same principles of influence that Danny Meyer uses to generate lavish hospitality.

Throughout this book, we'll explore the details of Rich's, Danny's, and other influencers' strategies for influencing human behavior. It takes over 200 pages to share their knowledge and techniques. However, the short explanation for why they're successful is that they see themselves not simply as owners, managers, or leaders but as full-time influencers. In fact, it's how they characterize themselves. Talk with them and you'll soon learn that they think intentionally about their ability to help others act in unprecedentedly effective ways. They think about influencing behavior, talk about it, and practice it, and all of them have created remarkable changes in domains where failure has been the norm—often for decades.

Now, unlike Rich or Danny, you probably don't work in a software development firm or a restaurant, but you probably *do* face challenges you'd like to overcome, not to mention the many stretch goals you'd love to achieve. Perhaps you'd like to help a troubled son who has just returned from his third drug rehab experience. Unfortunately, the program has failed twice before—and nothing has really changed since the last failure. This calls for influence. Or maybe you want to assist your work group in moving from being *decent* in on-time delivery to being *best in class*. Or perhaps you're working with a high school with a horrible dropout rate, and you want to see the students not only make it through high school but also to graduate from college. You want the best.

## A DEARTH OF INFLUENCE

Fortunately, there's good news in this call to learn more about influence. Learning how to motivate and enable others to change their actions may be the most important skill you'll ever acquire. It's not merely curiously engaging (and it is); it also sits at the center of what ails most of us. The lion's share of the problems that really bother us don't call for additional technology, theory, philosophy, or data (we're up to our necks in *that*); instead, the problems call for the ability to *change what people do*. And when it comes to this particular skill, demand far exceeds supply.

Given the versatility and importance of knowing how to get other people to act differently, you'd think that at every backyard barbecue or office party, you could find someone who is an expert in influence. In fact, you'd think we'd be so consumed with the topic of influence that our children would collect influence trading cards, complete with pictures of world-class influencers. As a result of all this study and passion, we would speak a unique language, carry a full array of models, and master a specialized set of skills for both enabling and encouraging others to change their behavior.

Of course, none of this is true. At best, we chip away at the edges of influence—maybe we attend a seminar or two—but we don't routinely study the topic, and we are not good at helping others to change. Unlike Danny Meyer, Rich Sheridan, and the other influencers we'll soon meet, most of us can't verbalize our personal theory of influence, we don't see ourselves as influencers, and we most certainly don't have a successful record.

For example, when was the last time you saw a change attempt conducted at your place of work yield anything more than the occasional t-shirt or mug emblazoned with the name of the effort? If your answer is "never," you're in good company. Our review of the past 30 years of change literature reveals that fewer than one in eight workplace change efforts produces anything other than cynicism.

When it comes to creating changes in behavior, we're equally challenged at home. For instance, every year we spend millions on diets and lose little more than our money. Fewer than 10 percent of us succeed when setting out to change our excessive spending, inadequate exercise, and other bad habits.

Communities fare no better. Two-thirds of the felons who are released from our "correctional" system return within three years—completely uncorrected—while having earned an advanced degree in crime. Stopping the spread of AIDS and other diseases requires people to cooperate in order to succeed; yet millions of individuals are infected every year because we humans are bad at cooperating, and we're not getting any better.

As a result of all of these failed influence efforts and unfulfilled dreams, most of us grow impatient. We ask: "Why aren't people doing what they should be doing, and why can't I get them to change?" Eventually we settle on the strategy recommended by essayist David Sedaris, who suggested: "I haven't got the slightest idea how to change people, but still I keep a long list of prospective candidates just in case I should ever figure it out."

But there *are* influencers out there.

## FINDING INFLUENCERS

Our visits with Danny Meyer and Rich Sheridan should give you a hint as to what we did to expand our understanding of how to influence human behavior. We studied people who had succeeded where others had failed. Actually, we didn't start there. As most researchers do, we began by reading. Our research team pored over more than 17,000 articles and books to find scholars and practitioners who have mastered various aspects of influence. From these we identified those who had succeeded at influencing rapid, profound, and sustainable changes in ways that most of the world thinks are impossible. Next, we tracked down these rare individuals and closely examined their work.

For instance, we learned that Wiwat Rojanapithayakorn has saved over 5 million Thai citizens from contracting HIV/AIDS from a position of little to no power, by influencing the behavior of his 60 million fellow Thai citizens. That was certainly worth examining. Dain Hancock, president of Lockheed Martin Aeronautics, influenced remarkable behavior change across a cynical and resistant 13,000-person workforce, helping him land a $1 trillion contract. Ethna Reid routinely enters schools that are last in their district in reading comprehension, and she propels them to the top—in less than a year. Martha Swai has helped reduce spousal abuse across the entire nation of Tanzania through the use of, of all things, a very influential radio program. Other notable influencers have eradicated a disease, saved thousands from dying from hospital errors, and turned convicted felons into productive citizens—to name but a few of their accomplishments.

So we tracked down these successful individuals and studied what they did—once again, looking for commonalities. It takes the rest of this book to explain what we learned from them, but we can offer some encouraging news. Influencers exist, and what they know and do is learnable. In fact, hundreds of thousands of people have read what we learned from them, and they have applied the principles and skills to their own challenges, put the ideas to work on their own aspirations, and they have made remarkable progress. And so can you.

So it's time to roll up your sleeves and get started. Go get that list of prospective change candidates you've been keeping for so long, and let's see what it takes to help them change.

# 2

# The Three Keys to Influence

*I wanted the influence. In the end I wasn't very good at being a [university] president. I looked out of the window and thought that the man cutting the lawn actually seemed to have more control over what he was doing.*

—*Warren Bennis*

So far we've claimed that influencers don't randomly succeed at creating impressive and lasting changes in human behavior. The good news is that if they did rely on chance, we wouldn't have a clue how to replicate their efforts. But they don't rely on chance. Instead, they count on three keys to success—keys that all influencers adhere to and that you can use to your own benefit:

1. **Focus and measure.** Influencers are crystal clear about the result they are trying to achieve and are zealous about measuring it.
2. **Find vital behaviors.** Influencers focus on high-leverage behaviors that drive results. More specifically, they focus on the two or three vital actions that produce the greatest amount of change.

3. **Engage all six sources of influence.** Finally, influencers break from the pack by *overdetermining change.* Where most of us apply a favorite influence tool or two to our important challenges, influencers identify all of the varied forces that are shaping the behavior they want to change and then get them working *for* rather than *against* them. And now for the really good news. According to our research, by getting six different sources of influence to work in their favor, influencers increase their odds of success *tenfold.*

## KEY 1. FOCUS AND MEASURE

To shine light on this first influence key, we'll fly to Atlanta, Georgia, where we'll meet with Dr. Donald Hopkins, a physician, the vice president of healthcare programs at the Carter Center—and a real influencer. Hopkins originally attracted our attention because he has taken on one of the most amazing influence challenges in history. His goal is to banish a horrendous disease from the planet without finding a cure.

And just what is this daunting disease Dr. Hopkins is attacking? To answer this question, take a look at a rather disgusting sample Hopkins keeps on his desk. If the enemy could stand, she would be three feet tall. But alas, she has no skeletal system. She's a worm. More specifically, she's a Guinea worm. Hopkins keeps his sworn enemy in a jar of formaldehyde as a reminder of the challenge he and his team have decided to confront. Helping individuals who have contracted Guinea worm disease is an enormous challenge because once someone has it, it will inevitably run its painful and ugly course through the host's body. Medical science offers no hope of relief. None. There are no medicines, surgeries, or magical techniques. Once you have the worm, it will cause havoc every single time. So Hopkins, in order to solve the seemingly intractable problem, became a social scientist.

When Dr. Hopkins came on the scene, over 3 million people in 23,000 remote villages in 20 countries were contracting Guinea worm disease every year. The disease begins when villagers get a little more in their drink of water than they bargained for. Hiding within the fetid ponds that many use as a water source lie the Guinea worm larvae. Drink the water, ingest the larvae.

And then, it gets really ugly. The larvae soon hatch into worms that eventually burrow out of the body by whatever route they choose—through the muscle and skin on an arm, leg— well, you can imagine the other options. This journey causes such enormous pain and suffering that the host eventually rushes to the nearest water source and plunges the emerging worm into the water to find a moment of relief. At this point, the dreaded worm ejects thousands of eggs into the pond— guaranteeing next year's crop of Guinea worms—when the awful process begins again as it has for thousands of years.

Hopkins took an interest in the Guinea worm because he concluded that it could literally be eradicated from the planet. All he had to do, he told us matter-of-factly, was change the behavior of 120 million people spread over 10 million square miles.

Think about it. How would you approach this kind of problem? With a team of two dozen people and a few million dollars in the budget, how could you even *think* about getting millions of strangers to change?

The difference between Dr. Hopkins and the rest of us is that he (like all the influencers we studied) knows how to think about these kinds of problems and how to develop predictably repeatable and effective strategies to solve them.

The first thing influencers do is *focus and measure*. They clearly articulate the goal they are trying to achieve. They know that fuzzy objectives are anathema to influence. Equally important, they know that clear, consistent, and meaningful measures ensure that they'll actually track their efforts and genuinely hold themselves accountable. This act alone sets them apart from the crowd. In fact, of the hundreds of influence attempts we've studied over the years, the vast majority of them fail at the outset by neglecting this first key. Unsuccessful agents of change make one of three early mistakes that undermine their influence:

1. **Fuzzy, uncompelling goals:** They begin with only a vague sense of what they'll achieve ("Empower our employees," "Help inner city kids," or "Build the team").
2. **Infrequent or no measures:** Even when they have a somewhat clear result in mind ("Develop a culture of candid communication"), unsuccessful individuals rarely develop credible measures against which to match their intentions.
3. **Bad measures:** And finally, even when they do take measures, folks who fail often drive the wrong behavior by measuring the wrong variable.

## Fuzzy, Uncompelling Goals

You'd think that if people only got one thing right when trying to create a change, it would be the way they define their objective. Their objective, after all, is the voice that calls out for change in the first place. "We have really poor customer service." "Our inner city kids need help." "Our quality is mediocre, and we want to be the best."

The goals associated with each of these cries for change seem obvious. Leaders need to improve customer service, help inner city kids, and push quality to new heights. Such goal state-

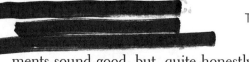
ments sound good, but, quite honestly, they are too vague to exert any real influence. Heaven only knows what they actually mean. "Improving customer service" could be interpreted as everything from answering the phone by the second ring to giving customers a free monkey with every purchase over $10.

Fortunately, not everyone fouls up the goal-setting part of their change process by providing vague objectives. For example, consider the near legendary work of another powerful influencer, Dr. Don Berwick, the former CEO of the Institute for Healthcare Improvement (IHI). In spite of IHI's diminutive size and Berwick's complete lack of position power in the $2 trillion U.S. healthcare industry, he is universally described as one of the most influential people in the field and a fine example of making strong use of clear and compelling goals.

"I think it's unacceptable," Berwick told us, "that the sixth leading cause of death in the United States is healthcare. . . . We inadvertently kill the equivalent of a jumbo jet filled with passengers every day of the year. We know how it happens, and we know how to avoid it. The challenge is influencing people to stop it from happening."

Now watch how Berwick uses a clear and compelling goal to lead change. One December day in 2004, Berwick stood in front of a group of thousands of healthcare professionals and issued an audacious challenge by setting a crystal clear and compelling goal: "I think we should save 100,000 lives. I think we should do that by June 14, 2006." Pause. "By 9 a.m."

Berwick's intent was to influence the behavior of hundreds of thousands of healthcare workers in order to save lives from medical mistakes. The success of the 100,000 Lives Campaign is now in the record books. By galvanizing the attention and efforts of thousands of people across an entire country, Berwick and his team beat the 100,000 lives goal.

How did he accomplish such a feat? He used all three of the keys to influence. To begin with, as our first key suggests, Berwick started with a crystal clear goal. He and his team weren't just going to "try to reduce problems." They weren't going to "improve safety." They weren't going to "help a bunch of people within the next few years have better lives." They weren't going to save an impressive number of lives "as soon as they could." They were going to save 100,000 lives by June 14, 2006—by 9 a.m.

There's no lack of clarity or room for misinterpretation here. Notice how compelling Berwick's goal statement is. Then notice the difference between these two statements:

- "We will reduce preventable harm in hospitals."
- "We will save 100,000 lives from medical mistakes by June 14, 2006. By 9 a.m."

You can actually *feel* the difference. The second goal statement contains clear, compelling, value-based language. You're saving lives, not simply changing numbers on a chart. And you know exactly how many and by when.

Clear goals aimed at a compelling target can have an enormous impact on behavior because they engage more than simply the brain. They also engage the heart. Research reveals that a clear, compelling, and challenging goal causes the blood to pump more rapidly, the brain to fire, and the muscles to engage. However, when goals are vague, no such effects take place.*

---

*http://www.sciencedirect.com/science/article/pii/S0887617701001135. A German study has shown that even brain-damaged patients perform arithmetic better when they have been given a clear and challenging goal than when they have been given a vague "do your best" challenge.

http://psycnet.apa.org/journals/apl/77/5/694/. This study has shown the heart rate as well as the cognitive and behavioral effects of the presence of a challenging goal.

We saw firsthand what happens when a leader uses the influence of a clear and compelling goal. This time we visited with the influencer Martin Burt who started Fundación Paraguaya 30 years ago. Initially his goal was to provide Paraguay's poor with access to credit as a means of helping them climb out of poverty. Unfortunately, after spending 30 years trying to meet that goal, Burt became concerned that many people were getting access to credit, but too few were emerging from poverty. As Burt and his leadership team learned the importance of creating both a clear and compelling goal, they made a stunning change. No longer would they focus on how many loans they processed (a somewhat uncompelling goal). Instead, they announced the following: beginning in April 2011, "Our goal is to help 5,000 poor families to earn $5 per day per person [the national poverty line] or more before the end of the year." (This goal, by the way, was not only clear but it was also at least 10 times more challenging than simply making loans and collecting payments.)

The effect of providing this clear, compelling, and time-bound target was immediate. It started a whole chain of events that virtually redefined the organization. It influenced the way people saw their jobs. It influenced the skills loan officers would need to work with clients. It influenced a million conversations that happened between Fundación Paraguaya employees and their clients over the next eight months. And, best of all, it generated enormous pride when on December 31, 2011, Burt announced that over 6,000 families had achieved this goal. Later on we'll explore how all this happened, but for now take comfort in knowing that it all started with a new clear and compelling goal—the first key to influence.

So, influencers don't merely start their change efforts with their ultimate goal in mind. They take care to craft that goal into a clear and compelling goal statement. Such statements can provide focus and inspiration to families, communities, and even whole countries as individuals rally around a compelling cause.

## Infrequent or No Measures

We'll start this concept with a government example. It's their turn to shine—or maybe not.

When the commander in charge of the Coast Guard boot camp located in Alameda, California, asked the authors to help him design an entirely new training experience, we leapt at the chance. Hundreds of young people were passing through the training center monthly where they were exposed to whatever the leaders could come up with to transform them into perfect, newly initiated "Coasties." It was an irresistible influence challenge.

"I worry about the amount of verbal and physical abuse we heap on these young people," the commander began. Having seen and heard about the rather frightening boot camp experience, we understood his concern. In fact, only meters outside the commander's cinder-block office, petty officers were shouting at their recruits, forcing them to drag around huge anchor chains, making them lie on their backs with their arms and legs squirming above them as they acted the part of a dying cockroach, and otherwise causing the recruits to regret their decision to join such an outfit.

"The theory," the commander continued "is that you break them down, and then shape them into what you want. You get them used to taking orders, and then later on when you tell them to do something dangerous or frightening, they'll do it without pause. But I don't know if it works. To me it seems like we're doing more harm than good."

"But we see such progress," interjected the chief petty officer in charge of instruction. "For one, we help improve their confidence."

Wondering how having them play a dying cockroach helped improve their confidence, we asked how they knew that confidence improved.

"Well, take last week's graduation," the chief enthused. "One of the recruits' parents attended the ceremony, and within minutes the fellow introduced me to both his mom and dad."

"And that shows that confidence is improving?"

"Heck yeah. Before going through boot camp, the kid wouldn't have had the confidence to handle a family introduction like that."

"And how do you know that?"

"Why, if you'd seen these kids before we put our boot to them, you'd know what I'm talking about."

This discouraging example highlights a new challenge. You can talk about results all you want, but they remain nothing more than ideas until you decide exactly how you're going to measure them. This seems simple enough when you're looking at something like weight or profits. You merely stand on a scale or calculate income minus expenses. However, when you're trying to track morale, employee engagement, customer satisfaction, or, as was the case with the boot camp, confidence, such items have to be operationalized into something you can measure. You have to pick something to represent the idea.

Now, these well-intended boot camp leaders aren't the only ones who fail to create a clear measure. The people with whom we routinely consult often leave out this step—not on purpose, but because they think they already have a firm grasp on the results they care about. But they don't. Their conclusions are based on anecdotal evidence and gut impressions rather than reliable measures.

We've all made this mistake. Perhaps we've set a goal of consuming X number of calories per day, and then we track our efforts by keeping a running guesstimate in our heads. Later when we log our exact food intake, we learn that our estimates were off by as much as half. Or maybe we think the morale in our office is just fine because everyone seems happy enough. Nobody has caused a scene or anything. And then one day we're surprised to see someone quit because he or she "hates the place." Then another person takes a job across the street for less pay and worse benefits. "What's that all about?" You wonder, but you don't know because you don't measure.

Surprises like this often take place in corporate settings because leaders see satisfaction, engagement, and other human metrics as not only difficult to measure but as "soft." Meaning, they don't believe the measures matter in the grand scheme of things, and they don't trust the measures. So leaders don't take "soft measures" more often than, say, every two years. This schedule is typically kept against a backdrop of measuring quality every 10 minutes and discussing cash flow measures every two hours. *A measure won't drive behavior if it doesn't maintain attention, and it certainly won't maintain attention if it's rarely assessed*—especially if other measures are taken, discussed, and fretted over a hundred times more frequently.

For example, what do you think would happen if our friend Danny Meyer measured restaurant revenues daily but customer experience only annually? Revenue would drive management attention, and customer experience would get a ritualized yearly review—as is the case in most of Danny's competitors. If you want a measure to influence behavior, it must be refreshed frequently.

Of course, frequently gathering data consumes enormous resources. Leaders often complain that it takes as much effort to measure an influence campaign as it does to deploy the campaign itself. And within this complaint lies the real problem. Leaders assume measurement is completely separate from influence. It isn't. Measurement is an integral part of the change effort, and done correctly, it informs and drives behavior.

## Bad Measures

Not everyone forgets to take measures and to do so frequently, but people still fail to create measures that generate the right kind of influence. They do so by measuring the wrong variable. For instance, during the Cold War, Soviet leaders didn't have or measure such a capitalistic thing as profits, and nobody tracked customer satisfaction (who even cared about such nonsense?), so they decided to improve productivity—something they did measure—by tracking weight. In short, production facilities were required to produce more tonnage. Nail factory leaders responded to this demand by switching production from the nails that were sorely needed for construction to huge railroad spikes that are heavier but weren't really needed. When the party bosses saw the results, they changed the measure to the number of units, and the nail factory leaders started producing tiny, mostly useless brads by the billions.

Or how about this? For years, charities have measured their success by how many services they provide. The more people they serve, the better they are doing, right? This, of course, leads agencies to focus their efforts on activities rather than results. (Imagine FedEx bragging in an annual brochure about how many miles its drivers had driven!)

Now, this all sounds pretty obvious, so let's look at an example where it takes careful analysis to uncover what you should be measuring. And by way of warning, this particular example is both complicated and heartbreaking.

Make no mistake. Senior officers of the U.S. Army find sexual assault repugnant to everything they stand for. And no one is more intolerant of it than Lt. General Tom Bostick—the Army's head of personnel. If you leave a conversation with General Bostick believing anything less, then you weren't paying attention. At a recent briefing, he described in shocking detail how a particular soldier deployed to Afghanistan was allowed to rape one fellow soldier after another. There were seven victims before the perpetrator was finally identified and arrested. General Bostick talks about these victims with as much emotion as he would have discussing his own children.

However, Bostick and his colleagues have yet to make a dent in the problem. They've poured enormous leadership and financial resources into reducing and preventing sexual harassment and assault with almost nothing to show for the effort. Last year there were over 3,000 assaults *reported*. The common belief is that this number represents as little as 10 percent of the violence that actually occurs. If that is true, then the real cost of this perpetual calamity is 30,000 damaged lives every year. And it's not getting any better.

How could the best intentions and focused efforts of so many people amount to so little influence? The first reason is that the Army measures the wrong thing. The only measure they track frequently is the number of sexual assaults. That might seem like exactly the *right* thing to measure, but it only seems so when you don't think about the measures you take as part of your influence strategy.

Let's speculate for a moment. What do you predict would result from the following strategy? You tell every military officer, "Look, we're now tracking reports of sexual harassment and assault. Your job is to make that number go down in your unit."

The number will drop. You give your senior military leaders a serious command, and they will move heaven and earth to "make it happen." But if the number drops, it won't necessarily be good news. If it's true that as many as 90 percent of assaults go unreported, then the first sign of making progress might be that the number actually goes *up*. An increase could mean that you've made it safer to speak up and then go get help. Assaults are decreasing, but more are being reported more frequently so, in the net, the number increases.

But how can you know whether the increase is good news because reporting has gone up or bad news because the actual incidents have increased? By measuring the *real* target you need to change: people's thoughts and actions. A useful measure would tell you (unit by unit) how safe people feel. It would tell you (1) if they feel safe *from* harassment or assault and (2) if they feel safe *reporting* harassment or assault. If you gather these numbers frequently, you're in a much stronger position to properly interpret an increase or decrease in reported assaults. Which, to their credit, is why the Army is currently revisiting what they'll measure and how they'll measure it as they work feverishly to resolve this horrendous problem.

From these examples we learn that good measures don't merely inform us. They also drive the right behavior. Sometimes it may take awhile to figure out exactly which measures you should be taking, but it's worth studying in detail. The measure of a measure is its actual influence. If there's a chance that the very process of measuring results might drive the wrong behavior, then be sure to faithfully measure the actions you need to produce those results as well.

For instance, you want to improve innovation (as measured by the number of new product proposals per quarter), and you have decided that the reason you're not as innovative as you would like to be is because people aren't comfortable raising new ideas. You interview employees, and they tell you that they get ridiculed or otherwise punished when they make suggestions, so they clam up.

You put together a course that teaches individuals how to speak up in a way that's heard and makes it safe for others to do the same. Then you track two measures: innovations and instances of speaking up. If both increase (and a control group you measure doesn't increase), you can then conclude that your efforts are well placed, and you can move ahead with confidence. You know what behaviors to change, and you have a clear understanding of what strategies to implement in order to actually change those behaviors. (We call these actions that lead to important results *vital behaviors*.)

So, start every change project with a clear and compelling statement of the goal you're trying to achieve. Measure your progress. Don't leave it to intuition or hunches. Measure your measures by the behavior they influence. And finally, measure the right thing, and measure it frequently.

## KEY 2. FIND VITAL BEHAVIORS

Every year over 3,000 Americans drown, many of them in public pools. This problem remained unchanged for decades until a team of tenacious leaders from the YMCA and Redwoods

Insurance got serious about influence. It wasn't long before they had reduced the portion of these 3,000 deaths that happened at YMCA pools by two-thirds.

How did they do it? They studied tragedies and successes until they found one vital (high-leverage) behavior that made the difference. They discovered that traditional lifeguards were spending much of their time greeting members, adjusting swim lanes, picking up kickboards, and testing pool chemicals. (Doesn't sound much like *life guarding,* does it?)

However, when lifeguards do *10-10 scanning,* drowning rates drop immediately. This means that a lifeguard stands in a special spot and scans her section of the pool every 10 seconds, then offers assistance to anyone who *might* be in trouble within 10 seconds. Simple. And it yields incredibly high leverage. Kevin Trapani and his colleagues at Redwoods Insurance and YMCAs across the world have spared scores of families from devastating loss of life by identifying and implementing one *vital behavior* that has made all the difference.

Let's see how this concept of focusing on high-leverage actions applies to Danny Meyer, the restaurant mogul we visited. He didn't demand dozens of actions of his staff. Instead, he focused on one vital behavior captured in the acronym ABCD, or "Always Be Collecting Dots." Dots, in Danny's world, are pieces of information about a guest's needs and desires that his staff can collect by astutely observing and interacting with that guest. Danny found that the employees who were best at collecting dots were also the ones who were most capable of connecting them in creative ways to create unique and special experiences for their guests.

For instance, Danny's employees learn that a customer works in the publishing industry, and they seat him at a table near other publishers. They also look for food preferences, seat-ing choices, body language, emotions, special events, and other dots, and then use that information to create a customized guest experience. Consequently, one day when a distraught woman walks through the door of one of Danny's establishments without her purse, Gramercy Tavern employees pick up the dot. They then find out exactly what has her worried, and they take spectacular initiative to solve the problem.

Danny understands that in order to create profound change, you don't have to change 50 behaviors. You usually have to change only a couple of them.

In the next chapters we'll dig into how influencers go about searching for and finding vital behaviors as well as the methods they use to influence each. The good news is that the key of finding no more than a handful of high-leverage behaviors works with almost any problem. Change vital behaviors, and soon you'll achieve the results you've wanted all along.

## KEY 3. ENGAGE ALL SIX SOURCES OF INFLUENCE

The third and final key to influence lies in finding a way to get people to actually carry out the vital behavior you identify. You've identified what you want. You know what behaviors it'll take to get you there. Now you have to get people to adopt the new behaviors. This is no small trick. In fact, we'll spend the bulk of the book examining best practices for doing so. For now, we'll share the high-level principle: engage all six sources of influence. Influencers succeed in creating change where others fail because they *overdetermine success*. They marshall a critical mass of not one or two, but six different sources of influence that shape human action. And when they do this, change becomes not only more likely but almost inevitable.

For instance, consider the work of a couple of educational influencers, David Levin and Mike Feinberg. They didn't *stumble* into a way of getting tens of thousands of inner city youth to—and through—college. They *studied* their way into it. As of the date this book was written, the Knowledge Is Power Program (KIPP) system that Levin and Feinberg founded in 1994 had 133 free public college prep schools serving over 30,000 students. Their teachers are paid no better than public school teachers. Their budgets are no larger. Their work hours are much longer. And they go out of their way to recruit kids with the fewest opportunities. Eighty-five percent of their students are from low-income families.

And yet with all these challenges, a child attending a KIPP school is four times more likely to graduate from college than a child attending the public schools in his or her surrounding neighborhoods.

How do these two masterful influencers do it? If you've been paying attention, you already know two of the three keys. First, they are goal and measurement maniacs. They know the results they're after, and they measure them mercilessly. Second, they know their vital behaviors. "Work hard" and "Be nice" are veritable watchwords at KIPP. Everything teachers and administrators do is designed to enable every student to develop these habits to a high art. And the third key to their success lies in their ability to routinely *overdetermine their results*. To do so, they have studiously amassed six different sources of influence (used in combination) to help all of their kids practice their two vital behaviors. These powerful sources include the following.

## Source 1. Personal Motivation

We'll start with the source people most frequently include in their influence attempts: personal motivation. As you watch others not doing the right thing while repeatedly doing the wrong thing, ask: *Do they enjoy it?* In most cases—particularly with deep-rooted habits—this source of influence is an important factor in propelling and sustaining behavior. For instance, when it comes to education, far too many students find school both boring and pointless.

At KIPP, you'll find the opposite. Hard work is constantly connected with bright futures. People constantly talk about getting "to and through college." Children introduce themselves by saying, "I'm Clifton, class of 2018." With time and success, students learn to associate hard work with good grades, which makes the work more enjoyable. Most end up enjoying the act of learning itself because it's routinely connected with success. Plus teachers make the in-class learning fun. Walk into almost any classroom, and you're likely to hear times tables done in percussive rap rather than in morose drills.

### Source 2. Personal Ability

Of course, motivation isn't everything. When trying to understand why others don't do what they should do, ask: *Can they do it?* Just because individuals enjoy something doesn't mean they'll succeed. They have to have the skills, talent, and understanding required to enact each vital behavior or they'll fail. For instance, Levin and Feinberg learned that kids drop out not simply because they're more interested in hanging out in the neighborhood but because they're routinely failing their assignments and courses and they feel incompetent and bad about themselves. Dropping out is a sane response to persistent disappointment and repeated reminders that they're performing below average.

At KIPP the entire design of the learning process is to create a feeling of competence and mastery. Educators achieve this objective by providing students with informative and engaging deliberate practice experiences coupled with clear feedback. When Levin was asked how long it takes to see results from a new child, he smiled disarmingly and answered, "One hour. When they succeed, they want to repeat their success. And our whole goal is to help them experience success from day one."

## Source 3. Social Motivation

Next, you need to examine the social side of influence by asking: *Do others encourage them to enact the wrong behavior?* When half of your colleagues drop out of school, quitting becomes the *norm*. And this *is* the norm most low-income youth experience. Unless your peers value scholastic achievement, you're unlikely to value it yourself.

At KIPP, college pennants are ubiquitous. Not hypothetical ones—but pennants from the colleges students from their school are already attending. Students frequently talk about where they'll be going to college, why, and what they expect to achieve from their efforts. As entering students meet and interact with peers who value learning, try hard, aim for college, and achieve, they want to follow a similar path. At KIPP, new norms are established and trumpeted loudly from day one. This rising social tide lifts all students.

## Source 4. Social Ability

Others not only provide a source of motivation but they can also enable vital behaviors. To examine this important source of influence, ask: *Do others enable them?* Students who typically drop out have few resources to help, coach, and mentor them.

One of the strangest experiences parents and students have at KIPP takes place when they first meet the teacher. It happens in their home. The KIPP administrators want the family to know there is *nothing* they won't do to help the student succeed. So the teacher visits with the parents and child and concludes the visit by giving the family his or her phone number—his or her *mobile* phone number. Then turning to the child, the teacher says, "Your classmates will help you succeed. If you're stuck on an assignment, here are three you can call for help. And if they can't help you, call me. Now, repeat after me: 'Try three before me!'" More than one child described his or her disbelief at being given a teacher's cell phone number. So they did what any curious kid would do in such circumstances—they tried the number! Something happened inside them when the familiar voice answered. Something they hadn't felt before. Hope.

## Source 5. Structural Motivation

Most burgeoning change agents think about both individual and social factors, but they leave out the role "things" play in encouraging and enabling vital behaviors. To check for this source, ask: *Do rewards and sanctions encourage them?* There is little perceived incentive to stay the course at most at-risk schools. In fact, some inner city youth see far more benefits from getting a job (legal or illegal) than from getting an education.

At KIPP, fun rewards are offered to kids who have done everything on time for the month. For example, they get to attend the monthly "Attend-Dance"—an invitation-only dance for those kids who maintain certain levels of participation.

## Source 6. Structural Ability

Finally, "things" can either enable or disable performance. To examine this source, ask: *Does their environment enable them?* When your school is dismal, your learning tools are antiquated, and your home environment is insecure, you have a hard time focusing on abstract learning.

At KIPP both the home and school environments are seen as important parts of the learning experience. Levin, Feinberg, and others routinely visit homes, assessing what's helping and what's hurting learning, and then they take action. For example, Feinberg describes how a mother in a tough Houston neighborhood had a difficult time getting her daughter to do her homework rather than watch TV. Feinberg (who was the principal at the time) made a routine home visit to check on the girl. After hearing the mother's despair, he said, "Okay, let's get rid of the television!" "What? I can't do that!" the mother protested. "Well," Feinberg pressed, "it sounds like you've tried everything else. I guess it's TV or KIPP. Which is it?" Without hesitation the mother said, "KIPP." Minutes later Feinberg exited the apartment carrying a 36-inch television—and still another girl made it to and through college (and later got her television returned). KIPP teachers help parents and students think about how to organize the home environment to make study easier and more successful.

As you can see from this extended example, KIPP's Levin and Feinberg have embedded dozens of tactics that draw from six very different yet important sources of influence. They select one vital behavior, and then they purposefully examine each of the six sources—first identifying the factors that are working against them, and then turning these factors in their favor.

By using them in combination, they overdetermine success. The results speak for themselves.

So, there they are—the three keys to influence. Whether you're eradicating disease, improving customer service, or engaging struggling students, these three principles provide the foundation of all effective influence strategies. They aren't tricks or gimmicks. They aren't fads or the latest "things." They aren't quick fixes. But together they make up a *learnable* path to success. They are the science of leading change.

# 3

# Find Vital Behaviors

*It is not enough to do your best; you must know what to do, and THEN do your best.*

—*W. Edwards Deming*

A s you do your best to increase your influence, if you've been following the path of effective influencers, you've already used the first key: you created clear, compelling, and measurable goals. You know exactly what you want, by when, and how to measure it. So you're off to a good start.

Next you have to figure out what behaviors people need to change in order to achieve these results. Influencers are universally firm on this point. They don't create methods for changing behavior until they've carefully identified the exact behaviors they want to change.

This can sound like an enormous task. On any given day, how many behaviors does one enact? Thousands? Fortunately, when it comes to creating change, you don't have to identify thousands of behaviors. Not even a hundred or a dozen. Typically one or two vital behaviors, well executed, will yield a big difference. This is true because with almost any result you're trying to achieve, there are moments of *disproportionate influence*. These are times when someone's choices either lead toward great results or set up a cascade of negative behaviors that create and perpetuate problems.

And now for the really good news. These *crucial moments* are often easily spotted. For example, when Danny Meyer's restaurant guest has a problem, it's obvious that the actions of staff members in that moment will disproportionately affect that guest's overall experience at Gramercy Tavern. A physician enters a patient's room and doesn't wash his hands as he enters. That is a crucial moment: his failure to practice one simple behavior creates the potential for many serious problems to follow. A person carrying a Guinea worm feels an uncontrollable urge to thrust his infected arm into the local water source. What follows makes a big difference in perpetuating Guinea worm disease in the village for another entire year.

Even the most pervasive problems will yield to changes if you spot these crucial moments and then identify the specific, high-leverage actions that will lead to the results you want. These actions make up what we call the *vital behaviors* in any change project. Find these vital few behaviors, and you've found the second key to influence.

Let's see how this has been done by genuine influencers.

## THE KING'S BIRTHDAY PRESENT

Meet Dr. Wiwat Rojanapithayakorn (or, as he mercifully permitted us to call him, Dr. Wiwat). He learned the value of focusing on a few high-leverage behaviors the hard way.

When King Rama IX of Thailand turned 60, he gave the country a gift. Unfortunately, the king's well-intended present actually unleashed a horrendous plague on his people. Prior to the king's birthday, AIDS in Thailand had been found only in the prison population, and it occurred there because the prisoners passed the disease from one to the other by sharing used needles. For several years the disease stayed incarcerated with its hosts. But in 1988, in a birthday-inspired act of compassion (in keeping with a national tradition for momentous occasions), the king granted amnesty to over 30,000 prisoners. Released from its confinement, the AIDS virus celebrated its new freedom by rampaging through a much larger community of intravenous (IV) drug users. In just a few months almost half the users nationwide were infected.

The country's infectious disease experts watched in horror as month by month the disease spread from one community to another. Close on the heels of IV drug users, sex workers fell prey. Within only a year, as many as one-third of the sex workers in some provinces tested HIV positive. Next, married men carried the scourge home to their unsuspecting wives, who frequently passed it to newborn babies. By 1993 an estimated 1 million Thais were infected with HIV. Health experts worldwide predicted that in just a few years Thailand would lead the world in infections per capita—with as many as one in four adults carrying the virus.

But it never happened. Within two years the virus hit a wall, and then it retreated. By the late 1990s—largely because of a remarkable influence strategy implemented by Dr. Wiwat—new infections had been cut by 80 percent. The World Health Organization (WHO) has estimated that as of 2004, over 5 million people who *should* have been infected weren't.

But the solution didn't come easily, and it certainly didn't come after the first attempt. While AIDS was taking Thailand by storm, Dr. Wiwat battled the plague alongside a handful of his colleagues in the Ratchaburi province. His training had taught him that the key to fighting the spread of any disease lay in making the public "aware" of the threat. The experts who were advising Wiwat (people who had thought about the transmission problem but who hadn't actually solved it) argued that diseases thrive in ignorance; therefore, you have to spread the word.

With this idea in mind, Dr. Wiwat accepted a position with Thailand's Ministry of Public Health. Specializing in venereal diseases, he approached the task of informing an ignorant public in much the same way corporate executives try to improve quality, customer service, or teamwork. Wiwat's team distributed posters. They held education sessions. They convinced celebrities to broadcast television and radio spots.

Despite their best efforts, Wiwat and his teammates failed. After two exhausting, expensive, and deadly years, Thai researchers found that they had accomplished nothing. The problem had actually grown far worse. That's when Wiwat threw out the handbook. Rather than accepting the word of people who had never actually succeeded in eliminating the rapid transmission of the disease, Dr. Wiwat decided to conduct a more intensive search for a strategy. He started by poring over data about the transmission cycle of AIDS through Thailand.

It didn't take Wiwat long to realize that 97 percent of all new HIV infections were coming from heterosexual contact with sex workers. This statistic might seem a bit odd until you learn that Thailand has over 150,000 sex workers—about 1 for every 150 adult men. Wiwat's concern was that, when induced by low prices and abundant supply, the vast majority of Thai men periodically visited brothels.

This statistic gave Dr. Wiwat the focus he needed. If contact with sex workers was causing the pandemic, he had no choice but to focus his attention there—despite the fact that the government refused to admit that the massive sex trade industry even existed. With over a million HIV infections in Thailand, Wiwat decided the time for political sensitivity and social niceties was long past. If the problem was born in a brothel, the solution would be found there as well.

After continuing his search for a solution, Wiwat surmised that there was a crucial moment—one that disproportionately affected the spread or the stopping of AIDS. It was when a sex worker chose—or did not choose—to demand the use of a condom. Wiwat had uncovered (1) the crucial moment (the point at which if you acted differently, you'd avoid the disease), and (2) the vital behavior that needed to follow. If he could influence 100 percent of the country's sex workers to act differently in this moment, he could nearly stop the spread of HIV in Thailand. That became his primary strategy. He'd find a way to get every single sex worker to comply with the condom code. And much to the surprise of the world's epidemiologists, Wiwat's plan worked. He helped save millions of lives.

## MIMI SHOWS THE WAY

The idea of finding but a few vital behaviors is an important and unlikely enough concept that it deserves a second example. After all, the idea of attacking but a few actions and then expecting enormous results flies in the face of years of tradition and "common sense." To see how this might apply to something even more complex, let's look into an example that demonstrates quite nicely how identifying, creating, and maintaining a couple of high-leverage actions can provide the perfect beginning to the most challenging of change programs.

To do so, we'll travel to San Francisco and meet Dr. Mimi Silbert. She's the founder of Delancey Street, a one-of-a-kind organization with headquarters at an upscale address on San Francisco's Embarcadero. Silbert's company is part corporate conglomerate and part residential therapy. It consists of several dozen businesses.

What's unique about Delancey is the employee population. In Silbert's words, "They're nasty, racist, violent, and greedy. They're thieves, prostitutes, robbers, and murderers." Then she adds: "When we started 30 years ago, most were gang members. Today, many are third-generation gang members." According to Silbert, "These guys get letters from Grandma saying, 'Get back here—the gang needs you!' " Dr. Silbert's typical new hires have had multiple felony convictions. They've been homeless for years, and most are lifetime drug addicts.

But this doesn't stop Dr. Silbert from asking a great deal from them. Within hours of joining Delancey, they are working in a restaurant, moving company, car repair shop, or one of the many other Delancey companies. And other than Silbert herself, these felons and addicts make up the *entire* population at Delancey. No therapists. No professional staff. No donations, no grants, no guards—just a remarkable influence strategy that has profoundly changed the lives of 16,000 employees over the past 30 years. Of those who join Delancey, over 90 percent never go back to drugs or crime. Instead they earn degrees, become professionals, and change their lives. Forever.

### Meet James

One of the employees you might meet if you stop by the restaurant is a well-scrubbed, affable but steely-eyed fellow we'll call James. James's story is typical of Silbert's staff. Like many of the

500 residents living on the San Francisco campus, James was a career criminal and drug addict before coming to Delancey. And like most, he started young. After four years as a regular runaway, criminal, and drug abuser, James turned 10. By that time Illinois was fed up with his shenanigans. The state officials had tracked down James's father—who had abandoned him at age one. State justice authorities wished James good luck as they stood at a gate at the O'Hare airport while making sure he understood that he was no longer welcome in Chicago.

James flew to Oakland, California, where he took up residence with his father near the docks. The first lesson his dear old dad taught him was how to shoot heroin. The next 25 years consisted of an uninterrupted period of violent crime, drug abuse, and prison time. Six years ago he was convicted of yet another violent offense, and he was sentenced to 18 years with no hope of parole for 16 years. That's when he asked to join Delancey rather than serve his full sentence.

James changed in ways that are hard to imagine. Should you run into him at Delancey, you'll see that he is professionally dressed and has not used drugs or alcohol in years. To learn how Dr. Silbert influences this kind of change, we'll touch base with her work throughout this book. She draws from the principles and practices of every one of the influencers we've studied to date.

To see exactly how only a few vital behaviors played an enormous role in both causing and solving profound problems with people such as James, let's examine what Dr. Mimi Silbert does to help people turn their lives around. She learned early on that if you're going to work with subjects whose lives are an undifferentiated bundle of dysfunctional behaviors, you have to limit your scope of influence by identifying only a couple of vital behaviors and then working on them. Otherwise you dilute your efforts and eventually fail. As you chat with Dr. Silbert, she's quick to point out that if you want to help ex-cons change their lives, you need to focus on behavior, not values, homilies, or emotional appeals. Just imagine Mimi Silbert giving a value-laden lesson to James on his first day at Delancey.

James vividly describes what she'd be up against.

"When residents wake up in their nine-person dorm the first morning and you say, 'Good morning' to them, they say, '$%@^ you!' " A sermon on courtesy just isn't going to cut it in this venue.

So Dr. Silbert focuses on changing behaviors, not on preaching homilies. And, once again, a few behaviors, not dozens. In Silbert's words: "You can't succeed by trying to change 20 things at the same time!" So Silbert made a study of the behaviors that needed changing, hoping to find a couple that would provide focus and leverage in transforming criminals into citizens. After working with over 16,000 felons, Silbert is now convinced that just two behaviors open the floodgates of change. If you focus on these two, a whole host of other behaviors, values, attitudes, and outcomes follow. Silbert explains how it works.

"The hardest thing we do here is try to get rid of the code of the street. It says: 'Care only about yourself, and don't rat on anyone.' However, if you reverse those two behaviors, you can change everything else."

James elaborates: "Helping residents learn to confront problems is essential. We've got Crips, Bloods, white supremacists, Mexican Mafia, and every other gang here, and they're all bunking together. As you might imagine, the tension runs high. Everything we try to change in here is about getting rid of the gang culture."

With this in mind, Silbert targets two high-leverage behaviors that help residents talk in ways that eventually destroy the gang culture. First, she requires each person to take responsibility for someone else's success. Second, she demands that everyone confront everyone else about every single violation or concern.

To transform these ideals into realities, each resident is placed in charge of someone else the very first week. For instance, say you're a resident who was homeless and strung out on crack a week ago. During the seven days since coming to Delancey, someone who had been a resident for only a little longer than you would take you under his or her wing and teach you to set a table in the restaurant. A week later when someone even newer than you comes in, you're in charge of teaching that person to set the table. From that moment forward, people no longer talk to you about how *you* are doing. They ask you how *your crew* is doing. You are responsible for them.

Next, residents practice the second vital behavior: to speak up to people who are breaking rules, drifting off, becoming verbally aggressive, and otherwise behaving badly. For most ex-criminals, talking about these types of problems is like speaking a foreign language. Ultimately, Silbert helps residents change their values and attitudes—even their hearts—but she does so by focusing on two vital behaviors. Silbert has seen that if she can just get these two behaviors happening consistently among the 1,500 residents, everything changes.

Later we'll explore how Dr. Silbert influences a reluctant group to actually adopt these behaviors. We'll also see how Dr. Wiwat actually got sex workers to practice 100 percent condom use. Obviously, simply knowing the behaviors isn't enough. But for now, let's not miss this second key to influence. Most of us are in such a rush to influence others that we fail to stop and thoughtfully decide what behaviors we want to change. Influencers are scrupulously careful about identifying vital behaviors before setting off to create change.

Acting hastily can not only lead to failure but can also create costly side effects. With the spread of HIV/AIDS, the rush to action took the form of ineffective "awareness" campaigns that burned up resources and did nothing to stem the flow of a deadly disease. With convicted felons, the rush to action has led to so many failures that today's penal institutions make no claim on rehabilitation whatsoever.

## STAY FOCUSED

Wiwat's and Silbert's work provides us with a classic example of the Pareto Principle, the old 80-20 Rule. This rule suggests that for whatever your change topic may be, 80 percent of your results come from 20 percent of your efforts. This means that even for the most complicated problems, ones that are influenced by, say, 10 different behaviors, influencers should focus their efforts on the top 2—and only the top 2. If they spend time on the top 4 or 5 behaviors, or, worse still, on all 10 behaviors, they'll spread themselves too thin.

Think of all the ways Wiwat could have lost his focus. In Thailand, the sex trade is a seamy underside that most would rather ignore, and in polite Thai society, people don't discuss condoms. It would have been easy for Wiwat to have given in to pressure, to water down his approach by focusing on a whole array of positive social behaviors that are worth changing—like overturning sexual taboos, improving gender equality, or reducing the sex trade. Every one of these is a tremendously worthwhile thing to do. But Wiwat couldn't do everything. He had to identify the behaviors that were most vital to the result he was trying to achieve. It was Wiwat's laser focus on 100 percent condom use by sex workers that led to a disproportionate amount of change—saving millions of lives. Silbert's focus has made her efforts not only successful but also the model for criminal rehabilitation worldwide.

Now, let's see how this might apply to something even more local—say, your marriage or significant relationship. Let's say you're in a relationship that is good but not great. How do you improve it? Once again, there are dozens of behaviors and attributes you could say are keys to great relationships—spending time together, sharing interests, listening, sexual compatibility—to name a few. So here's the big question. Could it be that only a couple of controllable actions make most of the difference in a relationship?

To answer this question, we visited marriage scholar Howard Markman's Relationship Lab. After years of observation, Markman found that overcoming just four hurtful behaviors reduces the chances of divorce or unhappiness by over one-third. Markman and his colleagues can watch a couple interact for just 15 minutes and predict with 90 percent accuracy who will and who won't be together and happy five years later—simply by watching how the couple behaves during one crucial moment. The moment of disagreement.

These researchers discovered that staying happily married isn't about 50 things. Rather, they found that it primarily comes down to how people behave during the few minutes a day or week when they disagree. If a couple's disagreements include significant amounts of four behaviors (blaming, escalation, invalidation, or withdrawal), then their future is bleak. If, on the other hand, they learn to take time out and communicate respectfully during these few minutes, then their entire future will be far brighter.

The 80-20 Rule has proven itself across problems in areas as different as improving student test scores, maintaining oilrig safety, and preventing medical errors. Across all these domains, we find the same hopeful, and yet counterintuitive principle. A handful of high-leverage behaviors drives most of the improvement in any successful change effort. Discover these vital behaviors and change them, and problems—no matter their size—topple like a house of cards.

## ACT LIKE AN INFLUENCER

Judy B., a nurse manager, tripled her department's patient experience scores by focusing on just two behaviors: (1) Nurses lead meaningful discussions with each patient every morning, and then they write the patient's Goal for the Day and Plan for the Day on a whiteboard; (2) All of the caregivers, including the physicians, read the whiteboard, respond to what's written there, and then update the whiteboard before leaving.

## FIND THE VITAL BEHAVIORS

Knowing that you need to find high-leverage behaviors and focus your efforts on them raises these questions: How do you find them? What if they aren't obvious? If you're not careful, you could easily focus all of your attention on the wrong behavior and achieve no results. For instance, a graduate student working with renowned psychologist Albert Bandura once went to the effort to teach alcoholics how to relax. Why? Because he thought it would be an important behavior in an alcoholic's road to sobriety. After all, alcoholics experience a lot of stress in their lives, so the grad student concluded that teaching them relaxation skills might help them reduce their drinking.

It turned out that the alcoholics were excellent learners. In fact, they seemed exceptionally adept at developing relaxation techniques. But it didn't reduce their drinking one iota. At the end of the study, the grad student was left with a bunch of very relaxed drunks. Getting people to relax was not a vital behavior for reducing drinking.

Successful influencers escape such debacles. They avoid spending time and effort on the wrong behaviors by drawing from the following four vital behavior search strategies:

- **Notice the obvious.** Recognize behaviors that are obvious (or at least obvious to experts) but underused.
- **Look for crucial moments.** Find times when behavior puts success at risk.
- **Learn from positive deviants.** Distinguish behaviors that set apart *positive deviants*—those who live in the same world but somehow produce much better results.
- **Spot culture busters.** Find behaviors that reverse stubborn cultural norms and taboos.

## Search Strategy 1. Notice the Obvious

Back in the 1970s, one of the authors had a summer job with the Stanford Heart Disease Prevention Clinic. For this particular science project, researchers were trying to determine the behaviors that separated the healthy residents of San Jose, California, from their less healthy neighbors. This study was completed a long time ago, and you may have never visited San Jose, but can you guess what their findings were?

Hint: They're pretty obvious.

Researchers found three behaviors that made nearly all of the difference in the subjects' health. Healthy people exercise more, eat better, and don't smoke. And what do we, as budding change agents, learn from this? Finding these vital behaviors isn't exactly rocket science. Many vital behaviors are just this obvious.

So here's the first strategy for finding those oh-so-valuable vital behaviors. Look for behaviors that are both obvious *and* underused. These are actions that lead directly to the desired results and often come with a big "Duhhh!" But they are also typically underused—not because we're morons, but because the behaviors can be exceptionally difficult or unpleasant. You find these high-leverage actions either by simply applying what you already know or by doing a quick search of what experts say about the topic. If it's easy for you to see the big-hitting actions or if you can find quick consensus from experts, you have a vital behavior.

Now, influencing this kind of vital behavior will take all *six sources of influence*—and using all of them is the *third* key to influence. But don't underestimate the importance of getting the second key right. Even if the behaviors are obvious or they have already been discovered by experts, identifying and focusing on them are the keys to leveraging your influence efforts.

Here is a second example that looks at this obvious, but underused, category. Can you guess the three vital behaviors that drive success during students' first year in college? The dropout rates for first-year students at some colleges are as high as 50 percent, so academic leaders worry endlessly about influencing these students to succeed during their first crucial year. Dropping out is disastrous for both the students and the schools.

This time, since it may not be obvious to your average citizen, we'll rely on our second quick-search tool—experts. In this case, a quick Internet search put us in touch with researchers from a large Midwestern university who culled reams of data examining patterns of success and failure and identified three vital behaviors. If you want to make it past that first tremulous year: attend class, complete assignments (duh!), and make friends (really?). The first two sound pretty obvious, and they are clearly underused by the dropouts. But does making friends really separate the A's from the F's?

So we asked the experts why making friends was *vital*. They taught us about a rite-of-passage that often happens over the Thanksgiving holiday weekend. First-year students go home for their first real vacation from college, and many either break up with or get dumped by their high school sweethearts. These Thanksgiving breakups are so common that college counselors have given them a name: the "Turkey Drop." And college counselors welcome these Turkey Drops. The students return from Thanksgiving serious and a little depressed. They dig into their studies, and they begin to make new college friends. They cut their ties with high school, and they begin to identify with their new role. Students who don't make this transition to new friends and a new identity drop out at a much higher rate.

So, before you aim your efforts at the wrong behaviors, stop and look for candidates who are immediately obvious to you or have already been discovered by experts. Apply what you already know. Then, do an Internet search or talk with local experts, and see if you can find credible research that supports clear consensus on other high-leverage behaviors.

## ACT LIKE AN INFLUENCER

A bank executive bragged that he had identified the vital behavior for winning a Dragon Boat race. His bank sponsored a team that raced outriggers across Tampa Bay. The vital behavior he had in mind? Drum roll please: it's *paddling.* The executive laughed, but he was also serious: "In the middle of a race, people start to argue about strategies and tactics, and then somebody yells, 'Shut up and paddle!' That's when you win the race!" Often it's the obvious but under-used behaviors that prove vital.

## Search Strategy 2. Look for Crucial Moments

As you intensify your research for vital behaviors, you'll need to become quite familiar with a concept we only alluded to earlier—crucial moments. Most of us are mostly successful most of the time. This means our problems typically boil down to a few perfect storms when everything lines up against us. The behaviors that help us succeed in these few crucial moments become vital.

For example, while we were working with Noble Drilling, a world leader in offshore oil drilling and a leader in workplace safety, internal experts described their safety challenge in the following way: "In our company 98 percent of our people do 98 percent of the right stuff 98 percent of the time. *And that's not good enough!*"

Notice how this statement focuses the search for vital behaviors. If Noble Drilling could find the 2 percent of the times when 2 percent of their people did 2 percent of the wrong stuff, it would have tremendous leverage for improvement. And that's what the company leaders did. They looked for crucial moments. They studied safety violations, and they documented the times, people, places, and circumstances when they occurred.

It turned out that their employees followed nearly every safety regulation nearly all the time, with a few exceptions. One exception was when the rig was down—not operating. When a rig is up, it brings in about a quarter of a million dollars a day. When it's down, it brings in nothing, and as you might imagine, everyone goes into emergency overdrive. The sound of "We're not making money!" rings through the rig, and people respond by taking shortcuts and skipping safety steps in order to get the rig back to making money. Nobody *asks* them to take shortcuts or turn a blind eye to safety protocols. They just do.

The other exception was similar, but it involves the weather. When a big storm is approaching and workers have to button up and evacuate the rig, they again feel entitled to take shortcuts and skip safety steps.

The third crucial moment stemmed from the fact that offshore oilrigs provide a vertical environment. They don't have much of a footprint, but they soar hundreds of feet into the air. Thus the third crucial moment was whenever someone was working on or around ladders. The most common and hurtful injuries occur when people fall from ladders or drop things from ladders.

These three crucial moments suggested the vital behaviors the company needed to encourage and enable. Noble Drilling's vital behaviors became the following:

- When a rig is down or it is behind schedule, or when a storm is approaching, hold a safety meeting, and take extra care to follow every safety precaution.
- Whenever you are climbing above the deck, tie off the ladder, use a safety harness, and never carry items in your hands.

These weren't easy behaviors to implement, but Noble Drilling focused all of its efforts on these two. And focusing on these two vital behaviors saved dozens of lives.

Let's now move away from the oilrigs and into an environment you might be more familiar with—a fast-food restaurant. After working closely with the leaders of a large chain of fast-food establishments, we learned a great deal about the following not-so-obvious vital behaviors.

Suppose you're the owner of a burger joint, and you're looking for ways to improve customer service. Your first effort takes you to a training course where you invest in training the restaurant managers and staff. On the whole, the managers are happy with the training, and they believe it was helpful. The only problem is that their customer service numbers haven't improved.

Next you take steps to find your crucial moments and the resultant vital behaviors. First, you look for *failure modes*. In your case, customer service failures consist of ignoring a customer who is trying to order, taking too long to complete an order, and delivering a poor-quality order. Notice what your failures *don't* look like. No one is yelling or cursing or being rude. Employees are nearly always nice, but that isn't enough to create high customer satisfaction scores.

Next, you look for the times and circumstances (the crucial moments) when these particular failures happen. You do this systematically by mapping the problems by time of day, time of week, and restaurant conditions. Here's what you find. More than 80 percent of the problems occur during one of three conditions: when the restaurant is shorthanded (down by at least two people); when one or more of the restaurant's ovens is down; and when you have an unanticipated rush of customers that overwhelms the staff.

Then you look at your own and your staff's behaviors during these crucial moments. You discover that you yourself often contribute to the problem. When the restaurant is overloaded or an oven is down, you often step into an employee role. You work the cash register or try to fix the oven. This takes you out of the quarterback role, and it results in poor customer service. Based on what you learned about your failure modes and crucial moments, when the restaurant is overwhelmed due to a staffing or equipment problem, you focus on two vital behaviors:

- You stop whatever you are doing and bring in your on-call team members.
- You become the quarterback and run a quick practice with the new staff configuration until the customers are served the right food the right way.

Finding and influencing vital behaviors for these crucial moments produce dramatic improvements in the customers' satisfaction.

## Search Strategy 3. Learn from Positive Deviants

Do you consider yourself a deviant? Hopefully you are, at least sometimes. Here's why. A *positive deviant* is a person who, by all rights, ought to have a problem but for some reason doesn't.

## ACT LIKE AN INFLUENCER

We worked with an organization in which managers never brought their projects in on budget. We asked them to create a flowchart of their project planning and execution process, and then we asked them to pinpoint crucial moments when problems occurred. They discovered they were caught in a vicious cycle. Executives thought their managers were wasteful, so they routinely sliced 20 percent off of their budgets and demanded that they deliver with the reduced resources. So managers routinely padded their budgets by 20 percent because they knew the executives' tricks.

The padding justified the cutting, which in turn justified the padding. The cycle perpetuated itself, and it drove trust ever lower. So, what cycle-cutting behavior should follow these crucial moments? After meeting and brainstorming with the leaders, the team identified the following vital behavior: "Whenever you think a budget is unrealistic, speak up with honesty and respect." This behavior was vital because it forced people to talk about their real, not their inflated, estimates. It was a difficult behavior for the managers and executives to implement because their trust levels were so low. However, once employees began being honest with each other, the flywheel turned from a vicious to a virtuous cycle, and their projects began coming in on budget.

If you can find individuals who face the same challenges as your struggling group, yet have found a way to succeed, then you can learn from their solution.

Here's an example. We once worked with a hospital team that transcribed physicians' notes. Transcribers sat at computers wearing headphones, and they typed what they heard into files. But recently their jobs had been radically altered by technology when the hospital introduced a new voice-recognition system that did 80 percent of their previous work for them. Here was the dilemma. Despite the technological advances, their productivity had actually decreased, and their morale had nosedived along with it. These were proud and motivated employees who were doing their best to make the new system work, but they were growing impatient.

So where would you go to learn why results had deteriorated when they should have improved? The first step in any positive deviance study is to find individuals who have found a way to succeed despite the change in conditions. In short, see if you can locate positive deviants in your midst. The department manager did this and discovered three women whose productivity hadn't decreased but had actually improved tenfold.

The second step is to ask members of the standard community and the positive deviants to observe each other's behaviors to see what they might be doing differently—especially during crucial moments. A word to the wise is to ask the people themselves—in this case the members of the transcription team—to lead the observations. Evidence is more compelling when you discover it for yourself.

Here is what the transcription team discovered. The three outliers, their positive deviants, had each independently created keyboard shortcuts to make their jobs faster. These shortcuts were the vital behaviors that made all the difference.

The final step is to have these vital behaviors adopted across the population. In the case of the transcription team, the three positive deviants compared notes, picked the best of their shortcuts, and then created a short lesson for the others on the team. Within the week everyone's productivity had improved by a factor of 10, and morale was as positive as it had ever been.

## ACT LIKE AN INFLUENCER

It was late at night on one of those courtesy vans that take you to your hotel. A flight attendant was bemoaning a crucial moment that is the bane of all flight attendants' work life. That's when a flight carries a mob of screeching, crying, and out-of-control children. As the attendant complained about the fitful toddlers on his last flight, other flight attendants began to pile on. Pretty soon they were one-upping each other's tales of woe.

But one attendant just listened with a puzzled look on her face. Eventually, one of the others asked her what was up. Didn't she suffer these same experiences? "No," she said. "I've got these little toys that work for me." She opened her purse, and she passed around a bewildering variety of simple, inexpensive, novelty toys. Everyone looked at her as if she were a genius, and of course she was. She'd found a simple solution to a problem that vexes most flight attendants, parents, and other travelers. She was modeling the best of what it means to be a positive deviant, and everyone learned from her that night.

## Search Strategy 4. Spot Culture Busters

As you search for vital behaviors, watch for crucial moments that call for behaviors that are currently taboo or punished or that challenge cultural norms. Many unhealthy behaviors continue for years within organizations because confronting them openly simply isn't done. Speak honestly and you pay for it. For example, when Spectrum Health Grand Rapids worked to eradicate hospital-acquired infections, the company's leaders learned that the vast majority of these infections are caused by inadequate hand hygiene on the part of the staff. Consequently, they set a goal of having everyone wash or use a disinfectant every time he or she entered or left a patient care area.

Washing in and out requires people to scrub their hands hundreds of times each day. If you're at all normal, you're likely to slip up now and then. Consequently, to no one's surprise, in positive deviant units—those that had abnormally high levels of hand hygiene compliance—a tandem of vital behaviors was routinely optimized. First, whenever someone failed to wash his or her hands, a colleague reminded him or her to do so.

Here's where norms come into play. Speaking up is generally taboo within healthcare, especially when it involves reminding people higher in the pecking order. For example, a housekeeper is cleaning a patient's windows when he sees a surgeon rush in. He hasn't seen her wash her hands, but he isn't sure that she hasn't. Will the housekeeper speak up? The weight of the culture says "No." And if he tries this vital behavior once, what will predict whether he does it again and again—making it a new norm?

It depends on what happens after the *next* crucial moment. The instant the housekeeper issues the reminder, he feels incredibly vulnerable. But that vulnerability disappears if the surgeon enacts the second vital behavior by saying one simple thing: "Thank you." If she utters this potent phrase, the house-keeper heaves a sigh of relief, and he decides that speaking up is not only helpful in ensuring success but it also won't get him yelled at. Without this second vital behavior (thanking the person who reminds you to wash), the old norm will continue and hand hygiene problems will rage on at unacceptable levels.

Notice that these two behaviors are explicit reversals of the long-standing, yet unspoken, culture. They take an unwritten rule, and they turn it on its head with a written, trained, and practiced one. When these two new behaviors were first introduced at Spectrum Health, and later at the Yale New Haven Health System, they were so countercultural that many staff members doubted they would ever be adopted. In each case, it took all six sources of influence (our third key to influence), but they became the new norms. And when they did, hand hygiene improved dramatically.

By the way, if you've been paying attention, you may have noticed a pattern in some of the culture-busting vital behavior examples we've shared so far. In the hundreds of influence cases we've studied, one of the most consistent vital behaviors for driving change involves helping someone step up to some *crucial conversation*. In fact, our research into crucial conversation skills came from this consistent finding. Whether it's reducing AIDS in Thailand, criminal recidivism at Delancey Street, Guinea worm disease in Burkina Faso, or error rates in software development, one of the most potent behaviors for driving change is influencing people to speak up about a previously emotionally or politically risky issue. Watch for these crucial cultural moments as you look for your own vital behaviors.

**Collect Stories to Uncover Norms.** As you look into your culture to determine if long-standing traditions are going to go head-to-head with proposed vital behaviors, you could be caught by surprise. After all, cultural norms are frequently invisible to the very influencers who need to deal with them. The concept that "fish discover water last" applies here. Culture so quietly and invisibly surrounds us that we often don't recognize its unique norms, practices, and unwritten rules.

Of course, just because we don't notice them doesn't mean they aren't exerting a powerful force. Consequently, influencers' first job in seeking culture buster behaviors is to map their own culture, and the best way to accomplish this is by gathering stories. For instance, one of our projects had us working with truck drivers who drove for gold mines in Ghana and Indonesia. Our goal was to make the roads safer for both the drivers and their neighbors. The drivers knew the written rules of the road: the laws regarding speeding, passing, and leaving the scene of an accident. But everyone also knew that these laws were largely ignored. Consequently, to turn this around, we were more interested in the unwritten rules of the road: the norms and expectations that actually governed drivers' actions.

We collected stories (as opposed to opinions or suggestions) from hundreds of the drivers. We asked for stories about accidents and near accidents. For this project, we used a networking tool that allowed us to collect stories in the drivers' own words and languages. (You can also use traditional interviews and focus groups for this purpose.) Stories provide a window into the storytellers' culture. In this case, the narrative accounts revealed the unwritten rules drivers actually followed on the road—rules such as, "Obey speed limits—unless you're driving bosses who are in a hurry" and "Pedestrians never have the right of way." These were the unwritten rules the gold mining company's leaders would need to change. Once they surfaced these unwritten rules, they found vital behaviors to change them—and aimed all six sources of influence at nurturing these new vital behaviors. But none of this would have been possible if they hadn't first taken the time to surface hidden but powerful cultural norms by collecting stories.

## TEST YOUR RESULTS

The four methods we've discussed for finding vital behaviors provide a good starting point, but they aren't foolproof. They often call for subjective judgments. All four help surface vital behaviors that are plausible, but they may still need to be rigorously proven. Fortunately, this search methodology provides enough information to take your project to the next level. When stakes are high enough and resources are available, you can start a genuine research project of your own. That is, you can track both the vital behaviors *and* the results you care about to see if an increase in behavior leads to an increase in the result. Then, as appropriate, you can make changes and continue to conduct similar mini experiments until you've located the vital behaviors that yield the results you want. While it's true that you might not have the resources to complete such a study, it's nice to know that it can and has been done, even within traditional corporations.

### Meet Ethna Reid

To see how the search for vital behaviors is key to a rigorous influence project, consider the efforts of learning expert Dr. Ethna Reid. She has spent over 50 years doggedly observing teachers in order to identify the vital behaviors that separate the best from the rest. She has codified, gathered, and studied data on virtually every type of teaching behavior, compared these behaviors to the desired results, and discovered a handful of high-leverage actions that make all the difference.

One of the vital behaviors Dr. Reid has unearthed concerns the use of praise versus the use of punishment. (For some, this appears to be a no-brainer.) The best teachers reward positive performance far more frequently than their counterparts. A second vital behavior is that teachers rapidly alternate between teaching and testing. Then, when required, they make immediate corrections. Poor performers drone on for a long time and then let students struggle, often allowing them to repeat errors. By watching positive deviants (those teaching similarly challenged students who get substantially better learning) and discovering the actions they took that separated them from the pack, Dr. Reid has been routinely successful in uncovering the vital behaviors leading to improvements in everything from reading comprehension to vocabulary acquisition.

Of course, the real test of a vital behavior comes when scholars take newly discovered vital behaviors and teach them to experimental groups. If they have indeed found the right behaviors, experimental subjects show far greater improvement in *the desired outcome* than do control subjects who fail to implement the vital behaviors.

This is where Ethna Reid reigns supreme. Studies she has conducted in Maine, Massachusetts, Michigan, Tennessee, Texas, North Carolina, South Carolina, Nebraska, Washington, Virginia, Hawaii, Alabama, and California have shown that, independent of the topic, pupils, school size, budget, or demography, changes in the vital behaviors Reid has discovered improve performance outcomes that influence the entire lifetime of a student.

From this best-practice research we learn two important concepts. First, careful research is sometimes needed to weed out "good" behaviors from the vital few. And second, in many of the areas in which you'd like to exert influence, the vital behaviors research has already been completed for you. For example, if you want friends, children, or loved ones to live healthily with type 1 diabetes, you'll need to find a way to motivate and enable them to complete two vital behaviors that have already been found: they should test their blood sugar four to seven times a day, and they should adjust their insulin appropriately to keep their blood glucose in control. These two behaviors substantially increase the likelihood of a normal, healthy life. If you search carefully, you'll find that good scholars have already found the vital behaviors that solve most challenges that affect a large number of people.

## SUMMARY

Master influencers know that it takes only a few behaviors to create big changes in the results they care about. To do so, they look vigilantly for one or two actions that create a cascade of change. They move through this phase by using a combination of four search techniques. They look for obvious but often underutilized actions. They then seek confirmation of what seems obvious to them by examining the advice of experts. When tailoring their own change program and trying to see what will work for them (given their unique circumstance), they look not at the 98 percent of the time they're successful but the 2 percent of the time when they fail. They then use these crucial moments to inform the actions that need to follow. Often successful influencers surface these high-leverage actions by studying individuals within their organization or circumstances who face similar problems and yet have found a way to succeed. Finally, they watch for behaviors that might be needed to break free of a culture that sustains past problems.

So, you've identified the results you want. You've found the vital behaviors that should get you there, and now all that's left is to help people to adopt those behaviors. This, of course, is akin to saying, now all you need is a miracle. Because, of course, if it were a simple matter to get people to do what they should, persistent and resistant problems would have been resolved years ago. That's why we'll now devote the next half dozen chapters to creating methods that both enable and encourage people to enact those precious vital behaviors.

# Part

## 2

# Engage Six Sources

*Who shall set a limit to the influence of a human being?*

—*Ralph Waldo Emerson*

L et's say that you've identified some important result you want to achieve. You've developed an appropriate way to measure progress. And you've even found vital behaviors that will produce tremendous progress—if you can get people to do them. And that's the third key to influence: figuring out how to get everyone to actually *do* the vital behaviors.

As we saw in Chapter 1, the difference between influencers and the rest of us is that whereas most of us run helter-skelter from one influence tactic to another, influencers take a more thorough and thoughtful approach. They *overdetermine* change. They systematically identify how six unique sources of influence are promoting the wrong behavior, and they carefully develop ways to reverse that influence. They marshal a critical mass of all six sources of influence to support change. And when they do, change becomes virtually inevitable.

Most of us have our favorite influence methods—just pass a law, just threaten a consequence, or just offer a training program. The problem with sticking to our favorite methods is not that the methods are flawed per se; it's that they are far too simplistic. It's akin to hiking the Himalayas with only a bag lunch. There's nothing wrong with Gatorade and a granola bar, but you'll probably need a lot more. Bringing a simple solution to a complex behavioral challenge almost never works.

Nevertheless, people bet on single-source influence strategies all the time. For instance, ask leaders how they're planning to change their employees from being clock-punchers to quality zealots, and they'll point to their new training program—the same one that they're convinced drove General Electric's stock through the stratosphere in the 1990s. The training content might provide a start, but when it comes to creating a culture of quality, it'll take a great deal more than a course. Ask politicians what they're doing to fight crime, and they'll tell you that they're working hard to secure harsher sentences for felony convictions. Also not enough to have much of an impact. Ask community leaders what steps they're taking to stem the growing plight of childhood obesity, and they'll sing the praises of their latest pet project—removing candy machines from schools.

And let's be honest. How many of us haven't yearned for a quick fix for our own problems? A powerful phrase for holding people accountable, a magical marriage solution, a two-hour course that will change your work culture from a short- to a long-term orientation.

The simplicity of this hope is alluring. But a quick fix rarely works. If the behavior you're trying to change is supported by only one source of influence, changing that one might be sufficient to improve results. However, when you're facing long-standing, highly resistant habits, you're typically up against many—if not all six—sources of influence. So think about it: if six sources are driving a bad habit and you address only one, what do you predict will happen? If you answer, "Nothing," you're right. The problem is not a mystery. It's math. Five sources are usually stronger than one. And as you learn to think in terms of the six sources of influence, you'll learn to solve your math problems.

## MASTER SIX SOURCES OF INFLUENCE

We shared an example of how two educators used the six-source model. Now let's take a look into how the model actually works. Virtually all forces that have an impact on human behavior work on only two basic drivers of behavior. Not thousands. Just two. At the end of the day a person asks, "Can I do what's required?" and, "Will it be worth it?" The first question simply asks, "Am I able?" The second, "Am I motivated?" Consequently, no matter the number of forces that affect human action—from managing peer pressure in a junior high school to making citizens aware of the cost of illiteracy in a barrio to offering a class on anger management in Beverly Hills—all these strategies work in one of two ways. They either motivate or enable a vital behavior. Some do both.

*Motivation* and *ability* make up the first two domains of our model.

We further subdivide these two domains into *personal, social,* and *structural* sources. These three sources of influence reflect separate and highly developed literatures: psychology, social psychology, and organization theory. By exploring all three, we ensure that we draw our strategies from the known repertoire of influence techniques.

Let's quickly look at the range of influence sources effective influencers draw upon. Don't worry if they aren't crystal clear at this point. Over the next six chapters, we explain the various sources in detail. In fact, you're likely to see how many of them account for improvements you've made in your own life. But for now, you'll know how to consciously draw upon this robust set of sources any time you need to.

At the personal level, influencers work on connecting vital behaviors to intrinsic motives as well as building personal ability to actually do each behavior through deliberate practice. At the group level, savvy folks draw on the enormous power of social influence to both motivate and enable the new behaviors. At the structural level, they take advantage of methods that most people rarely use. They attach appropriate incentives or sanctions to motivate people to pick up the vital behaviors. And finally, they go to pains to ensure that *things*—systems, processes, reporting structures, visual cues, work layouts, tools, supplies, machinery, and so forth—support the vital behaviors. With this model at the ready, influencers know exactly which forces to bring into play in order to overdetermine their chances of success.

Pictorially, we can display these six sources of influence in the following model:

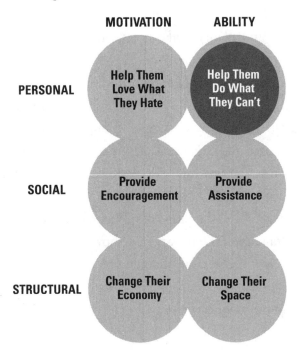

To better understand how each of these six sources operates, let's go to a village in Nigeria where we show up with visions of annihilating the nasty Guinea worm. We know that villagers are only three vital behaviors away from eradicating the worm. First, people must filter their water. How hard can that be? Second, should someone still become infected, he or she must not make contact with the public water supply until the infection has run its course. Just stay away from the water. And third, if a neighbor is not filtering water or becomes infected, the villagers must confront him or her.

Since we know the three behaviors that will eradicate the Guinea worm disease, it sounds as if our influence project won't be particularly complicated. However, before we start giving heartfelt speeches and handing out four-color pamphlets, let's see how each of the six sources of influence affects this actual project.

## Source 1. Personal Motivation

When the Guinea worm is exiting a victim's body, the pain is absolutely excruciating. Since victims can't merely yank the worm out of their arm or leg without the worm breaking then simply emerging elsewhere—or worse, causing a horrific infection, they're forced to wind the parasite around a stick and slowly edge it out over a couple of weeks—or even a couple of months.

There's only one source of relief during this prolonged ordeal, and that's for victims to soak their painful sores in water. That means that individuals are personally motivated to do exactly the opposite of one of the vital behaviors: "Stay away from the water." If you don't deal with *personal motivation*, your influence plan will fail.

## Source 2. Personal Ability

Naïve change agents assume that motivation is enough. For example, if Dr. Hopkins simply tells villagers how much pain and agony filtering their water will help them avoid, they will no doubt change, right? Wrong. Hopkins tells us, "Filtering is a skill. There are more ways to get it wrong than get it right." When they take the steps to filter the water, they carelessly allow the unfiltered water to splash here and there, which infects the filtered water supply and continues the infestation. Or they transfer filtered water into a pot that's still moist with unfiltered water. They'll need training to enhance their *personal ability*.

## Source 3. Social Motivation

Next, when you sit down with the locals to teach them how to eliminate the Guinea worm disease, nobody is going to pay very much attention to your advice. You're an outsider and as such you simply can't be trusted. You may be in good with the chief, but there are three tribes in the village, two of which resent the chief and will resist anything you offer *because* he's behind it. Unless circumstances change, you will have a serious problem with *social motivation*.

## Source 4. Social Ability

People within an individual community will have to assist each other if they hope to succeed. When it comes to an outbreak, nobody can make it on his or her own. If ever there were a circumstance in which the expression "It takes a village" applies, this is it. For example, if someone comes down with the Guinea worm disease, others may have to fetch water for him or her. And when it comes to filtering, locals often have to buddy up in order to have enough pots to both fetch and filter water. If locals don't enlist the help of others, you'll be missing the key factor of *social ability*.

### Source 5. Structural Motivation

Given the villagers' current financial circumstances (living hand-to-mouth), individuals who become infected can't afford to stay away from work. This forces them to labor in and around the water supply. Quite simply, to put food on the table, they'll need to fetch water for both their crops and livestock.

This means that the formal reward system is at odds with the three vital behaviors. Infected people earn money only if they work near the water source. If you don't deal with this incentive conflict, victims will be compelled to serve their families at the expense of the entire village. Try to move forward without addressing *structural motivation*, and your influence won't reach far.

### Source 6. Structural Ability

Last, locals don't have all the tools they need to filter the water or to care for their wounds in a way that keeps them away from the community water source. Worse still, the layout of the village makes access to the public water supply so easy and natural that it's enormously tempting for victims to merely plunge their aching arm or leg into the water—at the peril of everyone else. If you don't work on this last source of influence, *structural ability*, you're also likely to fail.

## MAKE USE OF ALL SIX SOURCES

Now that we've explored how all six sources of influence came into play with the Guinea worm project, it's easy to see why influencers take pains to address each source when going head-to-head with a profound and persistent problem. Leave out one source, and you're likely to diminish your chances for success. As of this writing, there are only a few dozen Guinea worm cases left in the world. This remarkable feat was accomplished because Hopkins and his team have helped villagers learn to engage all six sources of influence in order to foster the three vital behaviors. It's astounding when you think that a few intrepid influencers have been able to engage tens of millions in order to eradicate a disease for which there is no cure. The Guinea worm's defeat will not have come through medical science but rather through social science.

Throughout the remainder of this book—to demonstrate how the six sources can be applied in combination—we explore what Dr. Hopkins and a host of other influencers have done with each of these influence tools to create rapid, profound, and sustainable behavior change. For example, we'll apply the six sources to achieving influence in changing harmful social norms, lowering school dropout rates, and improving workplace safety. We'll ask you to pick a challenge of your own and read each of the six chapters with that problem in mind. Then fashion your own six-source influence strategy. Do it correctly, and like Dr. Hopkins and dozens of other successful influencers, you'll solve problems that have had you and others stumped for years.

## A LA CARTE IS OKAY TOO

Don't feel guilty if you get a single great idea from a chapter and decide to use it without addressing all six sources of influence. Much of the time you're just trying to persuade someone to attend a meeting, and you don't need to pull out the full influencer model and address all six sources.

For these simpler influence challenges, feel free to use ideas "a la carte" and see how they work. You don't always have to use all six sources of influence to create change. However, when simpler efforts fail, use the full model to diagnose the reason and to figure out how to supplement your effort to achieve greater success.

# 4

# Help Them Love What They Hate

## PERSONAL MOTIVATION

*Hard work pays off in the future. Laziness pays off now.*

*—Steven Wright*

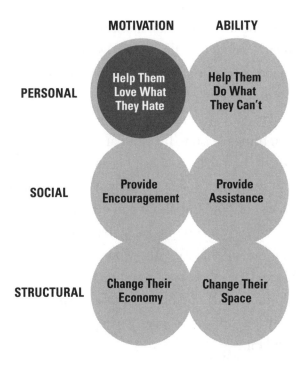

We'll start our exploration of the six sources of influence by examining tactics that address the first source, *personal motivation*. This important source of influence answers the question: Is the vital behavior intrinsically pleasurable or painful?

We'll start here because the first problem influencers often face is that good behaviors feel bad while bad behaviors feel good. For example, to eradicate the dreaded Guinea worm disease we mentioned earlier, change agents have to get 3 million people who are suffering the terrible agony associated with an emerging worm to avoid doing the one thing that would bring them immediate relief—soaking their infected limbs in the water. How could you possibly hope to convince others to do something so painful and difficult?

But it's not just Guinea worm disease eradication that demands that people find a way to do what they don't like doing. Think about it. The vast majority of the intractable influence problems we face or the stretch goals that we routinely miss are made more daunting because bad things are fun and good things aren't. The AIDS virus, for example, has been perniciously successful because the behaviors associated with its transmission bring pleasure. In a similar vein, tens of thousands of people die in hospitals each year because healthcare workers don't always wash their hands properly. Why? In part because it's tedious and boring. But also it can even be painful to do it for the eighty-seventh time in a day. Bathing chapped hands with alcohol isn't all that fun. And when it comes to influencer Danny Meyer, the New York restaurateur, he has to find a way to help thousands of employees take pleasure in going to extraordinary lengths to serve clients who are sometimes unruly or even petulant.

Is such a thing even possible? Can you help others *want* to do something that they currently *don't want* to do? Is it possible to help others learn to love what they presently hate? Let's take a look.

## TUESDAY AFTERNOON AT DELANCEY STREET

It's 3:17 Tuesday afternoon. Terri, a convicted felon, is carrying a CD loaded with financial data from the accounting office to the Delancey Street Restaurant. The manager asked her to bring it over ASAP, so she logged into her computer, burned the data onto the disk, and headed for the restaurant.

What surprises Terri is how quickly her feet are moving. She can't recall the last time they moved this fast. From the time she was nine, she had perfected a purposefully casual gait. She took great pride in her "I'm okay/you suck" approach to life. No matter that this attitude had landed her in jail for most of her adolescent years. No matter that it had earned her a manslaughter conviction after someone looked at her sideways in a bar. Nobody was going to tell her what to do. Nobody.

So why is Terri walking so fast now? It's been 19 months since she was offered a place at Delancey Street rather than serving her last five years in prison. Every semester, Terri has attended Delancey's graduation ceremony. It's a grand gathering where all 500 residents of the San Francisco campus crowd into the main hall to celebrate each other's progress. The first two times Terri was recognized for her accomplishments, she stared at the floor and ignored whatever they were saying about her. *"Who cares that I now know how to set a stupid table? This is all a pointless game, and I'm not playing it!"* When the applause for Terri had died down, she walked back to her chair, unaffected.

But last week they talked about her diploma and her promotion to crew boss. She looked over at Dr. Silbert, who was waving her arms and barking out Terri's amazing accomplishment. Terri made the mistake of listening to what Silbert said—just for a second. Then came the wave of applause. Terri looked around the room and caught the eyes of a few of her crew members. Then she looked quickly back down at the floor. Her legs felt weak when she walked back to her chair. "I'm not sure what that is," she mumbled to herself. "I'm probably just hungry." She ate a candy bar.

Now as Terri rushes to the restaurant, she looks down again, only this time at her legs. They're moving so fast it's as if they have a mind of their own. And then she lifts her hand to her cheek and feels something wet. *"I don't do this. What the hell is this?"* Terri is crying.

## MAKE PAIN PLEASURABLE

So, what has happened to Terri at this tender moment of an ongoing transformation? As Terri explained, she realized in that instant that she was feeling emotions she had never felt before. She was taking pleasure in accomplishing something. She was finding joy in her work. Better still, she has learned to care about something. In Terri's own words, "After thinking about it all afternoon, I finally realized, I was crying because *I cared.* I cared that I got the disk to Lionel. I cared."

If that's true, if Terri has found a way to take pleasure from something that she had previously disliked, what might your average person learn from this? For example, what mysterious trick might you pull in order to help your son enjoy doing his chores? Could this same magic potion help a team *enjoy* the work involved in reducing errors to below 3.4 per million? And can you use Terri's mystical elixir to make eating mini carrots as enjoyable as wolfing down a slice of chocolate cream pie?

Actually, people do learn ways to take pleasure from almost any activity, even if the activity isn't inherently satisfying. Psychiatrist M. Scott Peck makes this point rather bluntly: "Just because a desire or behavior is natural, does not mean it is . . . unchangeable. . . . It is also natural . . . to never brush our teeth. Yet we teach ourselves to do the unnatural. Another characteristic of human nature—perhaps the one that makes us more human—is our capacity to do the unnatural, to transcend and hence transform our own nature."

We're extending this argument even further. Humans don't merely find ways to act unnaturally. They find ways to enjoy activities that aren't inherently enjoyable. Depending on your point of view, hand washing in a hospital can feel like either a tedious distraction or a sacred duty. Finishing tasks on time can feel like either a bureaucratic bore or a demonstration of integrity. Changing a baby's diaper can feel like either a gruesome chore or a precious moment. The question is, how can you help vital behaviors feel like the latter rather than the former?

Influencers use four tactics to help people love what they hate:

1. Allow for choice.
2. Create direct experiences.
3. Tell meaningful stories.
4. Make it a game.

## Influence This

*A man convinced against his will, is of the same opinion still.*

—Benjamin Franklin

As part of a worldwide search to discover how influencers deal with a deficit of *personal motivation*, we found ourselves at the

Shake Shack in Madison Square Park. While it's true we were hankering for a burger, our primary errand was to see how the leader of one of Danny Meyer's more casual eating establishments is able to maintain extreme levels of customer service—in a burger place, no less.

Imagine that you are the manager of this busy burger joint. You've got an employee named Biff who just isn't into the whole customer-serving thing. You've been reminding him, coaching him, and even pleading with him to greet customers, thoroughly clean tables, and in other ways improve the guest experience. But today you look over the patio eating area where you see five filthy tables, and then your eyes land on Biff, who is sitting at a table, stuffing his face with French fries, and sending a text message. What will you do? Think about it. If you had to craft one sentence to influence Biff, what would it be?

**Read Your Lips.**   Now, examine your sentence. What method of influence did you employ? If you're like most of us, your sentence was some form of nag, guilt, or threat. Generally when we face a problem like Biff, we make an automatic assumption that he just doesn't care. In other words, we assume the problem is that he's simply not motivated because he takes no pleasure from doing the work. Then, without even realizing it, we make a second mental leap. We assume that the reason he's not motivated is because of some moral defect.

That may sound harsh, but think about it for a moment. When a doctor fails to wash his hands, we typically assume, "He's just concerned about his own convenience." Similarly, when Biff fails to exert himself for customers, we conclude, "He's just lazy." We attribute the problem not just to a simple oversight but to nothing less than a character flaw. And finally, when we do make this rather harsh diagnosis, we then respond with the only tool that might affect such a recalcitrant miscreant: coercion.

This proclivity to attribute others' worst behavior to some underlying character flaw is so common that psychologists have given it a special name. It's referred to as the *fundamental attribution error.* This is the belief that people do what they do merely because they enjoy it: "Why did that bozo just cut me off in traffic? Because he *wanted* to get where he wanted to go and didn't care about me! In fact, he probably enjoyed it." Whenever others cause us inconvenience or pain, we have a natural tendency to suspect they have selfish motives coupled with malicious intentions.

That's where influencers depart from the pack. Influencers are far more reluctant to conclude that others enact unhealthy behaviors simply because of a moral defect. Rather, they suspect the misbehavior might be caused by something less severe. In fact, they think the misbehavior may actually be curable. In their view, others don't suffer from a moral defect but rather, from *moral slumber.* The problem is *not* that these people are incapable of caring about others. It's that they aren't *thinking* about others—at that particular moment.

In other words, my neighbor who just survived a heart attack isn't eating the "Death by Chocolate" dessert (aptly named) because he's impulsive and doesn't care about surviving to raise his children. He's doing it because in this moment he isn't thinking about the relationship between his current consumption and his future relationship with his children. Similarly, the doctor who fails to wash her hands between patients may not be uncaring about patients. It could be that in this moment she's not thinking about germs and infections. She's thinking about examining a condition or perhaps even comforting a family member.

So if the problem with Biff is not moral defect, but moral slumber, what can you do to wake him up? How can you infuse a crucial moment—one in which he can act in a way to better serve customers (but in which it feels like he is just cleaning up a mess)—with moral significance?

## TACTIC 1. ALLOW FOR CHOICE

> *Your "yes" means nothing if you can't say "no." There can be no commitment if there is no choice.*
>
> *—Peter Block*

We've placed *allow for choice* at the top of our list of strategies because it is the gateway to all other methods of influencing personal motivation. Compulsion first replaces then erases motivation. You can never hope to engage people's commitment if they don't have permission to say no.

Think about how *you* yourself respond when people try to remove your agency. Your natural reaction is to resist. One of the deepest human drives stems from the desire to retain our will. The history of civilization frequently demonstrates that we would rather lose our lives than surrender our freedom. It almost doesn't matter how small the encroachment on our agency; we've been known to go to war over it.

Now, in principle this concept is easy to understand, but in practice it flies in the face of our most powerful impulses. When others appear to be willfully misbehaving, our native reaction is to nag, guilt, or threaten them.

"Biff! Get back to work!"

This knee-jerk response to coerce others into embracing our version of right living rarely works. In fact, the more we push others to comply, the less it works. This is particularly true with individuals who are *addicted* to their wrong behavior. They have already suffered through the impassioned speeches of their loved ones, listened to the clever podcasts from the experts, and squirmed in their pew as their minister has harangued them for their self- and other-defeating actions. And yet they continue in their weak and evil ways.

Do you really think your piled-on plea is going to get them to turn the corner? Most people do—even professionals. Turn on the TV and watch as degreed TV psychologists work with troubled addicts of all types. They start with gentle instruction, move to pleading, and end up with harsh "tell it like it is" lectures—while the audience hisses and boos. Switch to another channel and you'll find a competing television psychologist who uses the ultimate pile-on tactic. Since pleading doesn't appear to be working with their competitors, why not try an "intervention"? You know, bring in a whole host of friends and relatives who will take turns haranguing, shaming, and threatening? That'll work.

Lest we become convinced of our own innocence in this matter, consider our own history of verbal persuasion. Perhaps you have a grown child who comes to family events late—every single time. And when she walks in the door late, you say: "It's about time you got here!"—every single time. Or whenever your spouse bites into a fatty dessert, you give him the evil eye. Maybe when your neighbor rides by on her bike without wearing a helmet, you shout "Can you afford to crush your brain? I can't!" And then you smile as if making a joke. None of these tactics work for us, and yet we repeat them. Some call this insanity—applying the same tactic and expecting a new result—but a kinder explanation would be that we're desperate.

We want to convince others to change, but we have only one set of strategies—nag, guilt, and threaten. And since they're all we have, we use them over and over.

## William Points the Way

*I am not a teacher but an awakener.*

—*Robert Frost*

Fortunately, not everyone follows his or her natural proclivity to coerce others into changing. For instance, Dr. William Miller is an influence expert who has found a way to help addicts *want* to change without so much as a whisper of lecture. He knows how to transform from a lecturer who's trying to instill moral uprightness in others into an alarm sounder who helps awaken others from their moral slumber.

Dr. Miller stumbled onto this extraordinary technique by asking a simple research question: "What's better for addicts—more therapy or less?" Mental health professionals held their collective breath as he tallied his data, then went into paroxysms of denial when he announced that the length of time therapy lasted was irrelevant. Next he asked, "Is there one therapeutic technique that works better than others?" He found that the method didn't matter much either.

After offending almost everyone in his field by undermining the apparently irrelevant distinctions upon which people build careers, Miller stumbled onto an interesting finding. He found a distinction that *did* matter. It had to do less with what the counselor did than with what the counselor *didn't do*.

A reigning but inaccurate assumption in counseling—as evidenced by the TV gurus we referred to earlier—is that confrontation motivates change. Miller learned that forcing people to face their demons—and their friends, colleagues, and therapists who hated those demons—didn't work. In fact, in one study, he found that confrontation actually *increased* alcoholic bingeing. This led Miller in a different direction. He began to explore the opposite. What if the counselor merely helped patients figure out what *they* wanted rather than what their fed-up friends wanted?

With the new question, Miller discovered that the best way to help individuals align their behavior with their deepest motives was to stop trying to control their thoughts and behaviors. You must replace judgment with empathy, and lectures with questions. If you do so, you gain influence. The instant you stop trying to impose your agenda on others, you eliminate the fight for control. You end unnecessary battles over whose view of the world is correct.

This discovery led Miller to develop an influence method called *motivational interviewing*. Through a skillful use of open and nondirective questions, the counselor helps others reach their own conclusions about the values that are most important to them and the changes that might be required for them to live according to their values. When you ask thought-provoking questions and then listen while others talk, they discover on their own what they must do. Then, propelled by their own aspirations and beliefs, they make the necessary changes.

Dozens of studies have shown Miller's approach to be effective in helping people find the will to step up to the uncomfortable vital behaviors involved in recovering from alcoholism, smoking, drug addiction, HIV risk behaviors, and diet failures—and to stick to their healthy commitments. The additional good news is that the power of motivational interviewing isn't limited to therapeutic settings. Smart leaders accomplish the same results with everything from safety to cost cutting to productivity—when they replace dictates with dialogue.

For example, Ralph Heath, now president of Lockheed Martin Aeronautics, was tasked by the company to move the fifth-generation F-22 fighter jet from drawing board to production floor in 18 months. To do so, he had to engage 4,500 engineers and technicians and change their view of what it took to invent things. Heath had to convince them that results mattered more than ideas (a tough sell with engineers) and that engineering needed to bow to production (an even tougher sell).

So Heath didn't sell; he listened. He spent weeks interviewing employees at all levels. He tried to understand their needs, frustrations, and aspirations. When he finally began sharing directives, he framed them in ways that honored the needs, concerns, and goals of those he had interviewed. His influence didn't result from merely confronting problems but from listening to people and then framing the change process in their terms. The now legendary turnaround of the F-22 began when Heath helped people discover what they really wanted and how it related to corporate objectives—rather than simply issuing orders.

What William Miller teaches us is that a change of heart can't be imposed; it can only be chosen. People are capable of making enormous sacrifices when they have the agency to act on their own. For instance, healthcare professionals have known for decades that if you give patients control of their own IV-administered painkillers, they'll use less than when the painkillers are provided by a nurse. Give people a choice, and they'll step up to the plate. On the other hand, they'll resist compulsion on pain of death. Try to keep drugs from them, and they'll demand *more*.

Ginger Graham, the CEO of the medical devices company Guidant, learned this in a crisis. After the company introduced a new cardiovascular stent, sales went through the roof. Graham described this scenario in her April 2002 article for the *Harvard Business Review* titled, "If You Want Honesty, Break Some Rules." Almost overnight, good news turned into bad news as demand for the stent far outstretched supply. And all this hit as the holidays were approaching.

Executives figured that just meeting demand until new sources of production could come online would require three-shift workdays and seven-day workweeks. Graham could have simply mandated the work and required people to fill their obligations, but she knew that wouldn't work. Not only was it unfair to the employees to force this family-unfriendly schedule on them when they deserved time off, but it would also provoke resentment and just might hurt productivity.

So instead, Graham asked for help. At an all-company meeting, she praised the work that had brought about the wonderful success. She shared the sales data. She read success stories from doctors who were using the stent to avoid bypass surgery and save patients' lives. She then extrapolated the sales data and showed how many unmet needs would result if supply couldn't be stepped up substantially. And then she made a request: "We have the chance to do something [for patients and for ourselves] that no company has ever done in the history of our industry. We have an obligation to rise to the challenge. And if you'll rise to the challenge, we'll do all we can to make your lives easier during the tough times."

Within half an hour, employees had made a list of all the things management could do to help them through the holidays—including shop for their presents, wrap them, supply late-night taxis, bring in pizza, and so on. And with that, employees made a pact with management. Production hit new records, and the product was available on time for all patients who needed it. Total sales almost tripled in one quarter. Employees earned nice bonuses.

More importantly, the employees who went through this experience felt as if they were part of something special. Something important. A moral quest. And all because their leader knew better than to mandate a plan and, instead, allowed others to choose for themselves. When you swap coercive methods with personal choices, you open up the possibility of influencing even the most addictive and highly entrenched behaviors by gaining access to one of the most powerful human motivations: the power of the committed heart.

People can actually love engaging in behaviors that otherwise might seem obnoxious. But only if they're allowed the psychological freedom to choose them.

## TACTIC 2. CREATE DIRECT EXPERIENCES

> *That learning which thou gettest by thy own observation and experience, is far beyond that which thou gettest by precept; as the knowledge of a traveler exceeds that which is got by reading.*
>
> —*Thomas à Kempis*

We've just suggested that the first tactic for helping people find greater personal motivation is to avoid demotivating them by inviting choice rather than giving orders. With this in mind, let's return to our dirty doctor and reluctant employee. Obviously allowing them to make choices resulted in the one passing germs from patient to patient and the other cooling his heels and feeding his face rather than caring for customers. What next?

As we suggested earlier, people often make poor choices because they prefer the short-term benefits of their bad behavior over the long-term benefits of doing the right thing—chocolate today (love it for sure) versus the unknown likelihood of a stroke 40 years from now. Hmm. Pass the cake.

The most powerful way to help people recognize, feel, and believe in the long-term implications of their choices is to get out of their way and let them experience them firsthand. As Kempis suggests, travel trumps reading. And to no one's surprise, influencers help people go out into the cold, hard world and experience the consequences of their choices.

For example, healthcare safety expert Dr. Don Berwick once taught at a Harvard seminar for CEOs of some of the largest hospital systems in the world. The list of attendees was a literal Who's Who of patient safety. These leaders were sipping lattes, jotting notes, and in other ways having a delightful seminar experience as they examined ways to improve the overall healthcare experience—including eliminating costly hospital errors. And although it was a stimulating *intellectual* experience, Berwick had seen this happen so many times before that he knew the stimulating-lecture format would influence *no one*. All would return home, say they had a great time, e-mail their notes to their management team, and generate no real change.

"Then I had an idea," Dr. Berwick told us. "On the spur of the moment. I said, 'Look, before you come to the session next month, find an injured patient, someone who was harmed while in your hospital. And *you* investigate the injury. Do not delegate it. You find out what happened and come back and report it.'"

Berwick was unsure what would happen. Would the CEOs complete the assignment? Would they return with diagrams or data dumps? Or would it awaken passion?

Berwick's answer was emphatic: "Unbelievable!" he said. "I didn't know this would happen, but these people came back—I'm talking three-piece suit, high-end executives—and one by one they choked up and cried as they told their stories. They described the illusions they had about their systems and how fallible they now realized they were." As a result of this singular, poignant, firsthand experience, many of these leaders not only became champions for patient safety but they also remained champions *for the rest of their careers.*

What happened here? Like all of our influencers, Berwick operated on the belief that the problem with these leaders was not some moral deficiency. These were mothers and fathers, brothers and sisters—all of whom were capable of caring about human pain and suffering. However, the healthcare world around them shielded them from the human pain and suffering caused by the current behavior of their employees. Pain, suffering, and depravation had been turned into numbers, statistics, and charts—which sometimes inform but never inspire. So what did Berwick do?

Dr. Berwick trusted that if he set senior leaders loose inside an experience that would allow them to connect with the human consequences of their hospital's current behavior, they would truly *care.* Transform numbers into names, statistics, faces, and charts into human conditions, and everything would change. What seemed like an interesting abstraction would become a moral imperative. And it did.

With this in mind, it should surprise no one to learn that the gold standard of tactics for engaging personal motivation is *direct experience.* Let people feel, see, and touch things for themselves. Everywhere we've traveled we've seen influencers develop clever ways of helping connect people experientially with the consequences of their choices. And when they do, they change. They begin to feel differently about new and better behaviors.

## ACT LIKE AN INFLUENCER

Mike Wildfong, a general manager at TI Automotive, wanted to build a greater passion for workplace safety. To do so, he invited a work team to join him on a field trip. The team visited a former coworker who had been injured on the job. This man and his family were struggling to make ends meet, living on his disability check.

The team spent the day fixing the roof of the family's mobile home, building a swing set for their children, and laying sod around his yard. By taking part in a field trip, team members came face-to-face with the consequences of poor workplace safety. This volunteer day not only helped the injured worker and his family but also transformed the team's commitment to workplace safety. For this group, safety rules became more than rules. They became moral commitments.

### Invite People to Try It

Getting people to create their own direct experience is a powerful way to help them connect to genuine human consequences and ultimately find moral significance in vital behaviors. Field trips can do that. When you go out into the world on a field trip, so to speak, you can see firsthand what's happening. Rather than simply hearing impassioned speeches or clever words (that can be easily discounted), you see for yourself what's actually happening. You can feel the pain associated with the consequences you observe—all powerful tools in creating personal motivation.

But there's more.

Personal experience can be an equally important way to remove fears that keep people from doing the right thing. As you encourage others to create their own direct experiences—taking field trips, interviewing similarly addicted people, and so forth—it can be tough to get individuals to take that first step. This is true for a couple of reasons. First, people tend to resist new behaviors because they're crystal clear about what they'll lose by changing but uncertain about what they'll gain. Like it or not, when it comes to change, humans tend to overvalue what they're losing while undervaluing what they gain. So we don't eagerly embrace the verbally recommended strategy.

This cognitive limitation is worsened by the fact that we humans are notoriously bad at predicting how we'll feel in new circumstances—for example, predicting what will make us happier.

In fact, psychologist Daniel Gilbert has made a career out of demonstrating that human beings are downright awful at predicting their own likes and dislikes. For example, most research subjects strongly believe that another $30,000 a year in income would make them much happier. They feel equally strongly that adding a 30-minute walk to their daily routine would be of trivial import. Yet Dr. Gilbert's research suggests that the added income is far less likely to produce an increase in happiness than is the addition of a regular walk.

Dr. Mimi Silbert confronts this inability to predict happiness every single day. It's her job to ask new residents at Delancey Street to do things that, to them, sound painful, boring, or both. For example, lifetime criminals have no idea what a law-abiding life might be like. When they do try to imagine it, they make some very predictable errors. They assume that it will be very much like their present life—minus the fun. You know, cleaning toilets while giving up the excitement of crime or the stimulation of drugs. They're unable to imagine the pleasure associated with getting a raise, owning a home, or gaining any of a thousand other perks of a law-abiding life they've never experienced.

Silbert could spend a lot of time lecturing about the Delancey vision. "Trust me," she could say, "you're gonna love it. By the time you're out of here, you'll have a high school diploma. You'll be literate. You'll have gone to concerts and museums. You'll have mastered three different trades and tried a dozen others. You'll have a whole new set of friends. Just sign here."

Right.

These arguments are easy to make but hard to sell because they involve verbal persuasion, and the people you're talking to are very unlikely to understand the language you're using. You're describing activities and outcomes for which they have no frame of reference, and you're then asking them to make immediate sacrifices (no gang, no drugs, no freedom) in order to achieve them.

It won't work. It can't work.

Silbert realizes that it'll take awhile before new residents *personally experience* the benefits of a new life. She explains, "After they get their high school equivalent, we offer two-year college degrees through San Francisco State University. Some even get a BA. But early on, residents hate the discipline that it takes to study. We also go with them to museums, operas, and plays. Oh, believe me, they whine like crazy. They don't want to go. But I just keep saying, 'You can hate opera, but not until after you've *been to an opera.*' Coming in, our residents hate everything. But of course they've never done *anything!*"

So Dr. Silbert simply plods forward, demanding that residents try studying for a class, attending the opera, mentoring another student, and so forth. Experience has taught her that if residents try new behaviors, they end up liking many, if not most, of them. Okay, perhaps few become opera fans. Nevertheless, over 90 percent come to enjoy dozens of behaviors they never would have imagined they'd one day enjoy.

Silbert sticks with the strategy of asking residents to "just try it" until every single one has something similar to Terri's Tuesday experience in which she suddenly realizes that she now feels wonderful about something she once didn't understand or care about an iota. Dr. Silbert says it happens to virtually everyone at Delancey. In fact, the residents transform so many aspects of their lives that there comes a day when they become vastly different from the people who first walked in the front door at Delancey. They transform into people they've scarcely met before. They care. They take satisfaction in accomplishment. They've discovered the intrinsic satisfaction that comes with living a law-abiding life. And Silbert helps get them there by encouraging them to "just try it."

## TACTIC 3. TELL MEANINGFUL STORIES

The challenge in getting people to create direct experiences is that it's tough to create them for all of the people you need to influence. If you have few resources and limited time, yet still

## ACT LIKE AN INFLUENCER

Holding a job can't be fun, right? That's why they call it work. Many young people don't expect to like work, but then they quickly change their minds once they "just try it."

One of the authors has had several high school–age nieces and nephews spend summers with him and their auntie in Park City, Utah. Park City is fun in the summer, with lots of hiking and cycling, but there's a catch. In order to play in the mountains, these young people also have to work at a job for 40 hours a week—and it's a volunteer job, where they serve wounded vets and disabled children. A typical job involves belaying at one end of a climbing rope, while the disabled vet on the other end struggles up a climbing wall.

Most of these high schoolers rebel at the very thought of volunteering for such work. However, by the end of the first week, they can't wait to show up for their shift. They see the positive impacts they are having, and they love the feelings of fulfillment.

have a need to solve a personal motivation problem, what's an influencer to do? Plus, not everyone will attempt an action simply because you tell them to "just try it." Others won't buy in to your verbal persuasion; they won't do what it takes to create a direct experience, and your invitations to "just try it" will fall on deaf ears. Now what? Stated in the terms we've developed so far, is there something you can do that lies between verbal persuasion and direct experience?

## Snakes on a Campus

To answer this important question, we'll visit the chief theorist behind many of the influence principles we're about to discover: Dr. Albert Bandura. One of Bandura's many contributions to the science of influence was his remarkable work in the 1970s with phobics. His insights shined light on dealing with unmotivated—even terrified—subjects.

When Albert Bandura came on the phobic scene, the common treatment consisted of years on a couch. The accepted theory at the time was that the phobias originated in some critical childhood experience and the only way out of them was protracted efforts to resurrect and resolve those memories. Bandura took a different view. Rather than dredge up the past, he wondered if a more direct route would be to create influential, firsthand experiences in the present.

Phobics were a great test of some of Bandura's new theories of influence because they tended to resist every effort to verbally persuade them of the inaccuracy of their beliefs. He learned, as we suggested earlier, that when you try to convince others simply with words, they may not trust you, so they won't follow your advice. Either they believe you don't have their best interest in mind and what you're suggesting will not serve them well, or they don't trust your expertise. You may want what's best for them, but your ideas are wrong and will get them into trouble. Either way, verbal persuasion has feet of clay.

To find a different influence tool, Bandura began with a search for research subjects by running an ad in the *Palo Alto News* asking readers who had a paralyzing fear of snakes to descend into the basement of the psychology department to get cured. He was hoping that at least a dozen subjects would respond. Despite the creepy tone of the ad, hundreds of people

made their way to the research site. All had been seriously debilitated by their unreasonable fear of things that slither. Most had
horrible nightmares; many were veritable shut-ins; and since
their irrational fear extended to even harmless garter snakes, the
possible subjects suffered endless ridicule and indignity. It's little
wonder that they showed up for therapy—they were desperate.

Like any good influencer, Bandura began by defining the
result he wanted to achieve and how he would measure it. Success, he decided, would be achieved when subjects could sit
with a six-foot red-tailed boa constrictor draped across their lap.
Could a goal be clearer?

When they began, none of the subjects would so much as
enter the room containing a snake in a covered terrarium. In
fact, Bandura's very description of the objective caused some to
pass out.

Given these challenging circumstances, Bandura resisted
any effort to rush or coerce the subjects. At every step of the
way he offered options and allowed them to choose. If people
wanted to opt out, they could. If they wanted a simpler task, he
would devise one. They were in control at all times.

Bandura's strategy began with the "in between" influence
technique everyone had been searching for. He provided a
secondhand experience by asking subjects to watch a research
assistant handle a snake. He invited subjects to watch from the
doorway of the room—or if that was still too difficult, to watch
through glass—as the assistant walked into the room containing the snake, took a look at it, opened the terrarium, petted the
snake, and finally removed the boa and placed it on his or her lap.

After the subjects watched someone else handle the snake,
Dr. Bandura invited them to have a direct experience. First
they would simply walk into the room. But this wasn't enough

to put everyone at ease. Some of the subjects asked for protective gear—hockey goalie gloves, a baseball catcher chest protector and mask, and so on. Now, dressed like samurai warriors, subjects entered the room and stood next to the enclosed tank. Gradually, after several tries they worked up to removing the terrarium cover and then quickly retreated from the room. No harm done. After a bit more experience, they finally touched the snake. Later still they touched the snake without gloves and so forth. Eventually subjects sat in the room by themselves with the six-foot boa constrictor draped across their lap.

And now for the real miracle: the entire process took only three hours! People who had been debilitated most of their lives by a paralyzing fear were completely cured in a single morning. And the results lasted a lifetime. Once the phobics had a personal and positive interaction with the snake, they never regressed, and it improved their lives forever.

In Dr. Bandura's own words, "It was surprising to see how liberating it was for the subjects to be freed from the phobia. Their whole life seemed to open up before them now that they didn't have to worry about snakes. In addition, they gained confidence about their ability to make personal changes. Since they had been able to conquer their fear of snakes, perhaps now they could overcome other problems."

Take note of the influence technique we've just seen demonstrated. Subjects couldn't be talked into the room with the snake in order to create direct experience (without kicking and screaming), but they did choose to watch someone else interact with the snake. For the typical phobic, it was as if it were happening to them personally. The person was right in front of them, they couldn't deny what was happening, and the experience felt real and vibrant (many subjects actually hyperventilated). In short, Bandura had found the in-between tactic. He learned to create a vicarious experience, and through this method he helped subjects to the point where they could create direct experience and eventually become cured.

## How to Tell Influential Stories

> *Over the years I have become convinced that we learn best—and change—from hearing stories that strike a chord within us. . . . Those in leadership positions who do not grasp or use the power of stories risk failure for their companies and for themselves.*
>
> —John Kotter

Although it's true that Dr. Bandura had demonstrated the power of vicarious experience as a way of helping others see the world as it is, it still leaves us with the question of how your everyday person could use a similar technique—without the aid of an entire research team and university.

Dr. Don Berwick, the influencer we referred to earlier who aimed at saving a hundred thousand lives, shows the way. He walks to a podium to address an audience of healthcare leaders. They've been listening to speakers all morning and look a bit lethargic. Berwick isn't about speeches. He's about influence. He wants people to leave this room *behaving* differently. He wants them to take steps to ensure they and their colleagues save lives from the half dozen medical mistakes that most often kill or injure patients. In the allotted time, he can't have his audience of 800 investigate an injury. So what does he do? He tells them about Josie King.

Josie King was a little girl who loved to dance. She was 18 months old, had brown eyes and light brown hair, and she had just learned to say, "I love you." In January 2001 Josie stepped into a hot bath and burned herself badly. Her parents rushed her to Johns Hopkins Hospital where she was admitted into the pediatric intensive care unit. Much to her parents' relief, Josie recovered quickly. She was transferred to the intermediate care floor and was expected to be released within days.

But Josie's mom noticed that something was wrong. "Every time she saw a drink, she would scream for it, and I thought this was strange. I was told not to let her drink. While a nurse and I gave her a bath, she sucked furiously on a washcloth." Josie's mom told the nurse Josie was thirsty, and she asked her to call a doctor. The nurse assured her that everything was okay. She asked another nurse to check on Josie, but this nurse confirmed that everything was fine.

Josie's mom called back twice during the night and was at her daughter's bedside by 5:30 the next morning. By then Josie was in crisis. In her mother's words, "Josie's heart stopped as I was rubbing her feet. Her eyes were fixed, and I screamed for help. I stood helpless as a crowd of doctors and nurses came running into her room. I was ushered into a small room with a chaplain." Two days before her scheduled release, Josie had died of thirst. Despite her mother's repeated pleas for help, this sweet little girl died of misused narcotics and dehydration.

Now that medical mistakes have a face, a name, and a soul, now that the moral content of his topic is present, Dr. Berwick digs into the logic and order of the topic.

### What Influencers Do

The cynic in all of us can sit in Dr. Berwick's audience and wonder about the efficacy of a simple story. Certainly the emotions it evokes are ephemeral, right? We've all been in "motivational" sessions where we've felt a potent sense of conviction about doing something, only to have it wash off hours after the speech.

Although it clearly takes more than a story to drive change, when used in combination with other influence methods, storytelling can be a powerful tool in anyone's influence repertoire. In fact, the most convincing field experiment in the entire history of behavioral science research makes exactly this point. In 1993, Martha Swai changed the behavior of an entire nation by simply telling a story.

Swai was the program manager for Radio Tanzania. Her goal was to change the behavior of her fellow Tanzanians in order to strengthen families, improve the lot of women, and save lives from HIV/AIDS. Fortunately for her, televisions were not widely available in Tanzania, so, as a program manager for a radio station, she had access to millions of ears every single night. How could she leverage this tool?

Swai hired the best dramatic writers she could find. Then she and her team invited David Poindexter, a world's expert in *entertainment education,* to teach them how to craft a story for maximum influence. Swai understood that her task wasn't easy because those she was trying to influence held deep beliefs about how men should relate to women and about what causes AIDS and what cures it. For one, many thought that men could be cured of AIDS by having sex with a virgin.

When the time came to launch the radio show, disaster struck. Bureaucratic problems blocked Radio Tanzania transmission during the show's airtime to the large Dodoma region of central Tanzania. This programming barrier turned into a social science bonanza—as we'll shortly see.

In 1993 the show *Twende na Wakati* ("Let's Go with the Times") hit the airwaves. To demonstrate the cause and effect of AIDS, writers created a flamboyant, macho, and highly controversial truck driver named Mkwaju. He abused his wife, wanted only male children, drank excessively, engaged in unprotected sex with prostitutes along his route, and bragged about his escapades. His wife, Tutu (a model for female independence), eventually left him and succeeded in her own small business.

Over the course of many months, the philandering Mkwaju (who eventually died of AIDS) became so real to the listening audience that when the actor playing him went to a local vegetable market, villagers recognized his voice and women actually threw produce at him!

To see the emotional and behavioral impact firsthand, we interviewed several listening groups just outside Tanzania's capital city. One family group consisting of a father, mother, grandmother, aunt, and five grown children had religiously tuned in to the wild antics of Mkwaju and had been enormously affected. When we asked them exactly how the program had influenced them, the father explained that at first he had admired Mkwaju, but with time he concluded that the truck driver's reckless behaviors were causing pain to his wife, Tutu, and their children.

After tuning in to the show for several weeks, the father had come to sympathize with all the characters, and one day when sweet Tutu was hurt by her alcoholic husband, a light went on—his own wife was also suffering from similar treatment. Although this avid listener wasn't a truck-driving philanderer, he had abused alcohol. A part of him was Mkwaju. From that moment on he stopped abusing both alcohol and his family members. It seemed strange that this self-discovery would come through a contrived radio show, but as the transformed father finished his story, everyone in his family nodded in energetic agreement. He had truly changed.

This touching account, along with similar interviews, provided anecdotal evidence that *Twende na Wakati* was more than just a story. It created a poignant, believable vicarious experience. It didn't merely provoke emotions. It changed minds. It changed people's moral arithmetic about their choices in a way that led to lasting change. Or so it appeared in the interviews.

But is there more than just anecdotal support for the power of this influence strategy? The answer is yes, and we know with a certainty because *Twende na Wakati* was the first controlled national field experiment in history. Since the Dodoma region of Tanzania was excluded from the evening radio broadcasts, researchers could explore the effect of the vicarious models offered over the radio. From 1993 to 1995 all regions experienced a variety of HIV/AIDS interventions, but only half were exposed to the radio drama.

In their award-winning book *Combating AIDS: Communication Strategies in Action,* renowned social scientists Everett Rogers and Arvind Singhal report that one-fourth of the population in the broadcast area had modified its behavior in critical ways to avoid HIV, and they attributed the change in behavior to the influence of the program. The impact was so remarkable that the controlled experiment had to be stopped after two years in order to make the intervention available to everyone. Within a year, similar results were seen in Dodoma.

Rogers and Singhal proved with rare scientific certainty that exposing experimental subjects to believable models through powerful stories affected not only their thoughts and emotions but also their behavior. People who tuned in to *Twende na Wakati* were more likely to seek marital counseling, make better use of family planning, remain faithful to their spouses, and use protection than were their neighbors who didn't listen to the serial drama.

Change agents don't use stories to aim vicarious models only at audiences in the developing world. Readers may not be aware of how effectively the same methods have been deployed in the United States. Before David Poindexter (the founder and former president of Population Communications International) and his colleagues exported serial dramas to Africa, Poindexter met with Norman Lear—producer of popular TV sitcoms such as *All in the Family* and *Maude.* As part of their agenda to reduce population growth, Poindexter, Lear, and others routinely injected family planning messages into their programming.

It was no coincidence that in 1972, with 41 percent of those watching TV in America tuned in to his show, Lear created an episode ("Maude's Dilemma") in which the star—a middle-aged woman—announced that she was considering an abortion. This was the first time this topic was inserted into a primetime plot line, and it wasn't included by accident. Love it or hate it, it was part of a systematic plan of using compelling stories (complete with vicarious models) to influence social change. And according to public opinion surveys, it did just that, as have dozens of other programs that have since made use of poignant stories.

## Back to Biff

Storytelling isn't just for TV and radio. Time and again we watched influencers awaken people to the profound choices they were making by telling poignant, believable, and compelling stories that put a human face on people's actions. Independent of the industry—whether healthcare, IT, financial services, manufacturing, or telecommunications—leaders who helped build a sense of mission in their organizations were *always* storytellers.

---

### ACT LIKE AN INFLUENCER

While working with drivers for a gold mine in Ghana, the safety manager asked them to recall an accident or near accident they'd been involved in. He gave them 10 minutes to make a few notes, and then he asked them to tell the story of what had happened.

A volunteer raised his hand. "Can I tell my story?" he asked. "Sure," the manager replied. "Does it have a title?" The driver took off his hat, looked down at his hands and said, "Family man runs over and kills his neighbor's little girl." And big tears began to roll down his cheeks. This storytelling session immediately changed speeding from a legal to a moral issue.

---

However, when we decided to poke around Union Square Hospitality Group (USHG) restaurants, we thought we'd have to qualify our statement. Certainly you couldn't tell an emotional and touching tale about something as mundane as wiping down tables and cheerily greeting customers. Could you?

It turns out that storytelling is part of the DNA of USHG leaders. Earlier we retold Danny Meyer's story of the employee who tracked down a customer's purse. But that isn't where storytelling ends. Danny isn't the only one who tells engaging stories.

Here's what's likely to happen when Biff seems disengaged in the vital behaviors. His supervisor walks over to him and says, "Hey Biff, a few minutes ago a young mother walked into our patio area holding the hand of her three-year-old daughter. She set her daughter up on a chair and walked to the window to order their food. While her back was turned, her daughter began sweeping her hand back and forth across the table that was smeared with ketchup from a previous guest. Then she began licking her hand."

At this point, Biff cringes. He doesn't even wait for his boss to finish the *story*—but instead, he rushes to grab a rag and begins wiping down the tables.

What happened here? The supervisor made a connection. Rather than relying on verbal persuasion to nag, guilt, or threaten, she created a vicarious experience. She told a story that helped awaken Biff to the moral content of his actions. And that changed everything.

Now, is it possible that Biff may need more than this in order to become a hospitality zealot? Yes! The remaining chapters add just such richness. Nevertheless, the difference between influencers and the rest of us is that when influencers recognize that others aren't personally motivated to enact a vital behavior, they don't work *around* that problem. They work *through* it. They operate on the confidence that people are not morally defective, but morally asleep. When called for, they create vicarious experiences through telling compelling stories.

## TACTIC 4. MAKE IT A GAME

> *In every job that must be done, there is an element of fun.*
> *You find the fun, and snap! The job's a game.*
>
> —*Mary Poppins*

Let's look at still another way of transforming neutral or detestable vital behaviors into something enjoyable. Once again, an individual tries a new behavior but still doesn't like it all that much. Now what? Take hope from the fact that humans invest themselves in a wide variety of pursuits that, on the surface, don't look particularly engaging or rewarding. Yet somehow humans extract enjoyment from them. So, what's the trick?

It turns out that one of the keys to personal motivation lies in a force just barely outside the activity itself. It lies in the mastery of increasingly challenging goals. Mihaly Csikszentmihalyi, a researcher at Claremont Graduate School, has devoted his career to what he has come to call "flow," or the feeling of enjoyment that comes from losing yourself in an engrossing activity (something, he suggests, we all should be seeking with dogged determination).

Dr. Csikszentmihalyi has discovered that almost any activity can be made engaging if it involves reasonably challenging goals and clear, frequent feedback. These are the elements that turn a chore into something that feels more like a game. And we all like games. For example, imagine that you removed the scoreboard from a basketball court. How long would you expect fans to stick around without knowing the score? How long do you think the players would run breathlessly up and down the court? Much of what we do to transform intrinsically unpleasant behavior into something enjoyable is merely turning it into a game.

Consider the elements of an enjoyable game:

**Keeping score:** This action produces clear, frequent feedback that can transform tasks into accomplishments that, in turn, can generate intense satisfaction. The designers of many of today's video games have an intuitive feel for Dr. Csikszentmihalyi's research and have used it to create games that call for highly repetitive activities that end up being amazingly addictive as individuals strive for that next level of achievement.

**Competition:** Seeing numbers does more than provide data. It imbues the data with meaning: Am I doing better than *before*? (And certainly better is good.) Am I doing better than *others*? This element is more questionable (it can lead to unhealthy rivalry)—but to be honest, competition, especially with oneself, can help people take satisfaction from what would otherwise be a repetitive task.

**Constant improvement:** As you walk into fitness centers across the country, you'll note that many of the facilities' walls are papered with charts. A closer look reveals that each chart displays various members' personal progress. Some track weight. Others track measurements. Others track body mass indexes, bone densities, resting heart rates, and a whole host of other health indicators.

As you listen to experts talk with their clients—poring over the charts in detail—you'll often hear the word "slope": "The actual numbers," experts explain, "aren't as important as the overall slope. In what direction are you heading? You may not be improving at the rate you initially expected or you once achieved, but as long as you're headed in the right direction, time is your best friend." This also helps turn any regime into a game. Are you improving?

**Control:** Finally, game makers are careful to ensure that all earned points and rewards are in the participants' control. At work people often miss this element when their personal or team progress is folded into a larger, less successful unit's overall results. So employees lose any sense of control over their own contributions. Avoid this common mistake. Create and record measures over which individuals have complete control. Let them see the impact of their work. For many, the impact is far more rewarding than the job itself.

## SUMMARY: PERSONAL MOTIVATION

We often don't act in our long-term best interest because the short-term actions we currently enjoy are far more motivating than the remote and distant likelihood of suffering in the future. With persistent influence challenges, bad actions are generally real, fun, and now, whereas negative consequences are often fuzzy, maybe not so bad after all, and most certainly a long time off. To turn this around, influencers learn to help others love what they currently hate by allowing them choices, creating direct experiences, telling meaningful stories, and turning the tedious into a game.

# 5

# Help Them Do What They Can't

## PERSONAL ABILITY

*It's a funny thing, the more I practice the luckier I get.*

*—Arnold Palmer*

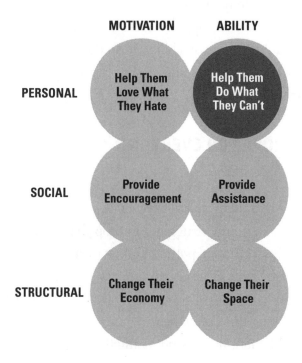

In Chapter 4 we examined strategies for tapping into personal values and emotions and, consequently, influencing vital behaviors. It's now time to examine source 2, *personal ability*. We, flighty human beings that we are, often forget this important source of influence, and corporate leaders are no exception For instance, managers frequently send employees to an intensive day of leadership training that inundates them with theories, models, and case studies—but the employees don't actually practice any of the skills being taught. Leaders mistakenly assume that *knowing* the training content and *doing* it are one and the same. Of course, they aren't the same. It's little wonder that participants frequently return from training and apply only a fraction of what they studied. When leaders and training designers combine too much motivation with too few opportunities to improve ability, they rarely produce change. Instead, they create resentment and depression.

Influencers take the opposite tack. They carefully invest in strategies that help increase ability. In so doing, they avoid trying to resolve ability problems by simply piling on one more motivational technique.

## THERE'S HOPE FOR EVERYONE

To see how easy it is to treat an ability problem as if it were actually due to a motivational deficiency, consider the case of Henry who is currently struggling to drop the 50 pounds he's added since his job started putting him on the road where, twice a week, he now eats at lovely restaurants—and packs it away. Henry has joined a team of coworkers who are collectively trying to lose weight (partly to keep their insurance costs in control and partly to feel better), but he's not doing that well. More specifically, one of Henry's vital behaviors—snacking on mini carrots rather than chocolate—is at risk. In fact, at this very moment, Henry is pulling the foil back on a partially eaten, two-pound chocolate bar. In Henry's defense, he didn't buy it. A colleague who knew of his deep affection for chocolate gave it to him. The tempting bar has been sitting on his desk for over a week.

Moments ago Henry decided to heft the hardy confection merely to see what two pounds felt like. When he did, he noticed that the adhesive holding the wrapper around the inner foil lining had failed. It appeared as if it were about to fall away, seductively revealing the beautiful red, shiny foil beneath it—the last defense before the chocolate itself.

Henry tugged at the wrapper playfully, and with almost no effort it came free. The next few seconds were almost a blur. Without thinking, Henry's hands peeled back the top flap of the foil and exposed the rich chocolate. In a rush, chocolate-filled childhood memories poured through his head as his fingers pried loose a single dark brown section—a modest, harmlessly small packet of pleasure. He brought the treat to his lips—and then it was over. The chocolate began its inexorable transformation from cocoa, fat, and sugar to cellulite.

Here's the problem. At the moment when Henry should be enjoying one of his secret pleasures, he's depressed. As he now gobbles down the chocolate, with each bite he is convinced that he has strayed from his diet because he lacks the proper strength of character. It's clear that he doesn't have moxie or willpower. In short, he's a weak person. Up until this sad indulgence, he had valiantly cut back on calories while sincerely promising himself to start an exercise regimen. This new, iron-willed Henry ruled for eight full days. And then the mere touch of the red foil lining brought him to ruin.

Henry wonders if he can overcome the genetic hand that he's been dealt. He has neither the self-discipline to diet nor the athletic prowess to exercise effectively. Surely he's doomed to a life of poor health. But then again, unbeknownst to Henry, a long line of research suggests that maybe he isn't doomed at all. There's a good chance that he can actually learn how to withstand the temptations of chocolate as well as how to improve his ability to exercise properly.

In fact, many of the stories Henry has been carrying in his head since he was a young man may be equally wrong. When his mother once told him that he wasn't exactly a gifted speaker and later when his father suggested that leadership "wasn't his thing," Henry believed that he hadn't been born with "the right stuff." He wasn't born to be an elite athlete; that's for certain. Later he learned that music wasn't his thing, and his interpersonal skills weren't all that strong. Later still he discovered that spending in excess, getting hooked on video games, and gorging on Swiss chocolate *were* his thing. But none of this is going to change because Henry, like all humans, can't fight genetics.

Fortunately, Henry is dead wrong. Henry is trapped in what Carol Dweck, a psychologist at Stanford, calls a "fixed mindset." If he believes he can't improve, then he won't even try, and he'll create a self-fulfilling prophecy. But Henry is in luck. Genes don't play the fatalistic role scholars once assumed they played in determining physical prowess, mental agility, and yes, even self-discipline. Characteristics that had long been described by scholars and philosophers alike as genetic gifts or lifelong personality traits appear to be learned, much the same way one learns to walk, talk, or whistle. That means that Henry doesn't need to accept his current status. He can adopt what Dweck refers to as a "growth mindset." Henry simply needs to learn how to develop a set of high-level learning skills and techniques that influencers use all the time. He needs to learn how to learn. Henry, like most of us, was actually born with the right stuff; he just hasn't figured out how to get it to work for him yet.

To illustrate this point, let's consider the lengthy hunt researchers conducted in a quest to find the all-important trait of self-discipline. Here was a personality trait worth studying. If the ability to withstand the alluring smell of chocolate or the siren call of hanging out with your buddies rather than studying for your night course—the ability to delay gratification—isn't a reflection of one's underlying character, then what is?

Professor Walter Mischel of Columbia University, curious about people's inability to withstand temptations, set out to explore this issue. Did certain humans have the right stuff while others didn't? And if so, did the right stuff affect lifelong performance? What Mischel eventually came to understand altered the psychological landscape forever.

## MUCH OF WILL IS SKILL

When Timmy, age four, sat down at the gray metal table in an experimental room in the basement of the psychology department, the child saw something that caught his interest. On the table was a marshmallow—the kind Timmy's mom put into his cup of hot chocolate. Timmy *really* wanted to eat the marshmallow.

The kindly man who brought Timmy into the room told him that he had two options. The man was going to step out for a moment. If Timmy wanted to eat the marshmallow, he could eat away. But if Timmy chose to wait a few minutes until the man returned, then Timmy could eat *two* marshmallows.

Then the man exited. Timmy stared at the tempting sugar treat, squirmed in his chair, kicked his feet, and in general tried to exercise self-control. If he could wait, he'd get two marshmallows! But the temptation proved too strong for little Timmy, so he finally reached across the table, grabbed the marshmallow, looked around nervously, and then shoved the spongy treat into his mouth. Apparently Timmy and Henry are kindred spirits.

Actually, Timmy was one of dozens of subjects Dr. Mischel and his colleagues studied for more than four decades. Mischel was interested in learning what percentage of his young subjects could delay gratification and what impact, if any, this character trait would have on their adult lives. Mischel's hypothesis was that children who were able to demonstrate self-control at a young age would enjoy greater success later in life because of that trait.

In this and many similar studies, Mischel followed the children into adulthood. He discovered that the ability to delay gratification had a more profound effect than many had originally predicted. Notwithstanding the fact that the researchers had watched the kids for only a few minutes, what they learned from the experiment was enormously telling. Children who had been able to wait for that second marshmallow matured into adults who were seen as more socially competent, self-assertive, dependable, and capable of dealing with frustrations; and they scored an average of 210 points higher on their SATs than people who gulped down the one marshmallow. The predictive power was truly remarkable.

Companion studies conducted over the next decade with people of varying ages (including adults) confirmed that individuals who exercise self-control achieve better outcomes than people who don't. For example, if high school students are good at exercising self-control, they experience fewer eating and drinking problems. University students with more self-control earn better grades, and married and working people have more fulfilling relationships and better careers. And as you might suspect, people who demonstrate low levels of self-control show higher levels of aggression, delinquency, health problems, and so forth.

Apparently, Mischel had stumbled onto the mother lode of personality traits. Kids who had been blessed with the innate capacity to withstand short-term temptations fared better throughout their entire lives. The fact that a four-year-old's one-time response to a sugary confection predicts lifelong results is at once exciting and depressing—depending on whether you are a "grabber" or a "delayer." You're either well fitted to take on the temptations of the world or doomed to a lifelong fate of enjoy now, pay later—as might well be the lot of our friend Henry.

But is this what's really going on in these studies? Are some people wired to succeed and others to fail?

One thing was clear from these studies: the ability to delay gratification did predict a large number of long-term results. That part of the marshmallow research nobody was arguing about. However, for years scientists continued to debate the cause of this strong effect. Did self-control stem from an intractable personality characteristic or something more malleable and thus learnable?

In 1965, Dr. Mischel collaborated on a study with Albert Bandura that openly challenged the assumption that *will* was a fixed trait. Always a student of human learning, Bandura worked with Mischel to design an experiment to test the stability of subjects who had delayed gratification. In an experiment similar to the marshmallow studies, the two scholars observed fourth- and fifth-graders in similar circumstances. They placed children who had not demonstrated that they could delay gratification into contact with adult role models who knew how to delay. The greedy kids observed adults who put their heads down for a nap or who got up from the chair and engaged in some distracting activity. The original "grabbers" saw techniques for delaying gratification. And to everyone's delight, they followed suit.

After a single exposure to an adult model, children who previously hadn't delayed suddenly became stars at delaying. Even more interesting, in follow-up studies conducted months later, the children who had learned to delay *retained* much of what they had learned during the brief modeling session. So what about those hardwired genetic characteristics or traits that had predicted so much?

The answer to this important question is good news to all of us and most certainly offers hope to Henry. When Mischel took a closer look at individuals who routinely held out for the greater reward, he concluded that delayers are simply more *skilled* at avoiding short-term temptations. They didn't merely avoid the temptation; they employed specific, learnable techniques that kept their attention off what would be merely short-term gratification and on their long-term goal of earning that second marshmallow.

So maybe Henry *can* learn how to delay gratification— if he learns tactics that will help him do so. But will that be enough to transform him into the physically fit person he'd like to become? After all, he's not good at jogging or weight lifting either. In fact, he's horrible at all things athletic. Surely factors as hardwired as body type, lung capacity, and musculature are predictors of good athletic performance. Henry has no hope of ever becoming one of those chiseled hunks you see hanging out at health clubs. Or does he?

## MUCH OF PROWESS IS PRACTICE

Psychologist Anders Ericsson has offered an interesting interpretation of how those at the top of their game get there. He doesn't believe for a second that elite-level performance stems from zodiacal forces or, for that matter, from enhanced mental or physical properties. After devoting his academic life to learning why some individuals are better at certain tasks than others, Ericsson has been able to systematically demonstrate that people who climb to the top of just about any field eclipse their peers through something as basic as *deliberate practice.*

We've all heard the old saying that practice doesn't make perfect; *perfect* practice makes perfect. Ericsson has spent his life proving this to be true. While most people believe that they are born with inherent limits to their athletic ability, Ericsson argues that there is little evidence that people who achieve exceptional performance ever get there through any means other than carefully guided practice—*perfect* practice. His research demonstrates that prowess, excellence, elite status—call it what you like—is not a matter of genetic gifts. It's a matter of knowing how to enhance your skills through *deliberate practice.*

For instance, Ericsson has described how dedicated figure skaters practice differently on the ice: Olympic hopefuls work on skills they have yet to master. Club skaters, in contrast, work on skills they've already mastered. Amateurs tend to spend *half* of their time at the rink chatting with friends and not practicing at all. Put simply, skaters who spend the same number of hours on the ice achieve very different results because they practice in very different ways. In Ericsson's research, this finding has held true for every skill imaginable, including memorizing complex lists, playing chess, excelling at the violin, and conquering every extant sporting skill. It also applies to more complex interactions such as giving speeches, getting along with others, and holding emotional, sensitive, or high-stakes conversations.

Before we move on, let's take care to avoid a very large and dangerous trap. The fact that improvements in performance come through deliberate practice makes all the sense in the world when it comes to activities such as figure skating, playing chess, and mastering the violin. However, few people, if any, would think to practice with a coach as a way to learn how to get along with coworkers, motivate team members to improve their quality measures, emotionally connect with a troubled teen, or talk to a physician about a medical error. Most of us don't think that soft and gushy interpersonal skills are something we need to study at all, let alone something we would study and practice with a coach.

But that's precisely what should be going on. Consider a common problem at hospitals. A surgeon has just committed a medical error. While performing a mastectomy, she has accidentally ripped a tiny muscle guarding the patient's chest cavity, but she doesn't notice her error. The anesthesiologist sees a gauge jump, so it appears as if one lung is no longer taking in air. Two of the nurses assisting the operation see similar signs of distress. If the medical team doesn't start corrective action soon, the patient could die. But before the action can be taken, either the surgeon needs to take responsibility or one of the other professionals needs to raise an alarm.

Let's focus on the staff members who are assisting and predict what they might do. Most would certainly hesitate for a few seconds before suggesting that the surgeon has just made a mistake. They'll hesitate because if they don't handle the situation well, they'll come off as flippant or even insubordinate. There are legal issues at play, which makes the discussion that much more delicate. Worse still, they've seen colleagues who've expressed a concern, turned out to be wrong, and then received a tongue-lashing. Better to let someone else take the risk. Precious seconds continue to pass.

This and tens of thousands of similar medical errors continue to happen because individuals who may have practiced drawing blood or moving a patient or reading a gauge dozens of times haven't studied and practiced how to confront a colleague—or even more frightening—a physician. They aren't exactly sure what to say and how to say it. They certainly lack the confidence that comes from having practiced.

Of course, healthcare isn't the only field in which a lack of interpersonal know-how has caused serious problems. Every time a boss expresses a half-baked, even dangerous, idea and subordinates bite their tongues for fear of being chastised, good ideas remain a secret and teams make bad decisions. Speaking up to an authority figure requires skill, and skill requires practice. The same is true for confronting a mentally abusive spouse or dealing with a bully at school or—here's a hot one—just saying no to drugs. Try that without getting ridiculed or beat up. Interpersonal interactions can be extraordinarily complicated, and most will improve only after individuals receive instruction that includes deliberate practice.

Consider the problem Dr. Wiwat Rojanapithayakorn faced when attempting to encourage young, poor, shy, female sex workers to deny services to older, richer male customers if the customers refused to use a condom. At first the young girls mumbled their disapproval, only to be intimidated by their vocal clients. Not knowing what to say or how to say it, they'd quickly give in and put themselves and thousands of others at risk.

Eventually Wiwat asked more seasoned sex workers to train young girls on how to defend their health. They shared actual scripts that helped them avoid offending the customer while at the same time holding a firm line. Equally important, the young women actually practiced the conversation until they had gained confidence in what they were going to say and how they would say it. They continued to practice and receive feedback until they had mastered their scripts well enough to actually use them at work. In this particular case, providing detailed coaching and feedback helped compliance with the strict condom code rise from 14 percent to 90 percent in just a few years—saving millions of lives.

Many of the profound and persistent problems we face stem more from a lack of skill (which in turn stems from a lack of deliberate practice) than from a genetic curse, a lack of courage, or a character flaw. Self-discipline, long viewed as a character trait, and elite performance, similarly linked to genetic gifts, stem from the ability to engage in guided practice of clearly defined skills. Learn how to practice the right actions, and you can master everything from withstanding the temptations of chocolate to holding an awkward discussion with your boss.

## PERFECT COMPLEX SKILLS

Let's return to a point we made earlier. Not all practice is good practice. That's why many of the tasks we perform at work and at home suffer from "arrested development." With simple tasks such as typing, driving, or playing golf and tennis,

## ACT LIKE AN INFLUENCER

Let's return to the leaders of the gold mine in remote Ghana who, as you may recall, were trying to reduce automobile accidents by asking their drivers to stop speeding. They discovered that most drivers didn't want to speed, but they felt they had to because of an awkward interpersonal situation. They were often asked to drive senior leaders to the airport, a two-hour drive, and these leaders were notorious for cutting it too close. They didn't allow enough time to catch their flight so their driver had to speed.

The vital behavior was for drivers to call the senior leaders an hour in advance to remind them of their scheduled departure time. For the drivers, this was a very awkward and countercultural call to make. It was an ability problem. So, they developed scripts. They practiced. They also practiced what they would say when leaders arrived late anyway. Then they invited the safety manager and several senior leaders in for a discussion, where they role-played the conversations with the actual senior leaders who sometimes terrified them.

These role-playing opportunities built both competence and confidence that helped drivers follow through on the vital behavior during very crucial moments in order to save lives. And equally important, they were a powerful way for senior leaders to provide encouragement (source 3) that it was okay for the drivers to hold them accountable.

we reach our highest level of proficiency after about 50 hours of practice; then our performance skills become automated. We're able to execute them smoothly and with minimal effort, but further development stops. We assume we've reached our highest performance level, and we don't think to learn new and better methods.

With some tasks, we stop short of our highest level of proficiency on purpose. The calculus we perform in our heads suggests that the added effort it'll take to find and learn something new will probably yield a diminishing marginal return, so we stop learning. For instance, we learn how to make use of a word processor or Web server by mastering the most common moves, but we never learn many of the additional features that would dramatically improve our ability.

When this same pattern of arresting our development is applied over an entire career, it yields fairly unsatisfactory results. For example, most professionals progress until they reach an "acceptable" level, and then they plateau. Software engineers, for instance, usually stop progressing somewhere around five years after entering the workforce. Beyond this level of mediocrity, further improvements are not correlated to years of work in the field.

So what *does* create improvement? According to Dr. Anders Ericsson, improvement is related not just to practice but to a particular kind of practice—something Ericsson calls *deliberate practice*. Ericsson has found that no matter the field of expertise, when it comes to elite status, there is no correlation whatsoever between time in the profession and performance levels.

The implications are stunning. A 20-year-veteran brain surgeon is not likely to be any more skilled than a 5-year rookie by virtue of time on the job. Any difference between the two would have nothing to do with experience and everything to do with deliberate practice. Surgeons who receive detailed feedback against a known standard develop far more rapidly than colleagues who practice their same old methods over and over again. Certainly, time is required (most elite performers in fields such as music composition, dance, science, fiction writing, chess, and basketball have put in 10 or more years), but it is not the critical variable for mastery. The critical factor is using time wisely. It's the *skill* of practice that makes perfect.

Most of us already have all the evidence we need to confirm that deliberate practice can have an enormous effect on performance levels. Just look at what's happened to our capacity to teach everything from mathematics to high jumping. Roger Bacon once said that it would take a person 30 to 40 years to master calculus—the same calculus that is taught in most high schools today. Today's musicians routinely match and even surpass the technical virtuosity of legendary musicians of the past. And when it comes to sports, the records just keep falling. For example, when Johnny Weissmuller of Tarzan fame won his five Olympic gold medals in swimming in 1924, nobody expected that years later *high school* kids would post better times.

What, then, is deliberate practice? And how can we apply the techniques to our vital behaviors and thus strengthen our influence strategy?

## Demand Full Attention for Brief Intervals

Deliberate practice requires complete attention. Deliberate practice doesn't allow for daydreaming, functioning on auto-pilot, or only partially putting one's mind into the routine. It requires steely-eyed concentration as students watch exactly what they're doing, what is working, what isn't, and why.

This ability to concentrate is often viewed by students as their most difficult challenge, enough so that elite musicians and athletes argue that maintaining their concentration is usually the limiting factor to deliberate practice. Most can maintain a heightened level of concentration for only an hour straight, usually during the morning when their minds are fresh. Across a wide range of disciplines, the total daily practice time of elite performers rarely exceeds five hours a day, and this is only if students take naps and sleep longer than normal.

## Provide Immediate Feedback Against a Clear Standard

The number of hours one spends practicing a skill is far less important than receiving clear and frequent feedback against a known standard. For example, serious chess players spend about four hours a day comparing their play to the published play of the world's best players. They make their best move, and then they compare it to the move the expert made. When their move is different from the master's, they pause to determine what the expert saw and they missed. As a result of comparing themselves to the best, students improve their skills much faster than they would otherwise. This immediate feedback, coupled with complete concentration, accelerates learning. Players know quickly when they are off course, and they learn from their own poor moves.

As you might imagine, sports stars require rapid feedback to improve performance as well. They tend to focus on small but vital aspects of their play and scrupulously compare one round to the next. Swimming gold medalist Natalie Coughlin completes each leg of her races with fewer strokes than her opponents, giving her a tremendous advantage in stamina. Her practice is focused on the minute details of each stroke. She explains: "You're constantly manipulating the water. The slightest change in pitch in your hand makes the biggest difference." At the conclusion of each lap, Coughlin is acutely aware of the number of strokes she took to complete it, and she adjusts her hand position for the next lap. This kind of focused, deliberate practice enhances performance more rapidly than does merely swimming laps.

This concept of rapid feedback stands traditional teaching methods on their heads. Many teachers believe that tests are painful experiences that should be given as infrequently as possible so as not to discourage students. Research reveals that the opposite is true. Ethna Reid taught us that one of the vital behaviors for effective teachers is extremely short intervals between teaching and testing. When testing comes frequently, it becomes familiar. It's no longer a dreaded, major event. It provides the chance for people to see how well they're doing against the standard.

Think about how deliberate practice with clear feedback compares with the way we currently train our leaders. Rarely do business school and management faculties think of leadership as a performance art. Faculty members typically teach leaders how to think, not how to act. So when would-be executives take MBA courses or graduate executives attend leadership training programs, they're routinely asked to read cases, apply algorithms, and the like, but there's a good chance that they'll never be asked to practice anything.

Granted, business schools typically offer a course in giving presentations and speeches where the performance components that students are asked to practice are so obvious. But this is not the case with other important leadership skills, such as addressing controversial topics, confronting bad behavior, building coalitions, running a meeting, disagreeing with authority figures, or influencing behavior change—all of which call for specific behaviors, and all of which can and must be learned through deliberate practice.

## Break Mastery into Mini Goals

Let's add another dimension to deliberate practice. Let's start with a test. How would you motivate patients to take pills that one day might prevent them from experiencing a stroke? If they've already had one stroke, you'd think it would be easy to get them to take the lifesaving pills. But let's add a confounding factor. The pills often cause leg cramps, painful rashes, loss of energy, constipation, headaches, and sexual dysfunction. So patients take a pill, and they will most assuredly suffer short-term negative side effects, but maybe they won't have a stroke until sometime way out in the future. This is going to be a hard sell. In fact, for years many stroke patients didn't take their pills because they didn't like the odds.

This all changed when researchers stopped focusing on long-term goals (avoiding another stroke) and created a regimen that helped patients set mini goals and then provided rapid feedback against them. Researchers gave patients packets of pills, a blood pressure monitor, and a logbook. Every day they took the pills, monitored their blood pressure, and recorded changes in the logbook along with other achievements. The change was dramatic and immediate. By setting small goals (daily monitoring and recording) and meeting them, patients now focused on something they could see and control. This enhanced their sense of efficacy, clarified the effect of the medicine, and motivated compliance. Now these patients take their pills.

Influencers have long known the importance of setting clear and achievable goals. First, they understand the importance of setting specific goals. Most people say that they understand this concept, but few actually put the concept into practice. For example, *average volleyball players* set goals to improve their "concentration" (exactly what is that?), whereas *top performers* decide they need to practice tossing the ball correctly—and they understand each of the elements in the toss.

As part of this focus on specific levels of achievement, top performers set their goals to improve behaviors or processes rather than outcomes. For instance, top volleyball performers set process goals aimed at the set, the dig, the block, and so on. Mediocre performers set outcome goals such as winning so many points or garnering applause. In basketball, players who routinely hit 70 percent or more of their free throws tend to practice differently from those who hit 55 percent or fewer. How? Better shooters set technique-oriented goals such as, "Keep the elbow in," or, "Follow through." Players who shoot 55 percent and under tend to think more about results-oriented goals such as, "This time I'm going to make 10 in a row."

This difference in focus is also borne out when players blow it. Researchers stopped players who missed two free throws in a row and asked them to explain their failure. Master shooters were able to cite the specific technique they got wrong. ("I didn't keep my elbow in.") Poorer shooters offered vague explanations such as, "I lost concentration."

The role of mini goals in maintaining motivation also deserves attention. With certain skills, people are deathly afraid that they won't succeed. And once they do fail, they fear that bad things will happen to them. As you might imagine, when people predict that their actions will lead to catastrophic results, these failure stories lead to self-defeating behavior. Individuals begin with the hypothesis that they will never succeed and that the failure will be costly, and then they look for every shred of proof that they're about to fail so they can bail out early before they suffer too much—which they do anyway.

When fear dominates people's expectations, not only do you have to improve their actual skill but you also have to take special care to ensure that their expectations of success grow right along with their actual ability. But how? As we learned earlier, simply using verbal persuasion isn't enough to convince them. ("Go ahead, the snake won't bite!") For example, in one line of research, scholars learned that you can teach dating skills to shy sophomores, but the students need to see proof of constant progress before they're willing to admit that they've learned anything useful or before they put the new skills into practice.

And where do people find this proof of progress? From progress itself. Nothing succeeds like success. As people succeed, they learn through personal experience (the real deal for changing understanding, which can be a powerful tool for changing minds) that they actually can achieve their goals. Unfortunately, skeptical people aren't likely to attempt behaviors that they perceive to be risky, so they never succeed. Now what's a person to do?

Dr. Albert Bandura (the father of social cognitive theory we introduced earlier and the scholar whose ideas have provided the theoretical foundation for most of the applied research we cite throughout this book) points out that to encourage people to attempt something they fear, you must provide rapid positive feedback that builds self-confidence. You achieve this by providing short-term, specific, easy, and low-stakes goals that specify the exact steps a person should take. Take complex tasks and make them simple; long tasks and make them short; vague tasks and make them specific; and high-stakes tasks and make them risk free.

If you want to see how to put short-term, specific, easy, low-stakes goals into play on a much grander scale, take a look at our friends at Delancey Street. The entering criminals and societal castoffs that Dr. Mimi Silbert works with are typically illiterate and completely unskilled. Not only do they not have job expertise or academic talent but they also lack interpersonal and social survival skills.

So what do you do when you have to teach residents dozens or even hundreds of skills? You eat the elephant one bite at a time. You select one domain—say, a vocational skill such as working in a restaurant—then choose a small skill in that area. For example, on the very first night, the senior Delancey residents teach the nervous newcomer how to set a table—maybe just the forks. Then, this novice who is very likely to be suffering from drug withdrawal along with culture shock and other physical and emotional problems practices placing the fork until he or she gets it right. Next comes the knife.

## Prepare for Setbacks; Build in Resilience

As important as it is to use baby steps to ensure short-term success during the early phases of learning, if subjects experience only successes early on, then failures can quickly discourage them. A short history of easy successes can create a false expectation that not much effort is required. Then if subjects run into a problem, they become discouraged.

To deal with this problem, people need to learn that effort, persistence, and resiliency are eventually rewarded with success. Consequently, the practice regime should gradually introduce tasks that require increased effort and persistence. As learners overcome more difficult tasks and recover from intermittent defeats, they see that setbacks aren't permanent roadblocks but rather, signals that they need to keep learning.

## ACT LIKE AN INFLUENCER

A group of senior executives had spent most of the day designing the rollout of a new quality initiative. As the team began to break up, one of the vice presidents commented, "You know, I believe we're all committed in this room, but unless we speak with a common voice to some of the cynicism out there, people will think it's just the flavor of the month." The group agreed. So, the group ended the session with a half hour of deliberate practice.

First, team members identified the four or five toughest questions they'd be asked. Then they broke into pairs, and they practiced responding to the questions in two-minute "elevator speeches." Their practice consisted of delivering their speeches, receiving feedback from their partners, and then delivering their speeches a second time. By the end of the half hour, the executives were confident they could answer people's concerns in a uniform, sincere, and effective way. This small investment in deliberate practice produced huge returns as executives delivered consistent messages across the organization. Employees sensed the commitment of the leadership team and engaged far more readily in embracing the new tools.

This capacity to tell ourselves the right story about problems and setbacks is particularly important when we're already betting against ourselves. When faced with a setback, we need to learn to say, "Aha! I just discovered what doesn't work," and not, "Oh no! Once again I'm an utter failure." We need to interpret setbacks as *guides*, and not as brakes.

Initially, failure signals the need for greater effort or persistence. Sometimes failure signals the need to change strategies or tactics. But failure should rarely signal that we'll never be able to succeed. For instance, you find yourself staring at a half-eaten ice cream cone in your hand. Should you conclude that you're unable to stick with your eating plan so you might as well give up? Or should you conclude that since it's hard to resist when you walk past the ice cream parlor on your way home from work, you should change your route? The first conclusion serves as a discouraging brake on performance, whereas the second provides a corrective guide that helps refine your strategy.

## BUILD EMOTIONAL SKILLS

Let's end our exploration into self-mastery where we began. Henry is staring down at his half-opened chocolate bar. His eyes, lips, and taste buds are prodding his brain to satisfy their demands. He wants chocolate. To see if Henry is doomed or if he can learn a skill to help him delay gratification, let's turn to research that helps us better understand the original marshmallow study.

Contemporary research reveals that human beings operate in two very different modalities, depending on the circumstances. However, as Mischel and Bandura informed us, these modalities or systems, rather than being character traits or impulses, are actually behaviors that can be regulated through skill. The first of these two operating modalities is referred to by contemporary theorists as our "hot" or "go system." It helps us survive. We stumble upon something threatening—say, a tiger—and as our go system takes over, our brain sends blood to our arms and legs, our heart rate and blood pressure increase, and like it or not, we start producing cholesterol—just in case we face blunt trauma.

More intriguing still, as our go system kicks in and blood flows out of the brain and toward our arms and legs, we start relying on a much smaller part of our brain (the amygdala) to take over the job of thinking. When the amygdala takes control, we no longer process information in a cool, calm, and collected way. Rather than cogitating, ruminating, and completing other high-level cognitive tasks, the amygdala or "reptilian brain" is made for speed. It's wired for quick, emotional processing that, when activated, triggers reflexive responses including fight and flight. The amygdala instinctively moves us to action. We see a tiger and bang, we're off and running. This hot or go system develops very early, and it is most dominant in the young infant.

The second system, known as the "cool" or "know system," serves us well during more stable times. It's emotionally neutral, runs off the frontal lobe, and is designed for higher-level cognitive processing. Consequently, it helps us thrive, rather than just survive. It's the part of the brain we're using as we're calmly picking blackberries while chatting with a friend. This system is very ill suited to dealing with the tiger that is just about to appear around the corner. Our know system is slow and contemplative, and it begins to develop at around age four—just about the time children are first able to delay gratification.

As terrific as it is to have two very different operating systems, each perfectly suited to its own unique tasks, when you have two of anything, you always run the risk of employing the wrong one given your circumstances. For instance, a tiger appears, and you remain emotionally neutral, marveling at the cat's amazing speed, while you carefully contemplate your options. "Let's see, if I climb that tree, there's a chance . . ."

Too late—you're tiger food. Too bad your know system wrestled control away from your go system.

To be honest, calling up our know system when it's our go system that would serve us better isn't all that common. It's the go system we call into service every chance we get. After all, it's better to run at the first sign of danger than remain mired in the know too long. Consequently, the go system often turns on at the mere hint that you're about to fall under attack. Heaven forbid you think complexly and clearly in such a case.

For example, an accountant who works with you makes fun of an idea you offer up in a meeting. This ticks you off. How dare this knuckle-dragging bean counter mock your idea! Of course, this isn't exactly a life-threatening circumstance you face; it's an accountant, not a tiger. Nevertheless, better safe than sorry. So, like it or not, your go system kicks in. In fact, it does so without your even asking for help. As your blood starts rushing to your arms and legs where it can do some good, your brain will just have to run off the amygdala. You're hot, you're ready to go, you're not the least bit contemplative, and you verbally tear into the poor fellow from accounting like an early human on a fallen woolly mammoth. What were you thinking? More to the point, what part of your brain were you thinking with?

This inappropriate emotional reaction is exactly the same thing that happens whenever your appetites or cravings kick in at a moment you would prefer that they remain less active. Your go system isn't designed merely for fight or flight. It's also designed to take charge whenever a quick, reflexive, survival behavior might suit you. For example, you smell fresh doughnuts as you walk by the company cafeteria, and an urge from within whispers, "Eat now before it's too late."

## ACT LIKE AN INFLUENCER

During a major economic downturn, leaders from a financial services company were worried about losing some of their high-net-worth clients to aggressive competitors. Research showed that one of the vital behaviors for high customer loyalty was candidly addressing emotionally risky issues with clients. For example, many wealth managers procrastinated sharing bad news about portfolio performance. Others would rather take a beating than discuss how their clients' failure to stick to their financial goals was hurting them. But those who handled these moments skillfully actually created deeper loyalty and won a larger portion of client business.

Wealth managers were trained to recognize when their emotions were impeding professional responses. They practiced skills for reframing these emotions: rather than ruminating on their fears, they thought about the positive potential consequences of addressing these issues respectfully. With a reasonable investment in deliberate practice, everyone learned to do what only some had known before. Many saw almost immediate evidence of deeper client loyalty and increased business.

So there you have it. Sometimes we switch into the wrong version of our two operating systems, and this change causes us huge problems. That's why in spite of the fact that we're committed to a vital behavior, we often crumble at stressful moments. If only we could learn how to wrestle control away from the amygdala when it's kicking in hard at the wrong time. Then perhaps we could be ruled by reason, and not let passion take charge. The good news is that this powerful self-management skill is *learnable*. And if you want to equip yourself or others to survive the tide of opposing emotions, this skill is pivotal.

## KICK-START OUR BRAIN

To learn how to take charge of our go system, let's return to the marshmallow studies. Once Mischel and others had divided their research subjects into "grabbers" and "delayers," they turned their attention to transforming everyone into a delayer. What would it take to help people survive immediate temptations in order to achieve long-term benefits? More importantly, they wanted to avoid the mistake of relying on verbal persuasion by simply telling people to gut it out, or to "show some self-control!" Instead, they wanted to teach people the skills associated with emotional management. But what were these skills?

Mischel discovered through a series of experiments with varied age groups and rewards that if subjects didn't trust that the researcher would actually return and give them the longer-term reward, they wouldn't delay. Why hold out only to be disappointed? Similarly, if subjects believed that they wouldn't be able to do what it took to withstand the short-term temptation, they also wouldn't delay. In short, Mischel confirmed what Bandura taught us earlier. People won't attempt a behavior unless

(1) they think it's worth it, and (2) they think they can do what's required. If not, why try?

In his original experiments, Mischel had observed that children who were able to delay gratification were better at distracting themselves from thinking about either the short- or the long-term reward. Delayers managed their emotions by distracting themselves with other activities. They avoided looking at the marshmallows by covering their eyes, turning their chairs away, or resting their heads on their arms. Some even created their own diversions by talking to themselves, singing, and inventing games with their hands and feet. One clever kid stood and traced the mortar seams in the wall with her finger. In short, delayers invented clever ways of turning aversive and boring waiting time into something that was more like a game.

When Mischel taught other children these same tactics—and thus helped them take their minds off the rewards and place them on something else—subjects routinely increased their ability to delay gratification. In similar studies where subjects were given specific tasks that would help them earn their long-term rewards, subjects who focused on the tasks as opposed to the rewards delayed longer. In contrast, individuals who glanced at the reward the most often were the least persistent. Researchers also found that distracting individuals by having them focus on the cost of failure, or thinking bad thoughts, did not enhance delay.

Finally, asking subjects to employ "willpower" by directing their attention to tasks that were difficult, aversive, or boring didn't work. Despite the fact most people are convinced that individuals who show poor self-control merely need to exert a stronger will—demanding that subjects dig down, suck it up, or show strength of character—research found the opposite. Telling people to hunker down didn't improve performance.

The far better strategy was to transform the difficult into the easy, the aversive into the pleasant, and the boring into the interesting. We examine methods for doing exactly this in Chapter 9. Suffice it to say that when industrial engineers began to find ways to help employees and others make their tasks easier and more pleasant, leaders learned that they didn't have to continually harangue people to stick to their unpleasant or boring tasks. And when leaders began to learn how to measure and focus on short-term goals, it took the pressure off having to continually motivate people into hanging on until the end.

Another effective way to manage emotions is to argue with your feelings. Psychologists call this particular strategy *cognitive reappraisal*. When emotions come unbidden through the go system, they can be dragged into the light of the know system by activating skills only the know system has. To do this, call out to your frontal lobe by asking it to solve a complex problem. That's right. If you ask your brain to work on a question that requires more brain power than the amygdala can muster, this mental probe can help kick in the know system and restore normal thought.

To start the reappraisal process, distance yourself from your need by labeling it. (I have a craving for a cream cheese–covered bagel. Bad.) Debate with yourself about it by introducing competing thoughts or goals. (What I *really* want is to be proud of myself after lunch when I write down what I ate.) Distract yourself (conjure up a potent image of the feeling you have when your belt feels loose). Or delay. That's right—the go system can often be outwaited.

For example, as a strategy to help obsessive-compulsives cope with their tendencies, therapists teach them to wait 15 minutes before giving in to a maddening mental demand—

such as washing their soap-worn hands for the hundredth time in eight hours. In the moment, we often believe that our emotions will not subside until they're satisfied. This turns out not to be true. If you delay your urge, within a fairly short period of time the brain returns control to the know system, and different choices become easier.

Active strategies such as classifying, debating, deliberating, and delaying can help change what you think. They do so by changing *where* you think. Your know system starts to kick in, and you transfer control from the amygdala to the frontal lobe. Once you change *where* you think, you change how you think, which in turn changes what you think. You're now able to carefully contemplate, ruminate, and take a longer-term view.

So, if, like Henry, you find yourself obsessing over the possibility of gorging yourself on chocolate—or maybe gambling or spending obsessively to the point where you can scarcely think straight—realize that there's a set of skills you can call into play if you want to take control of your urges.

## SUMMARY: PERSONAL ABILITY

Changing behavior almost always involves learning new skills. World-class influencers spend far more time engaging people in deliberate practice than the rest of us. If you want to succeed at influence, then spend more time than you suspect you'll need engaging people in practicing the new behaviors. Make sure that practice involves realistic conditions, coaching, and feedback. Break the vital behaviors into smaller actions that allow people to judge how well they're doing. And finally, help others practice how they'll recover from setbacks, should they fail in their early attempts.

And finally, be sure you help people develop not just the technical or interpersonal skills they need to succeed but also the *intrapersonal* skills. Engage them in practice in addressing emotions that might undermine their attempts to change. Help them learn to skillfully move from the *go* to the *know* parts of their brains so they can overcome impulses that might keep them from success.

Remember the good news here. Overcoming habits or developing complex athletic, intellectual, and interpersonal skills are not merely functions of motivation, personality traits, or even character. They all tie back to ability. Develop greater proficiency at deliberate practice as well as the ability to manage your emotions, and you significantly increase your chances for turning vital behaviors into vital habits.

# 6

# Provide Encouragement

## SOCIAL MOTIVATION

*I was part of that strange race of people aptly described as spending their lives doing things they detest to make money they don't want to buy things they don't need to impress people they dislike.*

—Emile Henry Gauvreau

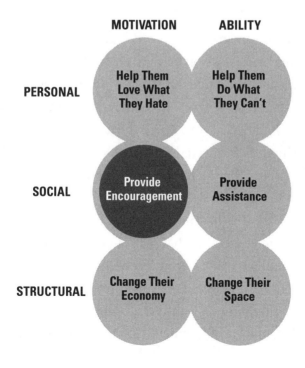

No source of influence is more powerful and accessible than the persuasive power of the people who make up our social networks. None. The ridicule and praise, acceptance and rejection, approval and disapproval of our fellow beings can do more to assist or destroy our change efforts than almost any other source. A raised eyebrow, curled lip, derisive look, or small shake of the head can wield more influence than the sum total of all the world's thundering speeches.

Smart influencers appreciate the amazing power humans hold over one another, and instead of denying it, lamenting it, or attacking it, they embrace and enlist it. They use the power of social influence to support change by ensuring that the right people provide encouragement, coaching, and even accountability during crucial moments.

## THE POWER

In 1961, when psychologist Stanley Milgram set out to find U.S. citizens similar in disposition to what most people believed were the crazy misfits, fundamentalists, and psychological wrecks who had marched Jews, Poles, Romanies, and countless others into the gas chambers at Auschwitz, the world was surprised by what Dr. Milgram discovered. In fact, Dr. Milgram's findings were so disturbing that he fell under attack from every corner. Nobody wanted to believe the data.

Mystified by what had happened in Hitler's Germany, Dr. Milgram was interested in what *type* of person could be compelled to annihilate his or her innocent friends and neighbors. Naturally, blind fundamentalists who followed unspeakable orders all in the name of political zealotry would be hard to locate in the suburbs of Connecticut. Nevertheless, Milgram was determined to track down a few of them and put them under his microscope.

Of course, as a respectable researcher, Milgram couldn't create circumstances under which his neighbors actually killed each other. But maybe he could trick subjects into thinking they were killing someone else, when in truth their victims would remain unharmed. To create these odd circumstances, Dr. Milgram ran an ad in the New Haven newspaper asking people to take part in an experiment that lasted one hour and for which they would be paid $4.50. Interested people reported to the basement of Linsly-Chittenden Hall on the campus of Yale University, where they were told that their job would be to take part in a study that examined the impact of negative reinforcement on learning.

While waiting for their turn to earn $4.50, subjects would chat with another participant about the upcoming job. This friendly stranger was actually a confederate of Dr. Milgram's who was working as part of the research team. Next, a scientist in a lab jacket would appear and ask each of the two participants to reach into an urn and draw out a slip of paper to determine who would perform which of the two jobs that were available. One would be a "teacher," and one would be a "learner." In actuality, both slips said "teacher," guaranteeing that the actual research subject would take the role of the teacher.

The teacher would then accompany the learner and the researcher into a small booth where the learner was invited to sit down while the researcher applied special paste to his arms. "This," he explained, "is to ensure solid contact between your skin and the electrodes when we administer the shocks." At this point, the learner would matter-of-factly explain, "A few years ago in the veterans' hospital I was told I had a bit of a heart condition. Will that be a problem?" To which the researcher would confidently say, "No. While the shocks may be painful, they are not dangerous."

After strapping the electrodes to the learner, the researcher and teacher would close the booth door and move to the adjoining room. There the teacher would see a frightening piece of electrical machinery with which he or she would deliver shocks to the learner. To reassure subjects (the teachers) that the machine was pumping out real electrons, each teacher would be given a 45-volt burst from the machine as a sample of the initial shock the learner in the other room would receive during the experiment. It hurt.

The stated goal of the experiment was to measure the impact of negative reinforcement on learning. To test this, the teacher would read a list of paired words loud enough for the learner to hear in the adjoining room. The teacher would then read the first word in each pair, and the learner would try to recall the second word. Should the learner get the word wrong, the teacher would throw a switch that would shock the poor learner with the heart problems. With each subsequent missed word, the teacher would raise the voltage, flip the switch, and give the learner an even larger shock.

Despite the fact that the teacher thought he or she was increasing the voltage with each new error, the learner received no electric shock whatsoever. Instead, with each throwing of the switch, the researcher would play a prerecorded audio clip that the subject could hear through the wall. With the first shock came a grunt. The second shock produced a mild protest. Next, stronger protests. Then screaming and shouting. Then screaming and banging on the wall with a reminder that he had heart problems. Eventually, when the voltage levels exceeded 315 volts, the teacher would hear nothing but silence as he or she read the words, raised the voltage, and cruelly flipped the switch.

Of course, Dr. Milgram knew he would have to experiment with a lot of subjects before he'd find anyone who would keep cranking up the volts. In fact, when Milgram asked a sample group of social psychologists to predict the results of this chilling study, they suggested that only 1.2 percent of the population, only a "sadistic few," would give the maximum voltage.

When you watch black-and-white film clips of Milgram's actual subjects taking part in the study, the hair stands up on the back of your neck. At first these everyday folks off the streets of Connecticut chuckle nervously as they hear the learner grunt in protest after being given a 45-volt shock. Some show signs of stress as they increase the voltage and the learner starts to shout. Many pause at around 135 volts and question the purpose of the experiment.

If at any time the subject called for a halt, he or she was told by the scientist in the white lab jacket that the experiment required him or her to continue—up to four times. If the subject requested to stop a fifth time, the experiment stopped. Otherwise, the experiment came to an end only after the subject had given the maximum 450 volts—to a learner who was no longer protesting, but who had gone completely silent—giving the teacher the distinct impression that the learner had either passed out or died.

Clearly the subjects who continued to send more and more volts to their protesting, screaming, and begging cohort took no pleasure in what they were doing. It's unnerving to watch clips as anguished subjects suggest that they should stop the torture. After offering their suggestions, they are immediately told that the experiment calls for them to continue.

Researchers watched and recorded the subjects, taking comfort in knowing that only a few subjects would administer much of a shock. As it turned out, "only" 65 percent of subjects would.

That's the finding that got Milgram in trouble. He hadn't discovered a tiny handful of Connecticut zealots and sociopaths who would gladly give their souls over to the totalitarian cause. He had found the vulnerable target within all of us. He had looked for the freak and found himself—and you and me. And nobody liked it.

What was going on? Why do human beings place such a high premium on the approval of others—often strangers? Certainly that's what you'd ask if you were a social scientist. As we suggested earlier, savvy students of influence ask how this amazing social force might work either for or against them as they do their best to lead change. Once they understand how social forces are working for and against them, they then use this power for their own purposes.

Savvy people know how to tap into this source of influence in hundreds of different ways, and they do so by following *one* rather simple principle. They ensure that people feel praised, emotionally supported, and otherwise encouraged by those around them—every time they enact vital behaviors. Similarly, they take steps to ensure that people feel discouraged or even socially sanctioned when they choose unhealthy behaviors.

The actual methods that influencers use to exploit the enormous power of "the fellow in the lab jacket" deserve a much closer look. Whole literatures are built upon the topic. Fields ranging from leadership to interpersonal influence to group dynamics sup at the table of social influence.

This being the case, we'll now narrow the field by examining how social influence can be harnessed for good. It's the part of the vast literature than can do us the most good. More specifically, we'll examine the three best practices that help magnify the power of social support: First, we'll look at "The Power of One," or how to magnify our own social influence by means of sacrifice and symbolic action. Second, we'll examine how to amplify your own social influence by partnering with opinion leaders. And third, we'll discuss powerful principles for engaging literally everyone in changing the existing social norms.

## THE POWER OF ONE

Stanley Milgram's research clearly revealed that one respected individual can create conditions that compel ordinary citizens to act in curious, if not unhealthy, ways. But he also found the opposite to be true. After discovering that he could propel people to act against their own consciences, he began exploring which variable had the largest impact. Was it the size of the room, the look and feel of the electronic machine, or the distance to the subject? After conducting tests with over a thousand subjects of every ilk and under every imaginable condition, Milgram concluded that one variable more than any other affected how people behaved: the presence of one more person.

Dr. Milgram learned that if a confederate sitting next to the subject either shocked the learner all the way to 450 volts or stood up to the authority figure, it dramatically affected how the research subjects acted. He could increase the already stunning 65 percent of all-the-wayers to 90 percent if only one other person—just an ordinary looking person from off the street who had agreed to cooperate with Milgram's team—gave a full dose of power just before the subject had a turn at the machine. Equally important, he discovered that the number who would administer the full shock dropped to a mere 10 percent if this confederate *refused* to do so. Either way, it just took one person to turn the tide of compliance.

This finding paints a much brighter picture of humanity and offers us a wonderful influence tool. To harness the immense power of social support, sometimes all you need to do is to find—or better yet, *be*—the one respected individual who flies in the face of what everyone else has done or is doing—and model the new and healthier vital behaviors.

Here's how this works. We once watched how one person acting in ways counter to the norm can have an enormous impact on everyone. In this particular case the CEO of a large defense contractor was trying to transform a rather timid culture into one in which individuals openly stated their differing opinions as a means of resolving long-standing problems. After months of lecturing, he faced a crucial moment. In a meeting of his top 200 managers, the CEO extended an invitation. "I've been told that I'm unapproachable," he began. "I am trying to work on it. But to be honest, I don't know what it means entirely. I'd appreciate feedback from any of you who would be willing to help me."

For a few seconds, the auditorium felt like a morgue. As the CEO scanned the audience for any takers, he was about to break the awkward silence and move on to a new topic when a fellow by the name of Ken raised his hand. "Sure, Bill. I've got some suggestions."

With that announcement, the CEO set an appointment to talk one-on-one with Ken. As you might guess, from that moment on most of the water-cooler chatter was about the foolish risk Ken had just taken. Pay-per-view could have made a fortune selling access to the private meeting between Ken and the CEO. But in the end, the entire story came out—from the CEO.

After meeting with Ken (and with Ken's permission) the CEO sent out an e-mail detailing the feedback he'd received. He made commitments to a couple of changes that he hoped would make him more approachable, and he was as good as his word. Equally important, the CEO sincerely thanked Ken for his candor. The CEO showed his genuine support of the behavior of being candid by not becoming defensive and by rewarding the person who had taken the risk to be honest—even when it hurt—and he then made personal changes to demonstrate his commitment.

The results of this incident were far-reaching. The CEO's and Ken's living examples of seeking and giving feedback emboldened the other 199 managers. Within months, candor among employees increased dramatically across the entire organization. Employees began to open up and successfully solve problems.

Although it's true that neither Ken nor the CEO wore white lab jackets, they did exert social influence. Both were respected individuals, and both demonstrated how to break from tradition and speak frankly. Had the CEO only given lip service to the proposed vital behavior, he would have doomed the change effort. Had he simply used verbal persuasion, his influence would have been equally limited. Instead, the big boss encouraged candor, embraced it, celebrated it, and rewarded the first person who had the guts to speak his mind.

When a respected individual attempts a vital behavior and succeeds, this one act alone can go further in motivating others to change than almost any other source of influence. But take note, the living examples of other humans' behaviors will exert power only to the extent that the person who is modeling the vital behaviors is truly respected. For example, when an HR manager at a midsize plywood mill we consulted with tried to put teeth into a training program she was touting, she videotaped the president of the company singing the praises of the new training. The president ended his short, energetic speech with, "I encourage each of you to take to heart the concepts taught in today's training."

When the HR manager showed the video clip at the beginning of the first training session, participants jeered, hooted, and mocked the president. It turned out that members of the audience despised anything coming out of headquarters. They thought the president was a raging hypocrite, and his ringing endorsement served only to harm the credibility of the training.

Some individuals can exert a great deal of influence on others; others can't—or worse still, actually poison the project. So, how can you make sure you're one of the ones who can set a positive example? Here are three best practices from influencers across the world.

## ACT LIKE AN INFLUENCER

A nurse manager begins staff meetings by sharing "the good, the bad, and the ugly" of what has happened during the last week. She usually begins with her own observations. In so doing, she models that it's safe to share bad news and failures, without any sugarcoating.

When others take the risk to share challenges and setbacks they've experienced, she responds with appreciation: "That's a great observation!" "Thanks for noticing that!" Her reactions show that it's safe to speak honestly. The team then uses these stories of failures and successes to improve future care.

## Lead the Way

The first place to look for social influence is in the mirror. When you ask people to take on new behaviors, the first question they ask is, "Why should I follow *you?*"

Think about it. When we ask people to change their actions, many of the new behaviors are far more physically or emotionally challenging than the actions required to maintain the status quo. You're asking people to step from a familiar, comfortable action into a world of uncertainty or difficulty.

For example, we worked with Mohammad Siddiqui, CEO of MTN of South Sudan, a telecommunications and digital services company. When Siddiqui took the job, he inherited a pretty cynical workforce. Due to political unrest and economic upheaval, local currency had lost 85 percent of its value. Thus, his workforce was living on 85 percent less than it had a year before. In addition, employees saw management as unsympathetic and demanding with their financial concerns.

Siddiqui was trying to solve a different problem. Employee engagement and productivity was unacceptably low. He was under the gun to dramatically improve results. He knew he would need the full intellectual engagement of his employees in order to make progress. So he started an effort to foster a new vital behavior. He wanted all employees to "speak up irrespective of the level or position of the person you need to address."

His employees were stunned. First, because this was counter to the country's culture. In South Sudan there is a strict sense of propriety about who speaks to whom—much less who *disagrees* with whom. And second, here was the man they partly associated with their unsatisfactory wages. He explained that the company would not survive if it gave substantial across-the-board pay increases. And now he is asking his employees to behave in ways that are terribly uncomfortable—even risky. Not a chance.

**The Sad Truth.** When you invite people to change, they begin to scan you for evidence of credibility (Siddiqui's employees certainly did). They consider your every move—past and present—in order to answer the question, "Why should I believe and follow you?" Not only that, but when your behaviors appear ambiguous, they rarely give you the benefit of the doubt. The sad truth is that in an environment of mistrust (i.e., the known universe), all ambiguous behaviors are interpreted negatively. And by the way, all behaviors are ambiguous.

For example, we worked once with Chris, the CEO of a financial services company. He had recently taken his company through a massive rebranding effort that coincided with an attempt to change from a heavily departmentalized culture to one of teamwork and cross-functional collaboration. To celebrate the change, Chris had his communication team create fancy new coffee mugs emblazoned with the old company name and slogan. When hot coffee warmed the cup, heat-sensitive chemicals in the coatings caused the new name to replace the old one. One morning he was riding the elevator with an employee who was holding the new cup. Chris pointed to it proudly and said, "So, what do you think of that mug?" The dour-faced employee muttered, "It means there will be layoffs!"

Chris was stunned. "How's that?"

"This mug is smaller than the previous one," the employee explained.

Still not getting it, Chris questioned, "I'm not sure I follow you."

"Isn't it obvious?" the employee continued, as though talking to a child. "If they're shrinking the cups to save a few pennies on coffee, we will have to cut headcount sometime soon."

All behaviors are ambiguous. People will interpret them as they see fit.

So here's the problem. When you ask people to step into a place of uncertainty and change, they look to you to take their cues. They look at your behavior. Unfortunately, they have a bias for interpreting your behavior in ways that confirm rather than disconfirm their existing concerns or mistrust. So, in order to encourage them to change, you have to generate clear, unambiguous evidence that they can believe you. But how?

**Sacrifice Breathes Life into Dead Values.** Some say that the limiting factor for building trust is time. The only way to build social influence, they suggest, is to slowly build a relationship of trust with those you lead. "Give it time," becomes a veritable mantra. But such a belief is an influence death sentence for someone like Siddiqui. He's a new CEO, from another country no less, who needs to influence change today—not 10 years from now.

Fortunately, the "time" theory is largely wrong. Within months Siddiqui built so much social influence with his team that behavior began to change in remarkable ways. What behaviors did he enact that made his stated beliefs both clear and credible—in an environment where people could draw negative conclusions about anything he did? Siddiqui learned that making a *sacrifice* can be a powerful influence accelerant.

The first thing Siddiqui did was unprecedented in South Sudanese culture. He listened and apologized. In public discussions with employees he listened carefully and attended to the pain they were experiencing due to the massive depreciation of their currency. He empathized with their plight, brainstormed ways he could help soften the blow, but ultimately explained that if the company was to remain viable (and they were to keep their jobs) there was little he could do. However, as employees left these remarkably candid sessions, more than one remarked that this was the first time they had ever heard a leader quietly, humbly, and sincerely say the words, "I am sorry." Something inside them began to stir.

Then the most shocking rumor of all began to spread across the organization. Apparently the previous weekend Siddiqui and his seven-year-old daughter visited the home of Jafar (not his real name)—a well-respected MTN employee. Jafar, positioned 10 levels below Siddiqui and holding the job of janitor, was stunned when the big boss and his daughter made a call. At the appointed time, Siddiqui arrived. He paid homage to the home. He warmly greeted Jafar's father and mother, who lived with Jafar. He inquired about Jafar's circumstances. He expressed gratitude for Jafar's long service and promised to do his best as a leader to earn his trust. Then he left.

Each weekend Siddiqui paid similar visits on other informal leaders from throughout the organization. In a matter of months, the talk about Siddiqui's invitations to change were no longer ridiculed. In fact, the widespread view was that this was a man they could trust. A man who *deserved* their support.

When you ask people to make changes that can be disruptive, difficult, and even frightening, they aren't likely to embrace your call to action if all you offer is a heartfelt plea. If you want to increase your influence with those you hope to help change—knowing full well that others can simply discount your speeches or misinterpret your actions—you're going to have to make some *sacrifices*. You must regularly demonstrate your sincerity by generating incontrovertible evidence that you believe in what you say. You say that openness is important and then sacrifice pride to prove your point. MTN employees had seen generations of leaders who valued being held in high esteem (even deferred to) above all else. Bosses are important.

Then along comes a man who is willing to sacrifice his own pride and be treated as a peer—and sometimes a servant. He calls for openness and candid dialogue. He listens. He apologizes. He enters humble homes. This is a man who lives up to the cliché—he walks the talk. More specifically, he sacrifices old values to demonstrate the importance of the new one. In a matter of weeks his colleagues recognized that, to Siddiqui, open discussion, results, and relationships are far more important than deferring to authority.

Given the importance of sacrifice in helping others interpret our actions—better still, believe in both what we say and do—let's take a look at four kinds of sacrifices that can act as a trust accelerant.

1. **Time:** Siddiqui's behavior was remarkable because it illustrated sacrifice on many levels. One of the most compelling sacrifices was with his time. When people heard about his personal visits to employee homes, they wanted *details*. They wanted to know what he said. How he behaved. Where he sat. But also, how *long* he stayed. We all know time is a finite commodity. No one has any more of it than anyone else. No one has found a way to create more of it. So we trust that it is a credible demonstration of our values. When you give of your time, you give of yourself—and, by the way, there is no such thing as *quality* time. Had Siddiqui made a brief and effusive five-minute visit, it would have sent an entirely different message than his hour-long conversation over tea spoke to everyone. If you want to persuade people that you are serious, sacrifice your time.

2. **Money:** We (the authors) became loyal customers of Hertz Rent-a-Car after 9/11. Two of us were in Dallas on

business when the attack came. Since all aircraft were grounded indefinitely, we were left with no way to get home to worried families. We placed a call to Hertz to ask how much it would cost to drive its car the 2,500 miles from Dallas to Salt Lake City. The agent replied, "Nothing. We've got this. You take the car wherever you need to go. You get home to your family. Turn it in at the most convenient Hertz location. There will be no drop-off fee. Take care." We were speechless.

That sacrifice at that tender time so moved us that our feelings about the company changed profoundly. We knew that Hertz talked about customer service. Its ads were full of such ideas. Now we believed that it actually did care about customers. Why? Because the company took a huge hit to the bottom line (at least in the short run) in order to do what was best to serve its customers in a time of crisis. Anyone who sacrifices money to serve customers cares about customers.

3. **Ego:** You're going to screw up. Just accept it. There will be times that you will lose it. You'll behave in ways that are antithetical to the vital behaviors you hope to foster. You'll be a hypocrite. But this isn't the end of the world. In fact, it can be a powerful opportunity for you to *enhance* trust. But how? By sacrificing ego.

For example, we once worked with a leader we'll call Liz. Liz was a facility manager in Kuala Lumpur. Her campaign to improve quality screeched to a halt one day at the end of a manager briefing when she responded to questions written on cards from the 200-person audience. One comment read, "Yesterday you and the execs from Japan were supposed to do a facility tour. My team spent all weekend preparing for the tour and you never showed up." Liz's face turned red. She slapped the card down on the rostrum. She removed her glasses, then said, "Yesterday I had a decision to make. I had to decide whether to spend two hours with our senior executives touring the facility, or discuss the future of the company. I chose the latter and would do the same today. Next question?" The session ended quite uncomfortably.

Liz was immediately repentant. She knew she had just damaged trust. She knew she had violated her own vital behaviors (which didn't include putting someone down in a meeting and becoming righteously indignant). Fortunately, it all changed the next week during a similar briefing. As Liz began, she stepped from behind the podium. She bowed her head. And she said with some emotion. "Last week I behaved despicably." She went on to describe what had happened. Then concluded with. "I beg your forgiveness. That was unacceptable. And I will not do that again." And she didn't.

Ironically, the apology had a more powerful effect on trust than if she had behaved perfectly in the previous meeting. In that moment of public contrition her team learned that her espoused value of openness and respect were more important than her ego. She was willing to sacrifice the latter for the former. And you can do the same. A mistake or two are not the end of the world. So long as you demonstrate what matters most by subordinating ego to integrity.

4. **Previous priorities:** There was a time when some employees at Lockheed Martin Aeronautics wrongly concluded their CEO, Dain Hancock, was all about image. When he had scarce capital dollars to spend, he invested them in a high-tech entrance to the company's facility rather

than installing much needed air-conditioning in the blistering hot receiving area. To these employees it appeared as though looking good to outsiders was more important to him than attending to employee needs—including listening to what they had to say.

This rather unflattering view changed one day when Dain was holding an employee feedback meeting. Fifteen minutes into the 90-minute session his secretary rushed in to announce: "The prince is here two hours early." Visiting royalty was scheduled to arrive following the session to discuss a multibillion-dollar order of F-16s. Dain paused, his expression inscrutable. Every employee in the room would have understood if he had canceled the session. Instead, Dain assigned his COO to send his apologies and greet the prince. Dain's decision to continue the feedback session over attending to the prince took mere minutes to ripple across the 13,000-person facility. By sacrificing what people previously perceived to be his priority (impressing outsiders), Dain's other stated value (listening to others) gained enormous credibility and went a long way in encouraging others to do the same. By sacrificing a previously important value for a newer one, the newer one gained credibility.

In summary, the first responsibility for creating social support for change lies in your own actions. You must ask yourself, "Why should others believe and follow me?" Then, to give weight to your talk about the importance of the vital behaviors you're espousing, make sacrifices. Sacrifice other key values. Nothing makes a new vital behavior seem more credible than when you sacrifice time, money, ego, and other priorities to demonstrate that what you say is important to you really is important to you. As you do, your social influence can grow rapidly.

## Engage Formal and Opinion Leaders

We've seen that one person can have an enormous effect on motivating others to enact vital behaviors. We've also seen that the influence of formal leaders (like the CEO and the fellow in the white lab coat) can have a remarkable influence on the behavior of those in their sphere of influence. So if you want to influence change, it's essential that you engage the chain of command. Smart influencers spend a disproportionate amount of time with formal leaders to ensure that the leaders are using their social influence to encourage vital behaviors. They develop specific plans for formal leaders to ensure they regularly teach, model, praise, and hold those for whom they are responsible accountable for behaving in new and better ways.

But the bosses are only half of what you'll need. It turns out that there's a second and often overlooked group of people whose social support or resistance will make or break your influence efforts. To find out who this group is and how to enlist it, let's take a look at the work of Dr. Everett Rogers. His contribution to influence theory remains one of the greatest in history, and it has important implications for how all parents, coaches, and leaders can best make use of social support.

After graduating with a PhD in sociology and statistics, Dr. Rogers took an intriguing job with the local university extension service. It was his responsibility to encourage Iowa farmers to use new and improved strains of corn. What could be easier? The new strains of corn Rogers was touting produced greater yields and were dramatically more disease resistant, and therefore, far more profitable than current strains.

As Dr. Rogers talked with local farmers about the terrific new seeds he was recommending, he quickly learned that his education and connection to the university didn't impress them. He wasn't exactly one of them. Farmers dressed differently; their hands were rough from physical labor; they read different magazines and watched different TV programs. Other than speaking the English language, they scarcely had a thing in common with Rogers.

At first, Dr. Rogers figured that this difference would actually work to his advantage. The reason the farmers should listen to his advice was because he *hadn't* done what they had done. He had made a careful study of the crops they should grow. He was now working for the experts in agronomy. In fact, Rogers figured that when he talked, farmers would be taking notes and thanking him for helping them increase their yields.

But it didn't work that way. It turns out that Rogers wasn't just different. In the farmers' view, he was the wrong kind of different. He was naïve. He was a city slicker. He had never plowed a field. Sure, he said he read books, but what if he was wrong? Who would dare put their annual harvest at risk by listening to a young fellow just out of college? None of the farmers. That's who.

After being summarily rejected by his target population, Rogers grew increasingly confused and desperate. What good is it, Rogers wondered, to invent better methods—in fact, *far* better methods—if no one will put them into practice? The very advance of civilization relies on citizens letting go of old, inefficient ways and embracing new, efficient ones. And Rogers just happened to know what those better ways were—at least for the farmers.

What could Dr. Rogers do if people didn't respect him (which they most certainly didn't)? The very fact that he was the one suggesting the new idea prevented people from listening to it. Perhaps Dr. Rogers could get a farmer to embrace the new strains of corn. Then a person from within the farming community could point to the better results, and everyone would be happy to follow. If Dr. Rogers could find a person who would be interested in trying the latest strains, he would be halfway home.

Eventually he enticed a farmer into giving the most current strains of corn a try. He wasn't much like the other farmers. He was a rather hip fellow who actually wore Bermuda shorts and drove a Cadillac. He had a proclivity for embracing innovation, so he tried the new strains of corn and enjoyed a bumper crop. Now his neighbors would see the better results and be motivated to change.

Only they weren't motivated.

The farmers didn't adopt the new corn because they didn't like the weirdo in Bermuda shorts who spurned their lifestyle any more than they liked the pretentious academic who had the nerve to tell them what to do.

This unvarnished failure changed the course of Rogers's life. He spent the rest of his career learning what happens to innovations as they move through a social system. He wanted to learn why some ideas are adopted and others aren't. He also wanted to uncover why certain individuals are far more influential in encouraging people to embrace an innovation than others.

As Rogers set to work, he examined every known study of change. He reviewed how new drugs catch on among doctors. He looked at how new technologies, such as VCRs, become popular. He studied the latest gadgets and discoveries. As he pored over the data, he was startled at how many great ideas simply die. For example, when Vasco de Gama made his triumphant voyage around the Cape of Good Hope, he took 160 men with him. Only 60 returned because the rest died of scurvy. Fortunately, in 1601, an English sea captain named John Lancaster discovered a cure for scurvy. He gave a little bit of lime juice to his sailors every day, and *no one* died of scurvy. And yet it took almost 200 years for the practice to spread. Initially the British were actually mocked for their curious practice, and the derisive term *limey* was born.

Rogers was shocked to discover that the merit of an idea did not predict its adoption rate. What predicted whether an innovation was widely accepted or not was whether a specific group of people embraced it. Period. Rogers learned that the first people to latch on to a new idea are unlike the masses in many ways. He called these people "innovators." They're the guys and gals in the Bermuda shorts. They tend to be open to new ideas and smarter than average. But here's the important point. The key to getting the majority of any population to adopt a vital behavior is to find out who these innovators are *and avoid them like the plague.* If they embrace your new idea, it will surely die.

The second group to try an innovation is made up of what Rogers termed "early adopters." Many early adopters are what are commonly known as "opinion leaders." These important people represent about 13.5 percent of the population. They are smarter than average, and they tend to be open to new ideas. But they are different from innovators in one critical respect: they are socially *connected* and *respected.* And here's the real influence key. The rest of the population—over 85 percent— will not adopt the new practices *until opinion leaders do.*

So it turns out that when the fellow with the Bermuda shorts used the new seeds, he didn't do Rogers a favor. As far as farming methods were concerned, Cadillac man was an *innovator.*

He was the first to adopt new ideas in his community, and like many innovators, his adoption cast suspicion on the "new ways" he endorsed. Since he was different from the majority of his peers in visible ways, and since much of what he did appeared to disrespect traditional methods, this made him a threat. He was neither respected nor connected.

As Rogers later explained, he learned that his recommendations would have fared better if he had carefully sought out opinion leaders to tout his strains of corn.

Given the boost opinion leaders can offer an influence strategy, it is no surprise to learn that the influencers we studied routinely use this powerful source of influence. For example, when Dr. Don Berwick and IHI try to influence the behavior of hundreds of thousands of physicians across the United States, they first engage the *guilds*, as they call them. These are the associations and research groups other physicians look to as credible sources. When the guilds talk, physicians listen.

Similarly, when Dr. Howard Markman tries to influence the communication behavior of couples across the country, he also looks for opinion leaders. He has found that if he trains members of the clergy to teach couples how to solve problems, the results are better than if an unknown outsider in Bermuda shorts swoops into town and offers training.

And how about the Guinea worm disease? Dr. Donald Hopkins and his team don't consider going into a village without first working with the village chief or drawing on the power of a respected official. From there, the local official or chief identifies respected village members from different groups or clans who will be listened to when they teach people the vital behaviors required to eradicate Guinea worm disease. Imagine what would happen if Hopkins recruited a person of no social standing to carry a lifesaving message that challenges old beliefs and norms. Such a person would probably be discounted in a heartbeat.

"The message," Hopkins reports, "is no more important than the messenger."

Interestingly, the power of opinion leaders is available even when you don't have *real* opinion leaders. The TV and radio heroes we referred to earlier *become* opinion leaders. For example, in the village of Lutsaan, India, a community action group made a solemn covenant to educate their daughters after listening to the wildly popular show *Tinka, Tinka Sukh* ("Happiness Lies in Small Things"). In this poignant TV drama, a beloved young girl dies in childbirth after being forced into an early marriage. After vicariously experiencing her death, audience members wrote over 150,000 letters in reaction to the episode. Listeners were so affected by what happened to the young girl that 184 Lutsaan villagers placed their thumbprints on a large public poster in honor of their fallen heroine in a gesture of solidarity and support.

"Of course I will not marry off my daughter before she turns 18," one listener told Dr. Arvind Singhal, who was commissioned to study the effects of the serial drama. "Prior to listening to *Tinka, Tinka Sukh*, I had it in my mind that I need to marry off my daughter soon. Now I won't, and I tell others as well."

Since *Tinka, Tinka Sukh* always featured an epilogue during which a respected person from the community asked questions, made a call to action, and encouraged public discourse, the show made double use of opinion leaders. The comments from the respected figure combined with the actions of the beloved characters made excellent use of social support as a means of promoting change.

To see how to work with opinion leaders, independent of other influence strategies, let's take a look at what Mao Zedong did 48 years ago. A terrible human being in most respects, Mao understood a thing or two about leveraging social influence to accomplish a bit of good.

On June 26, 1965, Mao lit a fire under the Chinese Ministry of Health, citing its poor record in improving health practices in the far-flung rural regions of China. Rather than wait for the stodgy ministry and medical institutions to solve the problem, Chairman Mao engaged 1.8 million change agents in the cause.

When deciding who would make up his population of change agents, he didn't go with existing health specialists. Instead, Mao zeroed in on locals who came from the villages they were to serve, who were recommended by their peers, who were committed to serving the people, and who had a basic level of formal schooling, which put them close to their fellow villagers but slightly above them in education. In short, Mao chose opinion leaders.

These "barefoot doctors," as they were later called, were given just a few months of medical training that covered basic preventive practices that could quickly and significantly improve public health in rural areas. They also learned how to treat the most common maladies. And to reduce risk, they were taught to refer more difficult cases to commune hospitals.

The results were immediate and dramatic. Health-related habits in rural villages improved overnight. Villagers adopted practices such as observing basic hygiene and boiling water; and they adopted these practices much faster than predicted. Mao broke from his traditional methods and didn't issue unilateral commands or create harsh policies because he knew they wouldn't have had much effect in rural China. Instead, he coupled support from the top with the actions of on-the-ground opinion leaders.

## ACT LIKE AN INFLUENCER

At one of Danny Meyer's restaurants, a server was asked by a customer if he knew where he could buy a good cigar along Madison Avenue. The server responded that, while he didn't know the answer to *that*, he *did* know one of the restaurant's staff had just returned from Puerto Rico and had a great "stash" himself. The server returned with the colleague seconds later and presented the guest with a gift of a fine cigar, pausing for a moment to tell about the family from which it was procured and the loving details about its preparation.

On hearing of this "hospitality legend," Danny invited the skillful server to become a mentor. Mentors are chosen from respected opinion leaders and then paired with newer employees in order to encourage them in the values and norms of Union Square Hospitality Group. Danny uses valued opinion leaders to provide encouragement for the vital behaviors that make his restaurants extraordinary.

Rogers's discovery offers enormous leverage to leaders, parents, and the general population alike. When it comes to creating change, you no longer have to worry about influencing everyone at once. If you preside over a company with 10,000 employees, your job is to find the 500 or so opinion leaders who are the key to everyone else. If you supervise 20 people, odds are 2 or 3 of them hold more sway over the team than others. Spend disproportionate time with them. Listen to their concerns. Build trust with them. Be open to their ideas. Rely on them to share your ideas, and you'll gain a source of influence unlike any other.

You don't get to decide whether or not you engage the help of opinion leaders. By definition, they will always be engaged.

They always observe and judge your influence strategy—that's what they do. Then they will give your ideas either a thumbs-up or a thumbs-down. And since they're respected and connected, they will exert their widely felt influence and decide the destiny of your influence strategy—whether you like it or not.

If you're interested in engaging opinion leaders in a large organization, the good news is that finding them is quite easy. Since opinion leaders are employees who are most admired and connected to others in the organization, simply ask people to make a list of the employees who they believe are the most influential and respected. Then gather the lists and identify those who are named most frequently. These are the opinion leaders. Once you know who they are, enlist them and partner with them in your efforts to institute change.

## Create New Norms

We once asked the crusty old warden of one of the most fearsome prisons in the world what he knew about influence. Here was a man who wielded more power within the walls of his institution than most anyone on earth. He had hundreds of armed guards at his command. He could detain, restrain, and shackle men at will. We asked him, "What's the fastest way to get people to change their behavior?" Without hestitating he answered, "Laugh at them."

## ACT LIKE AN INFLUENCER

A manufacturing manager wanted to improve quality and productivity across his plant. He decided to have two groups co-lead the initiative: plant foremen and union elected officials. The foremen were formal leaders; the union officials were opinion leaders. Of course, he had to convince the union leaders that their participation would be good for them and for the people they represented.

Once he'd gotten the union leaders on board, the training took off as no other course had ever done. The manufacturing manager said later that his favorite part was watching the union officials deal with skeptical participants. The officials had a kind of credibility no foreman could ever match.

There was deep wisdom in the warden's response. As we've seen in this chapter, small social cues (and laugher certainly fits in this category) can have a powerful effect on human choices —even to the point of driving most of us to ignore our moral sensibilities. A guy in a white lab coat simply saying "The experiment requires that you continue" is practically irresistible.

But why? Because embedded in that innocuous statement is a potent message. The message is, "compliance is *normal.*" The warden understood that derisive laughter is one of the most efficient ways to let people know they aren't *normal.* The shame we feel when we're laughed at can deter us from repeating a behavior—good or bad—ever again.

This being the case, it should be of little surprise to anyone to learn that one of the  greatest barriers to any change project lies in unhealthy norms. When behavior that you see as bad is seen as normal behavior to everyone else, you're in trouble. Deep trouble. You can muster every other source of influence to resist long-standing norms—but you're still likely to fail in your effort to create change unless you take direct action to create *a new sense of normal.*

But there's good news in this as well. Once you foster new norms, change becomes almost inevitable—raising the question: How do you create new norms? We'll suggest two methods.

1. Make the undiscussable discussable.
2. Create 200 percent accountability.

**Make the Undiscussable Discussable.**  Unhealthy norms are almost always sustained by what we call a culture of silence. You've probably been in one at one point or another in your life. Most people know that current behaviors carry an enormous cost—but no one talks about the issue.

For example, we found a terrible code of silence when conducting a multiyear study of healthcare in the United States, Thailand, Australia, and the United Kingdom. We began this particular study to discover why hundreds of thousands of patients contract infections *while in the hospital.** That can't be good.

When we asked neonatology nurses and doctors how infections find their way into the pristine environment of a neonatal

---

*For a full report of the healthcare study, visit www.silencekills.com.

unit, people would lower their voices, look both ways, and then relate very similar stories. First was the story of the physician who would periodically fail to gown up, glove up, or wash up as he or she should. The second story was of a nurse who, when starting an IV on a very tiny baby, would clip a finger out of his or her sterile glove to expose a fingertip. The nurse had a good reason for doing this; it's extremely hard to find a vein on a baby who can fit in the palm of your hand. Nevertheless, exposing the finger was an egregious violation of safety practices—a violation that helped spread infections to vulnerable babies.

Let's not lose the point here. The problem in this particular hospital was not merely that a doctor or nurse broke rules. The problem was that there was a conspiracy of silence held in place by powerful norms that kept people from speaking when colleagues violated hygiene, safety, or any other protocol. The existing social norm called for silence. In these hospitals the norm was "deferring to power players (like doctors or nurse managers) is more important than protecting patients."

Nothing could ever change in these organizations until the norm changed. In this case, the code of silence had to be broken. Once again: The fundamental problem was not that powerful people broke rules. The insurmountable barrier to improving safety was the widely shared norm of silence that sustained the problem. If you can't talk about it, you can't change it. And *nobody* talks about it.

If you're reading these examples but not wearing hospital greens, you're still not off the hook. We poked around in every type of organization imaginable, and we have found this same code of silence that sustains unhealthy behavior in every corner of business and government. For instance, we conducted an international study of project management where we explored the colossal failure rates of major high-stakes projects, programs, and initiatives.* Going in we knew that the vast majority of product launches, reorganizations, mergers, and improvement initiatives either fail or grossly disappoint. In all, roughly 90 percent of major projects violate their own schedules, budgets, or quality standards.

So we searched for the cause behind these embarrassing results. At first we learned that 88 percent of those we surveyed were currently working on projects or initiatives that they predicted would eventually fail—yet they continued to plod along. Most agreed that the expression that best described the state of their current project was "a slow-motion train wreck."

Then we learned the reason behind the reason: *fewer than 1 in 10 respondents said that it was politically acceptable to speak openly about what was going wrong.* Most suggested that problems such as weak sponsorship, unreasonable constraints, or uncommitted team members were eventually going to kill their efforts, but they said that no one—including the project managers themselves—could bring the issues out into the open.

So, what's the first step to changing norms? It's breaking the code of silence around the problem that *always* sustains the status quo. When you make the undiscussable discussable, you openly embrace rather than fight the power of social influence. Changes in behavior must be preceded by changes in the public discourse.

To see how to take this first step toward creating new norms, let's return to the Indian village of Lutsaan and revisit the mechanism through which the radio drama *Tinka, Tinka Sukh* affected public opinion. And although it's true that the villagers

---

*For a full report, visit www.silencefails.com.

weren't facing hospital infections or failed projects, they did run into a powerful social norm that caused many of them great pain, and their problem was also completely undiscussable.

In one of the *Tinka, Tinka Sukh* story lines, a beloved character was not allowed an education, she was forced to marry young, and she died in childbirth. As a result of the poignant episodes, the listeners in the village of Lutsaan were propelled to find a way to change the long-held practice of marrying young. But what actually brought about this tremendous change in norms? According to Dr. Arvind Singhal, the power of the show stemmed from its ability to force an undiscussable topic into the public discourse. Long-settled beliefs were suddenly opened to question and discussed at every corner, workstation, and shop— and eventually reshaped.

Before the airing of the episodes, millions of people had placed pressure on their friends, children, and coworkers to continue to honor the traditions of their past. This was peer pressure at its strongest. Some people had already changed their views on the treatment of young girls, but it was difficult for them to share their differing views openly without falling victim to public ridicule for not honoring their past. Many people were uncertain about the tradition and wanted to be able to talk it through, but once again, it just wasn't done.

Influencers applied the power of stories (vicarious experience) to the issue. They didn't preach the evils of the traditional treatment of girls because, as we all know, verbal persuasion typically leads to resistance. But the practitioners didn't back away either. Instead, they created a serial drama containing likable characters who talked about the social problem in the privacy of their home—while thousands listened in. The beloved family discussed the pros and cons of the tradition, and each show ended with the words of a respected narrator who merely asked questions.

As the radio family experienced its tragedy, family members began talking. They helped others first think about the issues and then talk about them with their friends, coworkers, neighbors, and family. As a result, the topic moved from the dark into the light. An undiscussable became a discussable, and what had remained underground for centuries wilted in the light of public discourse.

We've seen the same strategy work to reshape norms in organizations. For example, in one world-renowned academic hospital, leaders were struggling to engage their legendary physician leaders in improving the quality of patient care. Most seemed focused on *learning* about disease but seemed to care little about *treating* diseased people. And yet no one would admit it publicly.

This all changed one weekend when we presented the chief medical officer with a stack of 50 patient horror stories we had collected. She told us later, "When I returned home Friday night, I poured myself a glass of wine, sat in my reading chair, and read the first story. Three hours and 50 stories later I was emotionally overcome."

Beginning Monday morning, what had formerly been undiscussable became widely discussed. The stories were shared, read, and studied. What had been formerly only whispered was now openly debated. As the chief medical officer broke the code of silence—her formerly complacent organization took the first determined step toward change.

If you want to change an old norm, you have to talk about the old norm. You have to talk about the new norm. You have to talk.

## ACT LIKE AN INFLUENCER

Spectrum Healthcare did the impossible. The organization got over 90 percent of its doctors to use a new computerized prescription ordering system within a matter of days after the system went "live." One of the keys to this remarkable behavior change was enlisting physician leaders in making personal phone calls to every doctor who had not completed the mandatory training in the new system.

Previously, the norm had been respecting others' "professional prerogatives." When physicians didn't comply with new standards, their noncompliance was "undiscussable." Spectrum changed this norm by engaging influential doctors to communicate expectations. The message was clear, and the response was dramatic. New system adoption was almost immediate—translating into saved lives and safer patients as avoidable medication errors were substantially reduced.

**Create 200 Percent Accountability.** To introduce the second step to creating new norms, let's return to the influence lesson taught to us by the prison warden. "The fastest way to get people to change," he said, "is to laugh at them." While we don't ascribe to public ridicule as a reasonable source of influence, we have found that the pace of change is determined by the speed with which you can get everyone to hold everyone accountable (in ways other than poking fun or laughing). Whether through encouragement of the right behavior, confronting the wrong behavior, or a combination of the two, the strength of new norms is dependent on the consistency with which people are willing to speak up and defend them.

No one knows—or shows—this better than, Dr. Mimi Silbert. It's semester break at Delancey Street. All 500 residents in the San Francisco location have gathered in the family room where they quietly jostle and joke with one another. There's an air of excitement. After all, it's graduation day. This means that some of the residents are about to advance to more responsible positions. Others will move to a new job, and some will earn their GEDs. Even greenies may be ready to graduate from maintenance, where the requirements are pretty basic. But the accomplishment will be no less celebrated than that of the person who is about to receive a college degree—as a number will.

So here the residents sit, waiting for graduation to begin. Those who haven't been through the ceremony before look terribly uncomfortable. They know they will be singled out in front of 499 of their peers, and they have no clue how to deal with the moment. Then before you know it, their names are called. They stand up and are told that they have graduated from maintenance. They have done good work and are now assigned to food services. Congratulations!

All of a sudden new residents hear a sound that has never before been directed at them. They stumble forward to be acknowledged as they experience the most pleasurable wave of discomfort they've ever felt. Everyone is clapping for them.

"It's the most wonderful time," says Silbert. "They're crying. Huge clapping. You'll see this huge guy who doesn't know what to do with his arms because he's so uncomfortable. And it's the best thing in the world."

So what's going on here? Silbert knows how to gain an upper hand over her number one enemy. Previously enacted illegal, immoral, and antisocial behavior required a strong social system to support it. Criminals run in packs. The distinctly different and healthy behavior that Delancey will demand of each new resident will require an equally strong social system. So that's precisely what Silbert serves up. Delancey immerses residents in nothing short of a whole new culture composed of healthy expectations.

This means that from day one residents are hit by an unrelenting wave of social praise and social punishment. Remember, one of Delancey's vital behaviors calls for everyone to challenge everyone—and residents do. Silbert has gone to great pains to structure positive and negative peer feedback into every moment of everyday life. And since frequent and crystal-clear feedback comes from people who have lived the same life, it's hard for new residents to dismiss the data.

Part of Delancey's enormous force for change stems from the fact that there are 20 to 30 formal and informal leaders who know everything that's going on with each resident. "If your mom died," says Delancey resident James, "others learn about it, and all are saying, 'Are you okay?' We're all checking on each other all the time. If we don't watch out for each other in all regards, we'll go down."

Powered by an incessant wave of positive and negative feedback from people who matter a great deal to them, Delancey residents find that change is the path of least resistance. That's why 90 percent of those who graduate from Silbert's community stick with the changes they've made for the rest of their lives.

And yet it would be easy to escape the tendrils of the new culture. All the ex-cons need to do is walk out the door.

There's nothing to stop anyone from exiting; the locks keep people out, not in. But a strange, new, and powerfully magnetic pull draws residents into their new social network. For the first time in their lives, these former drug dealers, gang members, and thieves belong to a group of people who care about their long-term well-being. Sure, residents receive more direction than they're used to, and it's often served up pretty gruffly, but it always comes with their best interest in mind. And when residents hit their daily and weekly goals, they're embraced and praised.

Best of all, for the first time in their lives Delancey residents belong to a social unit that promotes pro-social behavior. Previous colleagues (usually gang members) wanted something *from* them, not *for* them, and they continually propelled them away from everyday society and into the hostile confines of state and federal prisons. Their new friends are *real* friends, rather than accomplices. They're hell-bent on shaping their coresidents into healthy people who can make it on the outside.

So here's a key to Mimi's success. Ensure that everyone understands that they are not just 100 percent accountable—but 200 percent accountable. Create an environment in which everyone is responsible not just to *enact* the vital behaviors—but to *hold others accountable* for them as well. When this happens, people make personal transformations that are hard to believe.

But the relevance of this concept extends far beyond the doors of Delancey. We saw it in action in Burkina Faso. It was pivotal in Boston. It's fundamental in Thailand—and everywhere in between. How do you get villagers to eradicate Guinea worm? By encouraging all of them to hold every neighbor accountable for staying away from public water supplies when they are infected. How do you get hand hygiene rates in a hospital from 50 percent to 100 percent? Get everyone to confront anyone who doesn't follow policy. How do you save millions of lives from AIDS in Thailand? Get everyone in the brothel—starting with the managers and opinion leaders—to hold others accountable to 100 percent condom use.

Old norms begin to fall when influencers bring the hidden costs of bad habits into the bright light of public discourse—for the first time. New norms take hold the instant people begin to defend them. When a critical mass of people practice 200 percent accountability, change is all but assured.

## SUMMARY: SOCIAL MOTIVATION

People who are respected and connected can exert an enormous amount of influence over any change effort. Under stressful and ambiguous circumstances, a mere glance from someone who is considered to be a respected official can be enough to propel people to act in ways that are hard to imagine. Fortunately, this "power of one" (often viewed as negative) can also be used to encourage pro-social behavior.

When a vital behavior is difficult or unpopular or possibly even questionable, you must lead the way. You must not just talk the talk, you have to walk it as well. However, people aren't likely to trust your words until you demonstrate your willingness to sacrifice old values for new ones. You'll need to create visible and believable evidence by sacrificing time, money, ego, and other priorities before people will take similar risks themselves.

While it's true that you must lead the way, you will also need the support of those who have more immediate contact with those you're trying to influence. It often takes the support of formal leaders and opinion leaders—to make it safe for people to embrace an innovation. Learn how to identify and partner with these important people. Ignore opinion leaders at your own peril.

Finally, sometimes change efforts call for changes in widely shared norms. You can do this in two ways. First, go public. You can't change norms without discussing them. Detractors will often suggest that it's inappropriate to hold such an open discourse, and they may even go so far as to suggest that the topic is undiscussable. Ignore those who seek silence instead of healthy dialogue. Make it safe to talk about high-stakes and controversial topics—including concerns about any proposed changes.

Second, to create new norms, invite everyone to hold everyone else accountable. Lead the way by praising and critiquing the presence or absence of vital behaviors. Enlist formal leaders and opinion leaders in doing the same. And ultimately create a widely shared norm of 200 percent accountability—where everyone is responsible not just to practice the new behaviors—but to communicate clear expectations to everyone they touch.

Remember, social influence—the deeply felt desire to be accepted, respected, and connected to other human beings—really pulls at human heartstrings. It often sits at the top of the heap of all sources of influence. Consequently, whether you're a manager, parent, or coach, it doesn't matter. The problem you're facing doesn't matter. Learn how to tap into the power of social influence, and you can change just about anything.

# 7
# Provide Assistance

## SOCIAL ABILITY

*Never run after your own hat—others will be delighted to do it; why spoil their fun?*

*—Mark Twain*

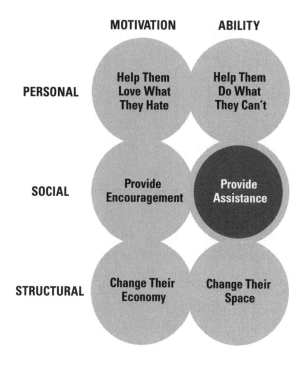

|  | MOTIVATION | ABILITY |
|---|---|---|
| **PERSONAL** | Help Them Love What They Hate | Help Them Do What They Can't |
| **SOCIAL** | Provide Encouragement | Provide Assistance |
| **STRUCTURAL** | Change Their Economy | Change Their Space |

A s we've just discussed, most of our actions are far more influenced by others than many of us imagine. That's why influencers take care to ensure that those they want to influence are sufficiently *encouraged* to adopt vital behaviors. But encouragement isn't enough. Offering a supportive smile is good, but when people need permission, information, coaching, or hands-on help, a friendly nod won't cut it. It's time to make use of source 4, *social ability.*

So we'll start this chapter with one of our favorite examples of an influencer who enables millions of people across half a continent to enact new vital behaviors by brilliantly leveraging the help of their friends.

Seated in a tight circle in a neat, tin-roofed building located in a small village in central India, we find five housewives—Tanika, Kamara, Damini, Payal, and Sankul. They're in the middle of the most important meeting they'll ever attend. They're selecting the first of five businesses they'll start (one each) through small loans from Ujjivan, a local microcredit firm that has set up shop in the region.

Despite the fact that none of these women has ever held a job outside the home or taken a single course in business, and despite the fact that all are caring for families of their own with little or no help from their husbands or ex-husbands, nobody will tell these five women what businesses to start. They will invent businesses on their own as a team.

Today Tanika plans to propose that she be the first of the five women to start her own business. She is desperate to get started because, like many women within a radius of several hundred miles, she lives in gut-wrenching poverty.

"Maybe I can start an egg business like my friend Chatri," one of the women, Payal, suggests with a shy smile.

"You can't start there," Sankul explains. "It takes three or four loans to work your way up to such a large investment. We have to think smaller."

"My cousin Mitali has enjoyed great success with the mini-van she rents," Kamara enthuses.

Once again Sankul sets her friends straight. "That requires an even larger investment. It has taken your cousin over five years to work her way up to a vehicle. We're beginners and have to start much smaller."

"I've got it!" Damini suggests. "I would like to make puffed rice. It takes very little money, and I've heard that many women in nearby villages are now doing well with similar ventures."

"That's the problem," Tanika says. "Too many people are in that business, and profits could drop."

"Then what do you think will work?" Damini asks Tanika.

Tanika makes her move. "I think I have a plan that will make money, even for a beginning person like me. You all know that I have earned money in the past by collecting hair from the local barber shops and making wigs."

"Yes, and they're beautiful," Sankul responds. "But you haven't been able to live off of that."

Tanika remains undeterred. The circumstances she faces are far too desperate for her to back away at the first sign of discouragement. Three months earlier when her husband sold his rice crop for far less than he expected, he came home one evening screaming obscenities, beat her, accused her of dragging him into poverty, called her ugly, and threw her and their three daughters into the street. Under normal circumstances in her village, a divorce such as this would have been a death sentence for Tanika and her children.

But these weren't normal circumstances. One day as Tanika sat in her tiny hut, worrying about her family's next meal, her neighbor Sankul approached her with wonderful news. A group of people from the city was starting to loan money to women such as her as a means of helping them start new businesses.

"It's our turn!" Sankul had said. "It's our turn to help lift ourselves out of poverty." Tanika liked the idea but had to admit that the radical words sounded like something Sankul must have heard from one of the strangers from the city. What did they know that she didn't?

*Who would loan money to a nearly starved woman of no means?* Tanika wondered. *How will I be able to come up with an idea for a successful business?*

As a gentle but unrelenting rain starts to beat its tattoo on the tin roof over the five Indian women, Tanika continues to articulate her partially formed idea.

"You're right; I can't count on wig making. But I know of a place that will buy hair and use the oil from the hair follicles to make health products. I was thinking that if I could find new ways to gather hair, I could sell it to that company and make enough money to feed and clothe my family."

"How do you propose to do that?" asked Payal, the shiest of the five would-be entrepreneurs. "I'll gladly give you the hair from my hair brushes. It does me no good," said Damini, offering her support. "So will I," Kamara chimed in. "And I bet we could get all of our neighbors to do the same."

Tanika had thought about asking her neighbors for the hair from their brushes and was encouraged to hear that her friends would support her.

"I was thinking that maybe I could hire people to gather hair from surrounding neighborhoods," she explained. "Yes,"

Sankul agreed, "but how would you pay them?" "Hire children," Kamara proposed. "You wouldn't have to pay them much, and surely children can gather hair."

"Toys!" Damini shouted. "Buy a batch of small plastic toys and offer them to any child who brings you hair. That way you'll get hair for almost nothing, and the money from your sales will be nearly all profit."

And with that final addition to her original idea, Tanika had all the elements of a business plan. Tanika secured a loan of $20 and immediately bought a bag full of inexpensive plastic toys. Then, much like an entrepreneurial Santa Claus, Tanika trudged with her sack of trinkets from village to village.

"I'll let you pick any toy you'd like from the bag if you'll bring me all the hair in your mother and sisters' hairbrushes," Tanika explained to the first group of waifs she encountered.

When the word got out that hair earned toys, our unlikely entrepreneur was inundated. Eventually Tanika sold the hair, repaid her loan, and had capital left over to expand.

A year has passed, and Tanika now has hundreds of women working for her. They gather hair in the villages using toys and sell the hair to Tanika, who then sells it again for a profit. She no longer worries about her family's next meal. And not only has she raised her family to a position far above the poverty line but Tanika is no longer the same shy, frightened person she was a year ago.

## LESSONS FROM A NOBEL LAUREATE

This example raises an interesting question. Why was Tanika able to succeed despite the fact that hundreds of millions of people just like her have failed to fight their way out of poverty? To answer this question, we need to spend time with a recent

Nobel Prize winner who just happens to be the genius behind Tanika's success. Meet the soft-spoken and brilliant Muhammad Yunus. He's the man who figured out how to help Tanika and another hundred million people out of poverty.

Here's the part of his amazing story that provides the central theme to this chapter. After leaving the United States with a doctorate in economics, Dr. Yunus decided to return to his homeland of Bangladesh to become a university professor. As he assumed his comfortable teaching position, he was horrified to discover that just outside the academic compound, hundreds of thousands of people were dying of starvation.

As Dr. Yunus investigated, it didn't take him long to discover that the root cause of Bangladesh's acute and chronic poverty was not the indolence of the poor. Everywhere he looked in neighboring villages he saw people who worked hard but who were still unable to earn a decent wage. After interviewing 42 people in one village, he was shocked to discover that the biggest barrier was not energy, but capital. Few in these villages had traditional jobs. Most were self-employed. If they weren't supported by their own small plot of land, they were the sole proprietor of a small craft or service business.

To finance their businesses, they needed capital. Usually it was just a few pennies. Since none had even this small amount, they were forced to turn to local loan sharks who charged over 1,000 percent interest. The interest rate was set at just the point to guarantee that each entrepreneur would exhaust his or her income repaying the loan and forever be locked in a cycle of indebtedness. Yunus was dumbfounded when he discovered that a woman who made beautiful handcrafted stools was held in poverty because she lacked the 5 cents she would need to buy supplies each day. Five cents!

Yunus ended his research with the conclusion that if he could enable one vital behavior (villagers' successfully securing and repaying a business loan), he could improve the financial fortunes of the 42 people he interviewed. In total, the 42 people he interviewed needed a paltry $27 to finance their businesses.

Yunus next turned to local banks and suggested that they offer loans to these 42 laborers at market rates. No takers. In fact, bank executives laughed him out of their offices. As far as they were concerned, no collateral, no loans! This harsh policy caused Dr. Yunus grave distress. In his own words:

> *Usually when my head touches the pillow, I fall asleep within seconds, but that night I lay in bed ashamed that I was part of a society which could not provide $27 to forty-two able-bodied, hard-working, skilled persons to make a living for themselves.*

Thirty years have passed since that tortured day, and Dr. Yunus now runs a multi-billion-dollar banking and business conglomerate known as Grameen Bank, which has started a revolution that has helped more than 100 million people like Tanika out of poverty. The microcredit group that loaned Tanika the starting cash she needed in neighboring India was formed as a direct result of Dr. Yunus's work.

What makes this story even more remarkable is that Dr. Yunus's methods not only helped Tanika but also her four friends who opened small businesses and succeeded—as do 39 out of every 40 people that Dr. Yunus helps. That's correct—98 percent of the people to whom Yunus loans money enact the second vital behavior for moving themselves out of abject poverty: they pay back their loans with full interest.

The majority of these successful business owners move their families out of poverty. They educate their children, and by now many of these children have earned advanced degrees. Once-starving villagers who at one time earned 2 cents for a day's hard labor now run profitable businesses while their children attend universities.

As inspiring as this story is, the key takeaway lies in learning how Yunus was able to ensure that his poverty-stricken clients were able to enact the vital behaviors that led to success. What influence magic does he work to ensure that noncollateralized loans are paid back over 98 percent of the time? Equally important, which strategies can you and I put into place as still another powerful tool in our influence repertoire?

As is the case with any complex intervention that claims to change people with long histories of painful failures, Dr. Yunus makes use of virtually every method we mention in this book. His task is too large to rely on a single influence tool, so he uses them all. Nevertheless, by watching Tanika and her colleagues in action, we can focus on yet another high-leverage influence tool: the power of *social capital.*

Dr. Yunus didn't merely ask Tanika to submit a business plan that he would review. He demanded that she form a team with four of her neighbors, each of whom would submit plans of her own. Each person from the team would eventually be granted a loan. And with the granting of a loan, each of the other four people would cosign for the debt! That meant that Tanika had to convince her four friends that her business idea would work. More likely, she would have to work with them to create a plan that they would first co-invent and then support.

What do you suppose happens when people who have never worked a job and who are currently inches away from the jaws of the grim reaper are being asked to cosign their new team-mate's note in case the business fails? They don't put up with any half-baked ideas. They create smart and workable plans by uniting the intellectual capital of all five people in the group.

## ENLIST THE POWER OF SOCIAL CAPITAL

In Chapter 6, we learned that other people can motivate us in profound ways. Now we add the second of the two social sources of influence: social ability. As the Beatles suggested, we're most likely to succeed when we have "a little help from our friends." These friends provide us with access to their brains, give us the strength of their hands, and even allow us to make use of their many other personal resources. In effect, they provide us with social capital. In fact, with a little help from our friends, we can produce a force greater than the sum of our individual efforts. But we can do this only when we know how to make use of social capital—*the profound enabling power of an essential network of relationships.* And Dr. Yunus has made use of this power as well as anyone alive.

Popular author James Surowiecki has explained why Tanika was able to come up with her successful business plan. Surowiecki was the first to suggest that the idea he proposes in his book *The Wisdom of Crowds* has been around for a long time. In his very first sentence, Surowiecki points to British scientist Francis Galton, who applied statistical methods to demonstrate that groups—made up of people at all intellectual levels—often perform better than any one individual.

When 787 local residents who visited a regional livestock fair guessed the weight of a slaughtered and dressed ox, Galton calculated the average score of the locals who predicted the weight to be 1,197 pounds. The ox eventually weighed in at 1,198 pounds. The group average wasn't merely close to the correct weight. It was almost exactly correct. The point Surowiecki makes about crowds is this: "Under the right circumstances, groups are remarkably intelligent and are often smarter than the smartest people in them."

Long before Surowiecki popularized the idea that groups can do better than the smartest individuals, Dr. Yunus put this notion to work in his microcredit enterprises. Consider the five women who had never held jobs as they were brainstorming ways to leverage Tanika's scheme. No one person came up with the final plan, but, by playing off each other's suggestions, they jointly came up with a method that succeeded. They were able to do so because they weren't merely pooling ignorance; they were inventing products and services that would sell in their own village, and they all knew their village.

## BUILD SOCIAL CAPITAL BY PROVIDING ASSISTANCE

Sometimes it's obvious that a profound change in behavior will require assistance from others. For example, if Dr. Don Berwick and his team want to save 100,000 patients from accidental death in U.S. hospitals, it's clear that they'll need to involve doctors, nurses, administrators, housekeepers, and others. The same is true with Dr. Silbert's work with ex-cons. She doesn't merely rely on a village to help her. She actually *creates* a village.

Sometimes it's not so obvious that your change strategy requires anyone other than yourself. For example, you might think that sticking with a diet is a matter of individual will. In the solitary moments when you're deciding between a deep-fried apple turnover and an apple, it's all up to you. But you'd be wrong to make the assumption that you're alone. While all vital behaviors are enacted by individuals and often done in private, an enabling group of individuals can make an enormous difference in influencing change.

For example, Dr. Wiwat succeeded at influencing vulnerable sex workers who can feel quite intimidated when facing a liquored-up client who demands sex with no condom. As we'll see shortly, although the sex worker is flying solo in these moments, scores of other people will find a way to help her succeed. Clever influencers always consider ways to ensure that individuals have sufficient social support to step up and succeed in crucial moments.

So, when exactly should you provide assistance to bring about challenging changes?

## When Others Are Part of the Problem

Consider the following common business problem. It highlights exactly when people need to rely on the help of others in order to succeed at work.

Meet Jess. At this very moment he's sweating like an Olympic boxer. That's because he's about to tell a lie, and he's afraid he'll get caught. Jess fears that he'll get caught because, unlike a good poker player who can bluff without giving off a clue, Jess has "tells" that he's powerless to mask. Right now in addition to sweating profusely, his left eye is twitching so violently that he's sure it must be visible from across the room. As Jess starts to speak, his throat constricts to the size of a straw—still another tell. After faking a coughing seizure, Jess eventually squeaks out the big, fat lie that's sure to get him in trouble.

"No problem," Jess mutters. "We're right on target."

Jess isn't the only fibber at the table. Everyone in this product development meeting is stretching the truth. In fact, at the 1,500-person software development group where Jess works, telling your coworkers and bosses that your work is on schedule when it actually isn't is deeply rooted in the culture. Lying about readiness is so common that Jess and his colleagues have given it a special name. It's called "project chicken."

Here's how the game is played. You say you're ready with your part of a project when you aren't, in the hope that someone else will admit that he or she will need to extend the deadline. The first person to lose nerve and say "I need more time" is the chicken. And like the vehicular version of the same game, once someone swerves, everyone else is safe. All the others are off the hook because they'll benefit from the new extended deadline, only they didn't have to admit that they messed up. In this particular meeting, most of the team leaders at the table, just like Jess, are dangerously behind. Yet none of them will admit it. Nobody swerves, the deadline isn't extended, and, as a result of their combined lying, a major product release will soon end in disaster.

When we (the authors) first started working with this particular software company, it was on the brink of bankruptcy. It had not met a product release date in years. And when the company finally did release products, those products typically cost twice as much as they should have. Morale was at an all-time low, so in addition to product problems, the company was losing far too many of its most talented players.

Mike, the newly appointed VP of development, was tasked with turning around this situation. He had already identified the vital behavior he had to influence. He knew that if he could find a way to both motivate and enable employees up and down the organization to speak up early and honestly about problems, the company would improve morale, reduce costs, and gain control of the schedule. But that was a big order.

When we first met Mike, he had already tried several strategies. He had implemented communication training. He had identified opinion leaders and asked them to help solve the problem. He had even created an anonymous survey to measure whether or not behavior was changing. Still, the organization was stuck. In fact, Mike told us that all he had to show for his effort was good solid data that the company was failing.

What Mike didn't realize until late in the game was that Jess and his colleagues were not isolated actors making independent decisions about how to talk about deadlines in meetings. Lying in order to look good had been reinforced by managers, directors, and vice presidents. Even Mike had unwittingly played a role in encouraging people to bring only good news to the table. And since the behavior was created by the group, the group would have to be involved in changing it. So how could he provide assistance?

To answer this, let's see how someone else dealt with a similar problem. We travel 9,000 miles to South Africa to study Garth Japhet. No one has thought longer, harder, or more carefully about how to build social capital than Garth Japhet. He's a master at turning a *me* problem into a *we* problem.

Dr. Japhet began his career as a medical doctor, but he wound a circuitous path to his current position as CEO of Soul City, a South African media brain trust that has led successful efforts to fight AIDS, infant mortality, and malnutrition. More recently, Japhet has turned his attention to preventing violence against women. Dr. Japhet has directed his attention to this particular problem because, within the borders of South Africa, the scourge of violence against women is nothing short of horrendous. One in nine women will be raped at least once in her lifetime. One in five will be physically or emotionally abused by her partner.

Dr. Japhet realized that he wasn't about to solve this deeply entrenched problem by teaching women individually to stand up on their own two feet and eventually overthrow the insensitive men who obviously deserved a comeuppance. Instead, Japhet realized that he'd have to find a way to include everyone who was *creating* the problem in *solving* the problem.

Japhet also understood that there were many in South African society who disapproved of the abuse—both women and men. And yet these people felt unable to exert sufficient influence to change the behavior they despised. So Japhet gave them a way. In his own words:

> *On the TV program* Soul City, *we purposefully created a well-respected teacher, Thabang, who repeatedly abused his likable wife Matlakala. Viewers—both male and female—quickly concluded that Matlakala didn't deserve the abuse as tradition had often indicated. She was pleasant, easy to get along with, and nothing more than an innocent victim. Equally curious, Thabang was mostly a reasonable and good person—much like themselves.*

Then the writers showed how interested friends and neighbors could be part of the solution. Dr. Arvind Singhal, who served as a research adviser to *Soul City*, reports: "On one episode the neighbors hear Thabang beating poor Matlakala, and they can take it no longer, so they decide to let Thabang know that his actions aren't going unobserved. But how? How could they let Thabang know without being too intrusive? How could they do it without putting themselves at physical risk? Saying something directly would be unacceptable and dangerous."

Dr. Singhal continues: "To send their violent neighbor the message that his behavior is neither private nor acceptable, the neighbors gather outside Thabang's front door and bang pots and pans. They don't say a word; they just bang pots and pans." In the program, Thabang becomes embarrassed and begins to change his behavior.

What happened after that was totally unexpected. People in several townships across South Africa, upon hearing the sounds of spousal abuse next door, began to stand in front of their neighbors' home and bang pots and pans.

The power of vicarious modeling worked its magic. The message was out. Men would no longer be allowed to abuse their wives with impunity. Violent behavior, and the collective silence that supported it, were not part of the new norm.

Here's the influence takeaway. Japhet realized that if bad behavior is reinforced by a web of players, all the players have to be engaged in influencing change. In this particular case, the neighbors had to help lead the change for good because neighbors who stood by and allowed obvious abuse to continue were a big part of the problem.

And that's also how Mike, the VP of development, finally eliminated "project chicken." He had first tried to solve the problem by confronting employees like Jess without addressing the role his managers, directors, and a host of others played in the problem. When he realized what was missing, he took a completely different tack. He asked the training department to teach people how to hold high-stakes conversations about project problems. Then he charged every one of his organization's leaders to be the teachers. It was a stroke of brilliance that changed everything.

Every two weeks the very manager who had previously sent subtle signals about suppressing candor taught a two-hour session on how to speak up about risky problems. In the first two sessions Jess listened passively and cynically. By the third session he raised a concern with his manager. In the context of the class, the manager felt a special responsibility to respond appropriately. By the sixth session many of Jess's peers had begun to open up. Within a matter of months powerful new norms emerged, and Mike's vital behavior of candor under pressure flourished. Within a year the organization had launched two product releases on time and on budget, and morale was at an all-time high.*

To see how providing assistance can apply at home, let's return to our friend Henry as he continues his lifelong quest to eat healthily and keep his weight down. He's learned that when it comes to coworkers, friends, and family members, most are full-out enablers, not helpers. Instead of acting like friends, they act like accomplices in the crimes against his body. They take Henry out to fancy restaurants, eat fatty and delicious food in front of him at work, give him gifts of the very food he loves but shouldn't eat, stock the pantry chock-full of all the wrong ingredients, and so on.

In fact, when it comes to losing weight, Henry can't think of anyone who is helping him in any way. One day when he asks his wife to stop buying bags of chocolate candy, she actually laughs out loud. She loves candy, buys candy, eats candy, and never gains a pound, so why shouldn't she buy candy?

---

*For more information on this and other case studies, visit www.vitalsmarts.com/corporate casestudies.aspx.

But Henry knows it's hard to go it alone. "Hey, look at me. I live here in the apartment with you. I smell all that delicious chocolate, and it drives me crazy!"

And it wasn't just his olfactory powers that clued Henry in about the importance of enlisting others' help. He had recently read a study (conducted by our friend Albert Bandura) about research subjects who were trying to lower their cholesterol. As both Henry and Bandura suspected, participants routinely achieved greater reductions in their cholesterol when their spouses took part in the program.

So Henry has to find a way to step up to his enablers and ask them to become helpers. This means that Henry will have to talk to others in a way that creates genuine dialogue rather than resistance and recrimination.

## When You Can't Succeed on Your Own

The poet John Donne was right: no man is an island. When the people surrounding you are causing or contributing to the problems, playing the role of enabler rather than helper, you need to fight the urge to attack your detractors for their contribution to your pain. Instead, co-opt them. Turn a *me* problem into a *we* problem. Provide assistance in order to help people turn vital behaviors into productive habits.

**Interdependence.** When a vital behavior requires several people to work in concert—where no one person can succeed on his or her own—you have to develop people's ability to work as a team. There was a time when highly skilled craftspeople worked alone producing pots, candles, jewelry, and the like. But today corporate success often depends on experts who are at least as specialized as their predecessors and who rely on one another to complete their tasks.

For instance, a typical software development team consists not only of code writers but also of designers, marketers, writers, and salespeople. At various stages in the development, all have to connect, bring their piece of the project online, and, at the interpersonal level, find a way to collaborate. Leaders who fail to appreciate this concept are regularly disappointed when their influence efforts bear no fruit.

We (the authors) once worked with a production team that had decided to lower costs by shifting to just-in-time inventory. This meant that no longer would the company maintain a stock of parts and works-in-progress as the product made its way through the production line. One expert would hand his or her finished work to the next expert instead of placing it in a stack that the next person would get to at his or her leisure. This new design, of course, called for impeccable timing (each person's job needed to take the same amount of time as the person's before and after him or her). It also called for genuine collaboration. If any one person slowed down, sped up, took an unscheduled break, or failed to meet a quality standard, it caused the previous and next person fits.

When we arrived to help with the project, the company had learned that the old style of stacking expensive inventory between employees had masked the workforce's inability to cooperate. Now that employees were immediately dependent on the person before and after them, they were constantly bickering, complaining, and asking to change positions in the line. Supervisors would routinely intervene to help their direct reports work through problems, but they ended up spending most of their time refereeing heated arguments.

It turned out that the company wasn't prepared to shift to a just-in-time system because it didn't possess the skills to collaborate. When executives purposely built interdependence into the work design, the new design quickly revealed that employees lacked interpersonal problem-solving skills along with the ability to hold one another accountable. Working in isolation had atrophied their ability to interact effectively. No longer did employees "work and play well" with their friends.

The company was unable to implement the new inventory system until each employee had been trained in interpersonal problem solving. Interdependence calls for individuals to share ideas, provide materials, lend a hand, subordinate one's personal needs to the needs of the group, and otherwise willingly and ably collaborate. Leaders who don't continually help interdependent employees learn new and better ways to work in tandem tend to routinely suffer from rivalry, and they are never able to make full use of their valuable social capital.

**Novelty.** Tanika's group demonstrates another circumstance that calls for the power of social capital. Tanika and the other members of her borrower group were certainly not specialists, and they faced problems that were completely new to them. Fortunately, the toys-for-hair plan the five came up with grew out of the best thinking of the group. No one person had exactly the right idea, but as one partial idea was added upon and then changed again, each person helped create a strategy that, if left to her own devices, none would have invented.

When facing changing, turbulent, or novel times—calling for novel solutions—multiple heads can be better than one. By demanding that no budding entrepreneur work alone, Dr. Yunus ensures that his microcredit clients always work in teams, think in teams, and meet every single week and brainstorm as teams. Grameen Bank counts on synergy through forced interaction.

**Risk.** As you might expect, among all the influencers we have studied, those who faced the biggest risks also worked the hardest to provide assistance as a means of influencing change during crucial moments. Toward the top of this list, of course, would be Dr. Silbert, whose job it is to transform hardened criminals into productive citizens. Think of what Silbert's wards do as a matter of their daily work, and you'll appreciate just how much risk she and her organization face.

Every day about a hundred of Silbert's San Francisco residents invade people's residences across the Bay Area and remove their valuables. This is something many of them did before joining Delancey. The difference now is that they are doing so as part of the Delancey Moving Company. That's right, people who had once made a living moving furniture and other goods illegally are now doing so legally. You'd think that this business strategy was far too risky given the employees' job histories. Nevertheless, every single valuable Delancey movers remove shows up at the new residence. Delancey is the largest privately owned moving company in the Bay Area for a good reason. The company has never had a loss or theft. Imagine what would happen if even one pearl necklace came up missing. Delancey's reputation would be lost, and the moving company along with its 100 jobs would simply disappear. In spite of huge risk, Delancey has *no* problems.

Equally astounding is the fact that in the Delancey restaurant, residents still reeling from alcohol or drug withdrawal serve alcohol to customers as part of their daily job. Hearing about this obvious incongruity for the first time, we asked Silbert how she deals with "relapses." Without hesitation, she answered, "We don't have relapse." When we pressed her, she thought back to the last instance of abuse and acknowledged that a year earlier one person had "gotten dirty." To fully appreciate what this means, we need to consider that the average rehab program has a very low success rate.

Silbert sends criminals into people's homes, and she asks alcoholics to serve drinks—with almost *no* problems. When you ask her why her influence strategy succeeds, she explains that a key lies in the complex, pervasive, and powerful social system of Delancey. The organization does not have a single in-house professional, but it does have a great deal of social capital. Delancey relies on a web of helping relationships that Silbert has constructed for over 30 years.

Here's how she provides assistance as a means of supporting vital behaviors. Silbert structures the entire Delancey experience around residents giving each other instruction, mentoring, and guidance. That means that a resident who has been onboard for a single day is likely to be asked to assist someone who has just arrived. And despite the fact that a resident may have shown up at the front door hungover, uneducated, and skilled only in criminal behavior, he or she will eventually earn the equivalent of a PhD in mentoring, coaching, and teaching—or nobody will make it out alive.

In Silbert's words, "You learn a little and then teach it to someone else—'Each one teach one.' For example, you're at Delancey a hot minute and someone newer than you comes in. So someone says to you, 'Do me a favor, take him under your wing.' From that point on, people talk with you more about how you're doing with the guys under you than about yourself."

To ensure that individuals assist one another, Delancey is structured with one goal in mind. From the moment a resident arrives at Delancey—frightened and suspicious—he or she is immersed in a culture and language system designed to maximize peer support. If you were a resident, here's how you'd be enriched with assistance.

When you first show up, you're assigned to a dorm of nine individuals of different races. Next, you're placed in what is known as a "minyan." A minyan is made up of 10 people from different dorms. The word *minyan* originates from Jewish tradition and refers to a congregation consisting of 10 adults. A full minyan is required to be present before public services can be held. So, the Delancey version of a minyan is a self-supporting group that's able to do what residents would be unable to do on their own. At Delancey, minyans practically print social capital.

Minyan leaders take primary responsibility for residents' growth, needs, and supervision. Minyans, in turn, are supervised by a "barber." (A good bawling out or scolding on the street is sometimes referred to as a "haircut." Hence, the title *barber* goes to those whose job it is to ensure that everyone in the minyan is challenging everyone else.)

Assistance comes in still more forms. For example, residents work for crews with crew bosses who are also peers. The average person arrives with a seventh-grade education, and each is required to leave Delancey with at least a high school equivalency certificate. And Delancey achieves this amazing result without hiring a single professional teacher. They provide assistance by tutoring each other.

To see how all this coaching, teaching, modeling, and tutoring plays itself out, consider the field of romance.

"We're not healthy," our Delancey resident James admits. "We shouldn't be in relationships until we can see the thing is more than sex. We tend to just say, 'The hell with it!' when the relationship gets tough."

So to prepare to go on dates (something they're not allowed to do for at least six months), residents attend couples' groups that, as you've probably guessed, are taught by resident couples who have been dating slightly longer than the new students. The more seasoned couples teach others how to behave on dates as well as how to talk about what's working and what isn't. And guess who will be going along with each new couple on their first few dates. A chaperone who is assigned by the barber to keep the two on the straight and narrow.

This is just a small sampling of how an organization that has virtually no professional resources provides interpersonal assistance as a powerful influence for changing people's behavior—and lives. Now, if a philanthropist left a billion dollars to Delancey so that the institution could afford to hire professional teachers, counselors, and coaches, do you think Dr. Silbert would allow it? Of course not. By helping others, residents help themselves even more. Teachers learn more than students, mentors more than mentees, and trainers more trainees, so why restrict all this important learning to outside professionals who have already been to school?

At the business level, more than one organization is beginning to understand how to reduce risk by making better use of social capital. For example, venture capitalists in Silicon Valley create "business incubators" as a way of helping new businesses survive the risky start-up phase. The incubators are systems through which specialists of all types freely offer expertise to companies when that advice is most needed.

From a personal career standpoint, the need to provide assistance by connecting with others has never been greater. Tom Boyle of British Telecom coined the expression *network quotient* (NQ) to highlight the importance of a person's ability to form connections with others. He argues that from a career standpoint a person's NQ is now more important than his or her intelligence quotient (IQ). Since you can't know everything, it's essential that you find people who can make up for your blind spots. A whole host of recent studies has revealed that today's most successful employees have networks of people they can go to for expertise, as well as networks of people they can trust with sensitive requests. Successful people not only refuse to see themselves as islands but they also carefully reduce their personal vulnerability by ensuring that they're valued members of hyperconnected networks.

All these examples deal with the same problem. Changing, complex, turbulent, and risky times require multiple heads to come up with creative solutions that no one person could ever invent. So take your lead from Dr. Yunus. When problems call for creativity and multiple views, place people in teams. To make the best use of your existing human resources and dramatically lower your risks, take your lead from Delancey by turning your more experienced employees into coaches, trainers, instructors, and mentors.

**Blind Spots.** Perhaps the most obvious condition that demands social support as a means of influencing vital behaviors comes with the need for feedback that can be offered only by a pair of outside eyes. Anyone who has ever tried to learn tennis on his or her own and then gone head-on with someone who has spent a similar amount of time practicing with the aid of a coach quickly learns that real-time feedback from an expert beats solo practice any day. This being the case, you'd think that most people would turn to coaches to help in key areas of their lives, but they don't. Only a few ask for feedback outside of sports arenas.

But there are exceptions. For example, in healthcare, where doctors are required to insert tubes in people's hearts and per-

**ACT LIKE AN INFLUENCER**

We often call for assistance when dealing with risky situations. For example: police officers call for backup before entering into danger; nurses ask for assistance before moving a heavy patient who could fall; recovering spendaholics bring their sponsor on shopping expeditions to keep them on budget; and new teachers pair up when dealing with difficult students or parents.

Think through the crucial moments when your vital behaviors are most at risk. Remember, these crucial moments are the times, places, people, moods, and circumstances when you are most likely to fail. Find a way to buddy up for protection in these few crucial moments.

form other such high-stakes practices, professionals long ago learned the power of real-time coaching. In many instances, physicians aren't allowed to merely watch others perform a detailed and dangerous procedure before they try it on their own. Instead, they must attempt the delicate procedure while a coach provides immediate feedback on what's working and what isn't.

When it comes to business and other lower-risk settings, leaders rarely think of using real-time coaches. Some of today's companies provide their leaders with call-in advisers who discuss what happened yesterday when the leader faced a challenge and didn't do all that well. But few provide real-time coaching. This should change.

For example, when we (the authors) worked with Lauren, a rather vibrant executive who was a terrible speaker, we provided her with a speech coach. It was amazing to watch someone once described as having "the uncanny ability to whip a crowd into a nap" be transformed into a solid speaker in a matter of a few hours. Lauren didn't take a course or read a book. She merely practiced giving a speech while receiving immediate feedback: "Pick up the speed by 10 percent." "Pause after the word 'successful.' " After four hours of guided instruction, Lauren learned what might have taken months without feedback.

Since you're on the wrong side of your eyeballs, you can't always see exactly what it is that you're doing that works or doesn't work. So invest in still another form of assistance: seek real-time feedback from an expert.

**Group Solidarity.** In a parable by William Forster Lloyd published in 1833, we first hear of a problem that is now known as the "tragedy of the commons." The parable describes how a town allowed farmers to graze livestock at will on common soil—soil often owned by nobility. This well-intentioned practice eventually led to a public disaster. The more successful a farmer became, the more sheep he grazed, until eventually there were so many sheep grazing on the land that "the common" was destroyed. What was good for the individual farmer was bad for the collective whole.

You might have faced a similarly constructed scenario. For instance, after plodding along for an hour in stop-and-go traffic, you come across the cause of the holdup. You discover that a large box lies in one lane, causing the snarl. On the one hand, what's good for you—zooming off immediately—is bad for everyone who follows. On the other hand, if you sacrifice

## ACT LIKE AN INFLUENCER

When Rich Sheridan of Menlo Software decided to redesign how his employees create software (from top to bottom), he wanted to make sure that individuals didn't feel alone, isolated, or cut off—or like the sole possessors of certain knowledge, which would make them indispensable and unable to take vacations. So Rich put code writers in teams of two—sharing one computer.

At first, this cramped everyone's style. Everyone wanted to sit in the driver's seat and write his or her own code. Soon the teams found that with one person typing and one co-designing and watching, they caught errors early on—cutting their time on fixing errors (something everyone hates) from 40 percent of their working time to no time at all. They also reduced "knowledge silos," situations in which only one person knew what was going on.

Now there were two or more experts working on every job. "Since then, we've never had to turn down a vacation request," Rich explains. By creating interdependent pairs (meaning everyone has someone to lean on), just about every measure has improved—including morale.

your own interest and step out of the car and remove the box, everyone else will benefit.

Under these conditions, individuals have to learn how to invest in one of the most powerful forms of social capital: solidarity. We must give ourselves up to the larger cause and act for the good of everyone else, or the plan will fail. For instance, we (the authors) were once charged with creating a leadership class that taught newly appointed frontline supervisors how to hold their direct reports accountable. To create the course, we looked for positive deviance. We watched those who succeeded where others failed in action, learned what they did, and then included their unique skills in an accountability class.

After completing the course, all the graduates were asked to put into practice what they had just learned by talking to people who broke rules, violated procedures, or otherwise behaved badly. But a few didn't put their new skills into practice. These "late adopters" waited to see if their colleagues were going to step up to the challenge before they gave their new tools a trial run. The majority who did confront their direct reports about deviations were soon ridiculed for being too tough. Hourly folks pointed to the supervisors who weren't setting the same standards for their employees and concluded that their own bosses were unfair or hard-nosed. Eventually everyone stopped applying what he or she had studied.

We learned from this incident the power of solidarity. From that point on, we secured the promise of every supervisor that he or she would step up to problems before we sent anyone into action. With that particular change project, asking employees to toe the line turned out to be an all-or-nothing deal.

To see the importance of solidarity on a much larger scale, let's look at how our friend Dr. Wiwat from Thailand engaged others' assistance to help stop the spread of HIV/AIDS. After failing to make a dent in the problem using traditional influence methods, Wiwat took a much more direct approach. Shutting down the sex industry in Thailand was the ideal, but leaders were unable to do so, and the vicious virus was spreading at unprecedented rates. So leaders turned their attention to stopping the spread of HIV/AIDS. Since almost all the new cases were coming from sex workers who weren't protecting themselves or their clients, Wiwat started a campaign of solidarity.

In Wiwat's view, one group of people—sex workers—could bring the spread of HIV/AIDS to a halt, but it would have to be done as a group. When a client offered money for sex and the sex worker demanded protection (a solution to the spread of AIDS), more often than not the client would simply go elsewhere.

But what if *every* worker demanded protection and always refused the financial incentive? Then there would be no place where clients could find sex workers who offered unprotected sex, and eventually every client would practice safe sex, thereby stopping the spread of AIDS. But once again, this plan called for an all-or-nothing deal. If one sex worker broke ranks or one brothel eased its demands, the game would be off.

To ensure that everyone complied, Wiwat held a meeting to which he invited all sex business owners. Then he held a meeting for all their workers. In both forums he explained the economics of why every single person had to participate in the plan or AIDS would eventually kill them all, along with their businesses. He then informed them of HIV growth rates and detailed what would happen if any individual or establishment refused to sign up for the program.

Eventually, when every worker bought into the plan and the entire population banded together by demanding protection, compliance rates increased from around 14 percent to over 90 percent. As a result of demanding solidarity and providing needed social support, an estimated 5 million people have been spared the horrific consequences of contracting HIV/AIDS in Thailand.

What role might solidarity play closer to home? When studying parenting, it doesn't take long to uncover the simple yet important notion that, with effective parents, no means no.

Effective parents help bring predictability into a child's turbulent life by letting him or her know that parents' word is their bond. If a child hits her sister, she'll pay a consequence. If a teenager comes home after curfew, it'll come with a cost. With two parents in the home, the expectation that *no* actually means *no* can of course be achieved only when both parents stand unified, shoulder to shoulder. Otherwise, the child plays one parent off the other, and anarchy prevails. When it comes to disciplining children—as is the case with many profound and pervasive problems—solidarity rules.

## ACT LIKE AN INFLUENCER

Researchers in a Pennsylvania homeless shelter discovered the key to eliminating bedbugs. It was solidarity. The shelter consists of three townhouses connected by shared walls. Thirty-nine people lived in 12 bedrooms within the townhouses.

Here is the problem: bed bugs are fast, tough, nearly invisible, and tenacious. If you make life uncomfortable for them in one bedroom, they'll simply move next door for a while. And then return. The solution was to convince the residents to work together—without a single person being out of step. Every bedroom in every townhouse was treated the same day; every piece of bedding and clothing was washed in hot water that same day; and every item that couldn't be washed was stored in a deep freeze for the day. The result of all of this cooperation and coordination? Bye-bye bed bugs.

## SUMMARY: SOCIAL ABILITY

In an interdependent, turbulent world, our biggest opponents—the mortal enemy of all families, companies, and communities—may well be our inability to work in concert. Since rarely does any one of us have all that's required to succeed with the complex tasks we face every day, we desperately need to build social capital. We need to provide concrete assistance during crucial moments in order to help people change.

However, that's certainly not the message we've been fed for years. The movie and TV heroes of the last half century have fought the enemy within—the big bosses, the establishment, "the man." This constant celebration of the rugged individualist has had an enormous dampening effect on people's willingness to draw on others to enable change.

Influencers know better than to turn their backs on social capital. They're quick to consider what help, authority, consent, or cooperation individuals may need when facing risky or daunting new behaviors. Then they develop an influence strategy that offers the social capital required to help make change inevitable.

# 8
# Change Their Economy
## STRUCTURAL MOTIVATION

*I can take any amount of criticism, so long as it is unqualified praise.*

*—Attributed to Noel Coward*

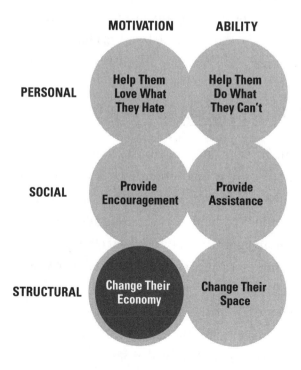

S o far we've explored both personal and social influence. Now we step away from human factors and examine how to optimize the power of *things* such as rewards, perks, bonuses, salaries, and the occasional boot in the rear. Most leaders need no convincing to align rewards with vital behaviors. They fully believe that incentives change behavior. So our advice here may surprise you.

Your goal with structural motivation and using incentives should not be to overwhelm people to change. Rather, it should be primarily to remove disincentives—to "change the economy" as it were. As we'll see, most leaders run the risk of relying too much on incentives rather than too little. If bad behavior is deeply entrenched, odds are that the current economic system people live in is positively encouraging what you don't want. Changing the economy means simply to ensure that positive and negative incentives aren't undermining the influence message you're trying to send. The real work of change must be done by sources 1 (personal motivation) and 3 (social motivation).

## USE EXTRINSIC REWARDS THIRD

We're about to step on dangerous ground. Stories of well-intended rewards that inadvertently backfire are legion. The primary cause of most of these debacles is that individuals attempt to influence behaviors by using rewards as their *first* motivational strategy. In a well-balanced change effort, rewards come *third*. Influencers first ensure that vital behaviors connect to intrinsic satisfaction. Next, they line up social support. They double check both of these areas before they finally choose extrinsic rewards to motivate behavior. If you don't follow this careful order, you're likely to be disappointed.

This particular concept came to the world's attention with a nursery school study that sent out a warning that won't soon be forgotten. In fact, in 1973 when Dr. Mark Lepper and his colleagues examined the effects of rewarding children (giving them their favorite snack) for engaging in activities that they already enjoyed (playing with their favorite toy), change agents, coaches, parents, and leaders all took note.

Dr. Lepper revealed that rewarding people for engaging in an activity that is already satisfying may work against you. Instead of increasing the frequency of the activity, once the reward is taken away, the subjects may do less of it. At least, once the favorite treat was taken away from the Bing Nursery School kids that Lepper studied, they played with their favorite toy less often than they played with it before they were rewarded for doing so.

Think of the implications. You want your daughter to learn to love reading with the same joy and fervor you and your spouse have. You notice that she's starting to pick up the habit on her own, so you decide to reinforce it. To encourage her, you create an incentive program. Every time she picks out a book on her own and reads it, you give her $5. She loves the plan and starts reading more, and after a while she spends her earnings on a new video game for her latest game system. In fact, it's not long until she's able to buy several games, for which she thanks you profusely.

After a while you think that you've rewarded reading enough and that the pure pleasure of soaking in the words of some of the world's best authors has become its own reward. So you pull away the incentive. Surely your encouragement has helped your daughter learn to love reading good books even more. Most certainly she'll now snuggle up with her favorite author's latest work without any encouragement from you.

But your plan backfires. The minute you stop paying your daughter for reading, she turns to her video game system and reads less than she did before you started the incentive program. Apparently she has learned to earn money to purchase video games, and the incentive you tried didn't leave the impression you wanted. She's just like those nursery school kids. Where did you and Dr. Lepper go wrong?

The explanation for this phenomenon, known as "the over-justification hypothesis," suggests that if people receive rewards for doing something they initially enjoy, they conclude the same thing an outsider watching them in action might conclude. When thinking about what's happening, humans recognize that they're doing something *and* getting paid a special bonus for doing it. They conclude that since they're being rewarded for the task, it must not be all that satisfying (why else would someone offer a reward?), and therefore they're doing it for the bonus. And now for the dangerous part. Once the reward is removed, the person believes that the activity isn't as much fun as he or she judged earlier, so he or she does it less often.

Generally people are perfectly happy getting rewarded for something they already enjoy. For example, imagine that you absolutely love playing the harp (a hobby you picked up in your forties) and your next-door neighbor asks you to play at his son's wedding reception—for a nice fee. You love playing, you love the attention, and you are really psyched about getting paid for doing something you already love doing. You can't believe your luck. For you, getting paid to do what you love doing doesn't diminish your affection one tiny bit.

Sometimes, however, making use of extrinsic rewards can be complicated. As Dr. Lepper learned, not every reward has its desired effect. Sometimes extrinsic programs can completely backfire and serve as a punishment. For example, a company's employee-of-the-month program is supposed to give special attention to people who have done something, well, special. They're singled out at an all-hands meeting and are given a plaque.

Comedian Demetri Martin summed up the way a lot of employees feel about such programs when he said, "I think employee-of-the-month is a good example of when a person can be a winner and a loser at the same time."

To many employees, being singled out in front of and compared to peers might not be all that rewarding. It could be just the equivalent of saying, "Congratulations! Here's a hundred dollars, a beautiful plaque with your name engraved on it—and four weeks of unrelenting ridicule from your coworkers!"

Organizational scholars have long found that many employees leave corporate award ceremonies not motivated and excited as intended but with exactly the opposite reaction. They exit demotivated and upset because they themselves weren't honored. In fact, many see the whole ceremony as a sham. Interviews reveal that typically half of those who attend corporate awards programs believe that they were far better qualified than the person who was honored but that they didn't get picked for political reasons.

And it's not just token awards that can go amiss. You could fill volumes with stories of how carefully considered incentive schemes have run amok. One hospital, for example, found that anesthesiologists who were paid based on personal production were less willing to jump in and help one another when someone else's patient was reacting badly.

Consider a couple of the former Soviet Union's attempts to dabble in incentive schemes. In the energy sector, rubles were literally being thrown away in the search for oil reserves because Soviet workers received bonuses according to the number of feet they drilled. It turns out that it's far easier to drill many shallow holes than to drill a few deeper ones—which is exactly what happened. Instead of following the geological advisories to drill deep to find existing reserves, workers were happy merely poking the surface over and over—turning up very little oil. After all, it's what they were rewarded for doing.

One woman we worked with—a manager at an internationally renowned company—decided that her employees weren't as innovative as they needed to be, so she instituted a simple suggestion program. What could be more innocent? To encourage creativity, she asked each work group to meet for at least a half hour per week to brainstorm new work methods, solutions to longstanding problems, and possible new products. To put teeth into the new program, she put together a committee that reviewed submissions and then awarded cash prizes to employees who came up with ideas that were judged as "real moneymakers."

Within a few months the cash-for-ideas program had completely broken down. In fact, members of one work group ended up beating up one of their own team members as a result of the program. It turns out the team came up with a really good idea, and Charlie, the aforementioned team member, promised that he'd take care of the paperwork. He then submitted the suggestion under his own name and kept the $5,000 bonus for himself. When his teammates found out about the deception, first they confronted him, then someone shoved him, then a melee broke out and Charlie ended up in the emergency room.

To avoid further injuries, the owner did away with the incentive program. Of course, she still invited suggestions, but none came in. Employees now believed that she was shorting them by asking for ideas without offering incremental pay. She had hoped to use the suggestion program to stimulate innovation, but she found that by paying people for their thoughts, she had inadvertently sent the message that making suggestions was outside a person's normal job requirements. Now employees believed that if they came up with a good idea, they deserved to be paid a bonus. Otherwise, they were being exploited.

What's a leader to do?

## USE INCENTIVES WISELY

Remember the principle we started with. Don't use incentives to compensate for your failure to engage personal and social motivation. Nevertheless, let's be clear. Influencers eventually use rewards and punishments. For instance, if you don't repay a loan to Muhammad Yunus's Grameen Bank, your borrower group has to pay it back for you. And remember, people there know where you live! If a person in a rural African village discovers that his neighbor is hiding a Guinea worm infection, and if that person brings it to the attention of village leaders, the good citizen is given an attractive t-shirt (emblazoned with a Guinea worm disease eradication logo).

So, the question is, how do you use incentives wisely?

Take care to ensure that the rewards come soon, are gratifying, and are clearly tied to vital behaviors. When you do so, even small rewards can be used to help people overcome some of the most profound and persistent problems. For example, Johns Hopkins Hospital completed a study of alcoholics who had been admitted to the hospital to, of all things, drink alcohol—but only in moderate quantities. The idea of the project wasn't to encourage the subjects to climb on the wagon or to go cold turkey but to learn how to drink in moderation.

To influence patients' behavior, each day staff members determined privileges on the basis of how much alcohol the patients consumed. If they drank too much, they were given pureed food instead of the normal offering. Their amount of consumption also affected phone privileges, visiting hours, and so on. When compared to control patients who were simply told how much to drink with no incentives, experimental subjects were 60 percent more likely to reach their target consumption level.

When you first hear that a simple incentive such as phone privileges can help patients break free from something as powerful as the steel grip of alcoholism, it's a bit hard to believe. Nevertheless, this example pales in comparison to the work of Dr. Stephen Higgins, who routinely uses vouchers to help direct the behavior of cocaine addicts. Cocaine addicts typically fail to make progress in recovery programs because they quit before the program starts to take effect. With Dr. Higgins's voucher system, outpatients are required to submit a urine sample three times a week. If all three samples test negative, the subjects receive a bonus voucher that they can exchange for goods and services provided by the research staff.

With something as tremendously addictive as cocaine, you'd expect that a simple voucher that could be traded only for a rather small prize wouldn't have much of an effect. In Dr. Higgins's own words: "It surprises many people that a stack of paper can outweigh the powerful urge to use cocaine, but it makes sense in terms of what we know about why people use drugs."

Obviously, vouchers alone wouldn't be enough to keep cocaine addicts clean. However, when used with subjects who are already morally and socially invested in giving up cocaine, and when they're combined with traditional methods, those who were given incentives benefited from the motivational boost. Of the patients who were given vouchers, 90 percent finished the 12-week treatment program, whereas only 65 percent of non-voucher subjects completed the program. The long-term effects were similarly impressive.

To show how small incentives can be powerful motivators for almost anyone, take a look at your luggage. If you're like millions of other travelers around the world, you're sporting a plastic tag that touts your status in your favorite frequent-flier program. It's almost embarrassing to acknowledge the way these programs have reshaped our behavior.

For example, a friend of ours recently took a trip from Salt Lake City to Singapore. If you were to take out a globe and draw a route from Salt Lake to Singapore, you'd pass through places such as San Francisco and Hawaii. But neither destination appeared on our friend's itinerary. Instead, he first flew two hours east to Minneapolis, Minnesota, before flying back west to Anchorage, Alaska, and Seoul, South Korea, on his way to Singapore.

Our friend added hours to his flight because it maximized his frequent-flier miles. This enormous inconvenience probably earned him a whopping $30 worth of benefits. But he wanted those miles. He needed those miles. In fact, flyers have become so obsessed with maximizing their miles that the dollar value of unused frequent-flier miles on the planet now exceeds all the cash circulating in the U.S. economy.

If you're still not convinced that small rewards can affect behavior, consider the following example. In a group home for troubled teenage girls, administrators noted an alarming trend. Suicide attempts among residents had increased dramatically. After administrators tried everything from giving emotional speeches, to holding group sessions, to enlisting the help of friends and family—all to no avail—they came up with, of all things, an incentive. They came up with an incentive that could be invoked on the spot, that was immediately motivating, and that was clearly tied to the desired behavior. This wasn't just any old incentive but one that on its face sounded crazy. Here was the incentive. If a teenage resident attempted suicide, she would be denied TV privileges for the next week. Suicide attempts dropped to zero.

Without going into the complex psychology of suicide attempts versus suicide gestures and then missing the point of the example, suffice it to say that small incentives that are immediately linked to vital behaviors can yield amazing results with some of the world's most difficult problems.

## If You're Doing It Right, Less Is More

From the examples we've provided, it should be clear that when it comes to offering extrinsic rewards, the rewards typically don't need to be very large—at least if you've laid the groundwork with the previous sources of motivation. Nobody's suggesting that corporate executives should ask employees to come to work without any compensation or that children should never get paid for helping out around the house. However, when you do want to provide a supplemental reward to help shape behavior, as the much maligned adage goes, it's often the thought, not the gift, that counts. That's because the thought behind an incentive often carries symbolic significance and taps into a variety of social forces that carry a lot of weight, much more so than the face value of the incentive itself. So, as you think of awards, don't be afraid to let the thought behind the award carry the burden for you.

Consider the work of Muhammad Yunus, "banker to the poor." When Dr. Yunus began to create a financial institution to administer loans to the working poor of Bangladesh, he discovered that some of the best young bank officers (who were often required to go door to door and meet with people living in the humblest of conditions) were former revolutionaries who had once fought to overthrow the government. Many put down their guns and picked up clipboards as they learned that they were able to effect more change through administering microloans than they could ever hope to achieve through violent means.

If you've ever visited any of the settings where these young people have worked their magic, you can't help but be impressed with the nobility of their work. Villagers who once lived on the edge of starvation—whose children were often born with severe handicaps resulting from the arsenic found in the unfiltered water, and who often died at a young age—now run small businesses. They also rear healthy children who, for the first time in their family's history, attend school.

Given the enormous intrinsic and social benefits associated with their jobs, what could possibly provide additional incentive to these erstwhile revolutionaries? Earning a gold star. An executive discovered this surprising fact almost by accident. To ensure that local branches were focusing on the right goals, one of the regional managers instituted a program where branches of Dr. Yunus's bank earned different-colored stars for achieving mission-central results—one color for hitting a certain number of loans, another for registering all the borrower's children in school, another for hitting profit goals, and so forth.

Soon it became the goal of every manager to become a five-star branch. Individuals who were doing some of the most socially important work on the planet—and already working diligently and with focus—kicked their efforts to a new level when faced with the opportunity of earning colored stars. Of course, there was nothing of tangible value in these ten-a-penny stars, but symbolically and socially they provided more incentive than anyone had ever imagined.

Once again, if you've done your work with both personal and social motives, symbolic awards take on enormous value. If you haven't, extrinsic rewards can become a source of ridicule and cynicism. Fortunately, in this case, bank employees' deep regard for Dr. Yunus, along with their commitment to serving the poor, made gold stars more valuable than money. In fact, if Yunus had offered large cash rewards, it might have undercut the moral and social motivation that already drove these employees every day.

Hundreds of executives showed this same high-energy response to a symbolic incentive when a large consulting firm in the United States decided to offer awards for completing training assignments. The plan was simple. Senior leaders would meet weekly in a world-acclaimed training program where they would be given specific behavioral goals to ensure that they put their learnings into practice. The leaders would then report back to their trainer when they had fulfilled their commitment.

Soon leaders were going to great lengths to complete their assignments, but in addition, in the event that they were called out of town, they'd e-mail their trainer to report on their progress. Senior executives jumped through these administrative hoops because, competitive souls that they were, they all wanted to earn the top award—an inexpensive brass statuette of a goose. Once again, it wasn't the cash value of the reward that mattered. It was the symbolic message that motivated behavior. It was the moral and social motivation that gave the token award supreme value.

Mimi Silbert, as you would guess, is a veritable master when it comes to making use of small rewards—one heaped upon another. Delancey residents quickly learn that with each new accomplishment they receive new privileges. Residents move from grunt work to increasingly complicated and interesting jobs. They move from a nine-person dorm to a five-person room, then through several more steps to the Brannon Building where they are awarded their own room. Eventually they arrive at Nirvana—an apartment of their own. Ultimately, probably at the top of the value chain, residents are given "walk-around money" (WAM)—and the privilege to use it.

Finally, when it comes to demonstrating the power of small rewards administered quickly and tied to vital behaviors, consider what happened at Cedars-Sinai Medical Center when Leon Bender, a urologist from Los Angeles, decided to pit a best practice he had observed on a cruise ship against one of the finest hospitals in the world.

Dr. Bender had noticed that each time passengers returned to the waiting cruise ship, someone squirted a shot of Purell on their hands. Crew members also distributed the disinfectant to passengers as they stood in the buffet lines. The good doctor began to wonder if it was possible that the cruise ship staff was more diligent with hand hygiene than the hospital staff he had worked with for nearly four decades.

The problems associated with poor hand hygiene, Dr. Bender realized, weren't restricted to remote islands or developing-world shopping bazaars. The acclaimed hospital he worked at (similar to all healthcare institutions) constantly fought the battle of hospital-transmitted diseases that are a product of poor hand hygiene. A healthcare professional picks up bugs from one patient and then passes them on to another. It happens all the time. Consequently, hospitals remain one of the most dangerous places in any community, causing tens of thousands of deaths annually. Find a way to get people to wash their hands thoroughly between patients, and you'd go a long way toward eliminating hospital-transmitted diseases.

When Dr. Bender returned home, he started a hand-hygiene campaign. He quickly learned that most doctors believed that they washed often and thoroughly enough. One study even found that while 73 percent of doctors said they washed effectively, only 9 percent actually met the industry standard.

According to Paul Silka, an emergency room physician at Cedars-Sinai, doctors often believe, "Hey, I couldn't be carrying the bad bugs. It's the other hospital personnel." Nobody believes that he or she is part of the offending majority.

To help set the record straight as well as propel doctors to wash effectively, administrators tried several techniques. First they deluged doctors with e-mails, posters, and faxes. That didn't work. It's likely that most physicians continued to believe that the problem was someone else's, not theirs. In fact, nothing worked until administrators stumbled on a simple incentive scheme. Staff members met doctors in the parking lot and handed them a bottle of hand disinfectant. Then Dr. Silka assigned a group of staff members to see if they could catch doctors in the act of using the disinfectant (choosing a positive over a negative approach).

Now here's where incentives came into play. When administrators "caught" physicians using the disinfectant, they gave them a $10 Starbucks card. That's it. They gave a $10 coupon to the highest-paid professionals in the hospital as an enticement for not passing on deadly diseases. With this incentive alone, compliance in that particular facility moved from 65 to 80 percent.

## ACT LIKE AN INFLUENCER

The giant trucks used at an open-pit mine were equipped with GPS systems that measured speed, acceleration, and braking. This information was combined to create "risky driving scores" for every driver every day. The drivers were grouped into five-person teams. A team's score consisted of whatever the worst score was for a driver on their team.

Teams with scores above a certain level won small weekly prizes—caps, t-shirts, and coffee mugs. These prizes were emblazoned with "Master Driver" logos. Notice how this highly successful incentive system tapped into both personal pride and peer pressure. It used rewards in moderation and in combination.

### Reward Vital Behaviors, Not Just Results

Earlier we learned that it's best to take complex tasks and turn them into small, achievable goals. Now we're adding another concept. Reward small improvements in behavior along the way. Don't wait until people achieve phenomenal results. Instead, reward small improvements in behavior.

As simple as this sounds, we're bad at it; especially at work. When polled, employees reveal that their number one complaint is that they aren't recognized for their notable performances. Apparently people hand out praise as if it were being rationed, usually only for outstanding work. Make a small improvement, and it's highly unlikely that anyone will say or do anything. Each year a new survey publishes the fact that employees would appreciate more praise, and each year we apparently do nothing different.

This is odd in light of the fact that humans are actually quite good at rewarding incremental achievement with their small children. A child makes a sound that approximates "mama," and members of the immediate family screech in joy, call every single living relative with the breaking news, ask the kid to perform on cue, and then celebrate each new pronouncement with the same enthusiasm you expect they'd display had they trained a newborn to recite "If" by Rudyard Kipling.

However, this ability to see and enthusiastically reward small improvements wanes over time until one day it takes a call from the Nobel committee to raise an eyebrow. Eventually kids grow up and go to work where apparently the words *good* and *job* aren't allowed to be used in combination, or so suggest employee surveys. There seems to be a permanent divide between researchers and scholars who heartily argue that performance is best improved by rewarding incremental improvements, and the rest of the world where people wait for a profound achievement before working up any enthusiasm.

## Reward Right Results and Right Behaviors

Perhaps people are stingy with their praise because they fear that rewarding incremental improvement in performance means rewarding mediocrity or worse.

"So you're telling me that every time a poor performer finally does something everyone else is already doing, you're supposed to hold some kind of celebration?"

Actually, no. If employees' current performance level is unacceptable and you can't wait for them to come up to standard, then either terminate them or move them to a task that they can complete. On the other hand, if an individual is excelling in some areas while lagging in others, but overall his or her performance is up to meeting expectations, then set performance goals in the lagging areas, and don't be afraid to reward small improvements. This means that you shouldn't wait for big results but instead should reward improvement in vital behaviors along the way.

For example, while working on a change project in a massive production facility in Texas, a member of the change steering committee abruptly informed the leaders that the culture was too negative. Apparently he had read the surveys. His exact words were: "Do something right around here, and you never hear about it. But do something wrong, and it can haunt you for your entire career."

With this in mind, the CEO asked all the leaders to keep an eye open for a notable accomplishment—something they could celebrate. For about a week nothing happened. Then one of the assembly areas set a performance record. The crew had assembled more units in one day than ever before. The CEO immediately called for a celebration.

While it seemed like a victory, the details the leaders uncovered as they researched this record revealed something quite different. It turned out that in order to set a record in production, the afternoon shift had reduced quality standards on the product. They had also focused only on producing, and not on replacing the stock they had used up, which left the morning shift with a lot of extra work. Finally, the workers had purposely underperformed the previous day in order to set themselves up to hit record numbers on the day in question.

In short, leaders were horrified to discover that they were inadvertently rewarding behaviors that ultimately hurt the company and morale. They had rewarded results without giving any thought to the behaviors that drove them.

## ACT LIKE AN INFLUENCER

When we asked our hospitality expert, Danny Meyer, how he uses incentives to motivate great customer service, he paused for a long time. "We don't do much with incentives," he concluded. "Well, we pool all tips, but lots of places do that. We believe that creating exceptional customer experiences requires an entire team. So tips are a reflection not just of one person's effort—but the whole team's. However, people don't serve customers just to get tips. They do it because they enjoy it and because they're part of a great culture that promotes it." Danny shows us that the heavy lifting of influence is done by sources 1 and 3. His goal is to ensure source 5 is simply aligned with the results and behaviors he wants.

### Reward Vital Behaviors Alone

In addition to the fact that rewarding results can be unwise if you're unable to observe people's actions, it's important to remember that behavior is the one thing people have under their control. Results often vary with changes in the market and other external variables. Consequently, influencers continually observe and reward behaviors that support valued processes.

For example, the book *Kaizen*, by Masaaki Imai, highlights the Japanese appreciation for the importance of rewarding effort and not outcome. Imai tells the intriguing story of a group of waitresses whose job it was to serve tea during lunch at one of Matsushita's plants. The waitresses noted that the employees sat in predictable locations and drank a predictable amount of tea.

Rather than put a full container at each place, they calculated the optimum amount of tea to be poured at each table, thus reducing tea-leaf consumption by half.

How much did the suggestion save? Only a small sum. Yet the group was given the company's presidential gold medal. Other suggestions saved more money (by an astronomical amount), but the more modest proposal was given the highest recognition because it captured what the judges thought was the best implementation of Kaizen principles. They rewarded the process, knowing that if you reward the actual steps people follow, eventually results take care of themselves.

## Watch for Perverse Incentives

People are so often out of touch with the message they're sending that they inadvertently reward exactly the wrong behavior. Just watch coaches as they speak about the importance of teamwork and then celebrate individual accomplishment. Kids quickly learn that it's the score that counts, not the assist, and it turns many of them into self-centered prima donnas.

Or consider the family whose son has a serious drug addiction. In their effort to express love and support, family members unintentionally enable his addiction. With their words they say, "You should really stop taking drugs." But with their actions they say, "As long as you're taking them, we'll give you free rent, use of our cars, and bail whenever you need it." They are, in fact, rewarding the very behavior they claim to want to change.

For years U.S. politicians have wrung their hands over the fact that Americans save so little money. For a time they looked jealously across the ocean at Japanese citizens, who save money at many times the rate of Americans. Some analysts speculated that there was just something different about Japanese character. Perhaps they were more willing to sacrifice. But then again, maybe the difference could be attributed in part to incentives. For example, in the United States interest earned on savings is taxable. For many years in Japan it wasn't. In the United States during that same time period, interest on consumer debt, like that from credit cards and home loans, was tax deductible. In Japan it wasn't. Maybe we were more alike than we thought.

Many organizations set up an entire reward system that, by design, motivates the wrong behavior. Dr. Steve Kerr first drew attention to this problem in his now classic piece, "On the Folly of Rewarding A, While Hoping for B." For example, some veterans and scholars were concerned about a phenomenon that had occurred in previous wars but that had increased significantly during the U.S. war in Vietnam. While still not the norm, U.S. soldiers in Vietnam were more likely to avoid conflict—even "fragging" their own officers to do so—than soldiers in previous wars had been. And instead of going on search-and-destroy missions, as had their predecessors, many learned to "search and escape." How could this happen?

Clearly soldiers in Vietnam labored under a set of conflicted emotions that had no corollary in World War II. It's hard to imagine how U.S. soldiers in Vietnam functioned at all, knowing how hostile many of their fellow citizens were to their mission. And yet, according to Kerr, there was more going on that influenced this behavior than a fuzzy mission and a hostile citizenry.

Examine the reward structure. Both generations of soldiers wanted to go home. That was a given. Nobody liked putting his or her life at risk. The typical GI from World War II knew that in order to go home, he and his comrades had to win the war. They'd never go home until the enemy was defeated. Avoiding a mission simply put off the inevitable and might well give the enemy more time to prepare.

Contrast their circumstances to those of their own children—the Vietnam soldiers. They were allowed to go home when their tour was over, not when the war was over. And if they disobeyed orders, avoiding immediate danger, rarely did anything ever happen to them. So, rational beings that they were, they avoided danger, broke regulations, caused problems, and otherwise did their best to stay out of harm's way. Their parents were rewarded for being heroes during World War II, while their children were rewarded for watching out for themselves during the Vietnam War.

So take heed. When behaviors are out of whack, look closely at your rewards. Who knows? Your own incentive system may be causing the problem.

## ACT LIKE AN INFLUENCER

Early in his career one of the authors was asked to help a consulting firm discover why many of its best consultants were leaving. When he arrived, his host invited him to their annual awards luncheon, which was being held that same day. The luncheon recognized the "Road Warrior of the Year" with a cash prize. This Road Warrior was the consultant who had spent the most days on the road that year, earning the greatest number of consulting days for the firm.

The winner bounded to the stage, grabbed the oversize check he'd won, and announced he'd use it to buy a Porsche Sidebarster. The prize was $50,000. This reward was plenty motivating, but here was the problem: for four years in a row, these "winners" quit the firm the same year they won the prize—citing work-life balance issues.

## PUNISHMENT SENDS A MESSAGE, AND SO DOES ITS ABSENCE—SO CHOOSE WISELY

Sometimes you don't have the luxury of rewarding positive performance because the person you'd like to reward never actually does the right thing. In fact, he or she does only the wrong thing—and often. In these cases, if you want to make use of extrinsic reinforcers, you're left with the prospect of punishing this person. Fortunately, since punishment is from the same family as positive reinforcement (half empty/half full), it should have a similar effect. Right?

Maybe not. Punishment far from guarantees the mirror effect of positive reinforcement. In virtually hundreds of experiments with laboratory animals and humans, punishment decreases the likelihood of a previously reinforced response, but only temporarily. Plus it can produce a whole host of other undesired effects. When you reward performance, you typically know that the reward will help propel behavior in the desired direction, but with punishment you don't know what you're going to get. You might gain compliance, but only over the short term. Then again the person in question may actually push back or purposely rebel. And there's a good chance that this person is not going to appreciate you for what you've done, thereby putting your relationship at risk.

Actually, punishment can create all sorts of serious and harmful emotional effects, particularly if it is only loosely administered. For instance, Martin Seligman, in his book *Learned Helplessness*, reports that if you place a dog on a metal grid and then shock the animal—randomly electrifying one part of the grid, then another, then another—eventually the poor animal cowers in one spot and doesn't even bother to move when the shock is randomly administered. When exposed to random pain, the unfortunate subject becomes helpless, broken, and neurotic. So take heed. When it comes to punishment, you must be very careful.

## Before Punishing, Place a Shot Across the Bow

One way to make use of punishment without actually having to administer it is to "place a shot across the bow" of those you're trying to influence. That is, provide a clear warning to let them know exactly what negative things *will* happen to them should they continue down their current path, but don't actually administer discipline yet. Then if they stay clear of the wrong behavior, they enjoy the benefit of the threat without having to actually suffer its consequences. This method may sound manipulative, but before you pass too harsh a judgment, consider a novel and effective police tactic that is currently being used with drug dealers and other perpetual criminals in North Carolina and other states. Here's how the method used by authorities makes use of warnings as opposed to merely tracking down offenders and throwing them in jail.

Traditionally, cops tried to put a dent in crime by implementing aggressive search-and-arrest strategies that focused on a targeted area. This blitz strategy tended to provoke public outrage and mobilize a community against the policing efforts, and it rarely created effects that lasted very long. As soon as the cops moved to the next area, new faces came in to fill the old positions, and the bad guys were once again in charge.

With the new strategy, authorities take a different approach. Police invite individuals whom they are about to arrest to attend an offender notification forum. The district attorney's office promises that attendees won't be arrested during a 90-minute meeting where authorities then make use of every source of influence imaginable.

For example, along with the offenders, authorities bring in the attendees' friends, family, and other community opinion leaders who ask the criminals to give up their ways and seek normal employment. Next, public officials clarify existing laws and likely consequences: if you get caught, here's the likely penalty. Following this formal approach, ex-offenders (usually former gang members and drug dealers) talk about what they're currently doing to stay straight. Finally, heads of public agencies explain choices the offenders can make in order to avoid falling back into their old habits, including job programs and what it takes to get signed up.

Then comes the fun part. What makes these second-chance meetings so effective is not merely that they employ so many sources of influence but also that the meetings do such a terrific job in making it crystal clear that the offenders *will* be convicted and *will* serve long sentences. Nobody does a better job of providing a warning. Unlike the *Scared Straight* program that focused on how bad jail is—leaving room for subjects to conclude that only saps get caught and sent to jail—with this new program, police make it abundantly clear that the offenders will indeed be caught and prosecuted.

After the first part of the meeting concludes, authorities invite the participants (who are often a bit bored with the sermon at this point) to a different room where they see posters tacked to the walls. Under each poster they find a small table with a binder on it. During previous weeks police have gathered evidence, including video footage of each of the attendees making at least one illicit drug sale.

As the drug dealers enter the new room, each is told, "Find your poster." When they do, they discover that the poster sports a high-resolution photo of them doing a drug deal. In the adjacent binder, they see all the case evidence the police intend to use to prosecute them. Next the invitees are asked to take a seat and watch a video. At this point the local prosecutor states: "Raise your hand when you see yourself committing a felony." One by one, they do. Next, authorities tell the offenders that they've been put on a special list and will be aggressively prosecuted when caught.

Combine this tactic with support from family and friends as well as job programs, and the results have been terrific. Small crimes have dropped by 35 percent in certain neighborhoods in North Carolina, and in the three neighborhoods where the initiative was implemented, 24 of 40 alleged dealers have stayed clear of the law. More importantly, community members have become far more active at reporting crimes and partnering with law enforcement officials.

All this is done without having to haul nearly as many people off to jail in order to catch their attention. Poignant, real, and immediate, threats of punishment help keep potential hardened criminals on the straight and narrow.

And to enhance the credibility of their efforts, the authorities never bluff. They invite drug dealers to the open forum, and those who don't come are immediately arrested and prosecuted for the crimes recorded on videotape. Those who go through the program and don't stay with their new job training or do commit a crime are also immediately arrested. Soon the word gets out that the authorities are serious about what they say. Then the mere threat of possible negative consequences becomes much more effective.

## When All Else Fails, Punish

The implications here should be clear. There are times when you're simply going to have to punish others. A shot across the bow hasn't been enough. You've also tried incentives, exerted social pressure, and even appealed to the other person's sense of values, but the immediate gratification associated with the wrong behavior still remains victorious. It's time to make judicious use of discipline.

Consider the poor safety record of workers in the oil fields of Russia. With the fall of communism and the influx of demand for oil, Russian leaders cranked up their petroleum industry. Unfortunately, many of the new employees had not been trained in safe work practices, nor did they appear to be the slightest bit interested in learning or applying them. Coming out of years of unemployment and depression, many new hires were drug and alcohol abusers. Combine poor safety practices, alcohol, and heavy equipment, and you have the perfect recipe for accidents.

Since the immediate danger was so high and employees had been used to heavy-handed methods before going to work in the fields (and they had not responded to encouragements or hollow threats), company executives decided to punish behavior that led to accidents. Leaders notified employees that they could be randomly tested for drugs and alcohol at work or while traveling to and from the job. Then authorities did exactly that and summarily fired anyone who was found to be under the influence. This direct application of punishment, coupled with safety training, helped dramatically decrease the number of accidents. Once again, the methods may seem harsh, but when compared to the loss of life or limb, leaders argue that it's worth it.

Consider the horrible cases of bride abduction in Ethiopia. Young girls were kidnapped on their way to or from school, raped, and then forced to marry the rapist in an effort to save face. This dreadful practice had survived in silence for generations. Nobody wanted to talk about or address the issue. However, that changed when a popular radio soap opera addressed the issue head on. Dr. Negussie Teffera—Population Media Center's country representative in Ethiopia—worked with a staff of writers and producers to create an enormously popular radio show titled *Yeken Kignit* ("Looking Over One's Daily Life"). In one story line, a much-admired character on the soap opera, a woman named Wubalem, was abducted and then eventually freed and able to marry the man she really loved. Immediately, this previously taboo topic became part of the public discourse. A letter from one female listener shows the impact the program had on the devastating problem in her community:

> *The story of Wubalem in your radio drama reflects clearly to the general public the harmful traditional practices in our country such as abduction and sexual violence. These practices have prevented us from sending our girls to school. . . . Our first child was married at the age of 14 after she was abducted. We were worrying for years as we thought that our second child would face a similar fate. At present, however, the radio drama focusing on abduction and sexual violence that you have presented to the public, and the discussions conducted on these topics, have aroused considerable popular indignation. The people have now strongly condemned such inhuman traditional practices. . . . Unlike in the past, special punitive measures have been taken by community people against offenders involved in such crimes. As a result, we have no worry in sending our girls to school. Our children go to school safely and return unharmed.*

According to Dr. Teffera, the problem has been solved in many places in Ethiopia once and for all—not simply as a result of the discourse but by also putting into place harsh punishment for what had previously been rewarded. Now if a man assaults a young girl, instead of being allowed to keep the victim as his wife, he is put in prison.

Finally, a corporate example. One of the first questions we (the authors) ask employees in companies that complain about a lack of accountability is, "What does it take to get fired around here?" Almost always the answers have nothing to do with poor performance. "Embarrass the boss" is a common response. Another is a sarcastic "Kill a really valuable coworker." In other words, only raging violations of ethics or political faux pas get the boot. When you hear these types of stories, you can bet that the *lack* of punishment for routine infractions is sending a loud message across the organization. The point isn't that people need to be threatened in order to perform. The point is that if you aren't willing to go to the mat when people violate a core value (such as giving their best effort), that value loses its moral force in the organization.

On the other hand, you send a powerful message about your values when you do hold employees accountable. For instance, the authors worked with a large consumer-goods company in Georgia where company leaders decided to take a harsh stance against racist behavior. To take on a norm that had lasted for centuries, the leaders decided to pick a common racist behavior and annihilate it through the judicious use of punishment. They started with something simple. No longer would the company tolerate racist jokes.

To put the plan into action, the leaders explained their stance, the first behavior they were going to eliminate, and the action they would take. Anyone who told a racist joke would be fired on the spot, without any warning or grace period. The leaders then told their employees that they would be looking to make an example of anyone who dared violate the policy, and the first time someone did, they fired him. That was the end of racist jokes in that company.

## SUMMARY: STRUCTURAL MOTIVATION

Administering rewards and punishments can be a tricky business. Consequently, when you look at the extrinsic motivators you're using to encourage or discourage behavior, take care to adhere to a few helpful principles. First, rely on personal and social motivators as your first line of attack. Let the value of the behavior itself, along with social motivators, carry the bulk of the motivational load.

When you do choose to tweak the economy, make sure the extrinsic motivators are immediately linked to vital behaviors. Take care to link rewards to the specific actions you want to see repeated. When choosing rewards, don't be afraid to draw on small, heartfelt tokens of appreciation. Remember, when it comes to extrinsic rewards, less is often more. Do your best to reward behaviors and not merely outcomes. Sometimes outcomes hide inappropriate behaviors. Finally, if you end up having to administer punishment, first take a shot across the bow. Let people know what's coming before you impose the punishment.

# 9

# Change Their Space

## STRUCTURAL ABILITY

*You are a product of your environment. So choose the environment that will best develop you toward your objective. Analyze your life in terms of its environment. Are the things around you helping you toward success—or are they holding you back?*

*—Clement Stone*

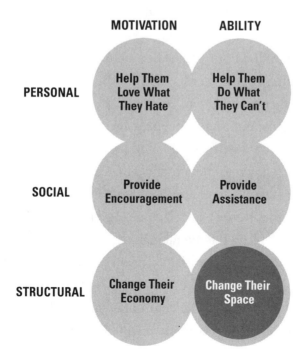

When it comes to *enabling* vital behaviors, we've already looked at two sources: improving personal mastery through deliberate practice and gaining assistance from others. For our third and final source for increasing our ability ("Can I do it?"), we move away from human influence altogether and examine how nonhuman forces—the world of buildings, space, sound, sight, and so forth—can be brought to bear in an influence strategy. To show how this might work, we start with an example that, when it comes to influence theory, is a genuine classic.

In the late 1940s, representatives from the National Restaurant Association (NRA) asked William Foote Whyte, a professor at the University of Chicago, to help them with a growing problem. As World War II came to an end, the United States was in a period of incredible growth and prosperity. Along with this flourishing economy, Americans began eating out in unprecedented numbers. Unfortunately, the restaurant industry wasn't ready for the surge of customers.

Along with the return of soldiers came an awkward change in the restaurant pecking order. GIs returned from battle to take over the higher-paying job of cook, one that, along with "Rosie the Riveter," women had occupied for the first time during the labor-starved war years. Many of the displaced cooks were forced to step down to the job of waitress, and they were upset with the new circumstance. When they shouted their orders to the kitchen, they weren't always polite. And the gnarled veterans weren't always pleased to be taking orders from these women.

Given the increased workload and growing social tension, loud arguments often broke out at the kitchen counter. The results were predictable. The commotion annoyed the patrons, and the power struggles often resulted in late or incorrect orders—sometimes out of confusion, often out of revenge. By the time Dr. Whyte entered the scene, both customers and employees were stomping out of restaurants in increasing numbers.

Dr. Whyte started his work by observing a sample of restaurants, doing his best to identify the behaviors behind the growing conflict. He noted that a waitress would rush to the counter, shout an order, and then rush back to her customers. If the order was not ready when she returned, she would urge the cook to hurry, shouting expressions of encouragement such as, "Hey, hairball, where's the breaded veal? You got a broken arm or what?" The cooks usually responded in kind. Later, when the waitress received an incorrect order, the two would exchange still more unflattering remarks. After being yelled at a couple of times, the cooks often took revenge by slowing down. Dr. Whyte even observed cooks turning their backs on the servers and intentionally ignoring them until they left, sometimes in tears.

While many consultants might have been tempted to alter this unhealthy social climate by teaching interpersonal skills, conducting team-building exercises, or changing the pay system, Whyte took a different approach. In his view, the best way to solve the problem was to change the way employees communicated.

And now for Whyte's stroke of genius.

Dr. Whyte recommended that the restaurants use a 50-cent metal spindle to gather orders. He then asked servers to skewer a detailed written order on the spindle. Cooks were then to pull orders off and fill them in whatever sequence seemed most efficient (though generally following a first-in, first-out policy).

Whyte's recommendation was tried at a pilot restaurant the next day. Training consisted of a 10-minute instruction session that was given to both cooks and servers. Managers reported an immediate decrease in conflict and customer complaints. Both cooks and servers preferred the new structure, and both groups reported that they were being treated better.

The National Restaurant Association distributed information about the new system to its membership. Whyte's spindle (which quickly transformed into the now-familiar order wheel) did not directly affect behavior. Whyte chose not to confront norms, history, or habit. Instead, he simply eliminated the need for verbal communication and all its attendant problems. He did so immediately, and the improvements lasted forever by changing not people, but *things*.

## FISH DISCOVER WATER LAST

If you didn't think of Whyte's solution, you're in good company. Rarely does the average person conceive of changing the physical world as a way of changing human behavior. We see that others are misbehaving, and we look to change *them*, not their environment. Caught up in the human side of things, we completely miss the impact of subtle yet powerful sources such as the size of a room or the impact of a chair. Consequently, one of our most powerful sources of influence (our physical space) is often the least used because it's the least noticeable. In the words of Fred Steele, the renowned sociotechnical theorist, most of us are "environmentally incompetent." If you doubt this allegation, just ask any of today's cooks and servers why they don't scream and curse at one another as did many of their predecessors a half century ago. See if any of them ever point to the order wheel as the source of their cooperation.

The impact of physical space and the things that occupy it on human behavior is equally profound within the business world, and as you might suspect, just as hard to spot. For example, the authors once met with the president of a large insurance company that was losing millions of dollars to quality problems that were widely known but rarely discussed. To turn things around, the president had decided to nurture a culture of candor within the organization. He declared: "We'll never solve our quality problems until every single person—right down to the newest employee on the loading dock—is comfortable sharing his or her honest opinion."

Despite the president's passion for candor, the heartfelt speeches he had given, the fiery memos he had written, and even the engaging training he had initiated, his efforts hadn't done much to propel people to share their frank opinions. When talking privately with his HR manager, he explained, "I keep telling people to open up, but it's not working." So he asked us (the authors) to help him come up with a plan to create a culture in which people, no matter their position or station, could comfortably disagree with anyone—particularly people in authority.

To reach the president's office, we had to traverse six hallways (each the length of an aircraft carrier), walk by hundreds of thousands of dollars of museum-quality artwork, and pass four different secretary stations. At each station we were visually frisked and subtly interrogated. Finally, we entered the president's office to find him seated behind a desk the size of a 1964 Caddy. Then, while seated in loosely stuffed chairs that slung us next to the floor and pushed our knees up and into our chests, we stared up at the president, much like grade-school children looking up at the principal.

The president's first words were, "I get the feeling that people around here are scared to talk to me." Perhaps he had missed the fact that his office was laid out like Hitler's chancellery. (Hitler demanded more than 480 feet of hallway so that visitors would "get a taste of the power and grandeur of the German Reich" on arriving.) Granted, there were several forces that had kept employees in this particular company from talking candidly. However, the physical features of the executive suite alone were enough to terrorize anyone.

"I'm not sure that you'll ever be able to overcome the intimidating effect of your office suite," one of us eventually shared, in a quivering voice.

From that point on, we developed a plan that contained a variety of features, starting with the strategy of placing decision-making groups in physical surroundings that didn't shout, "Behold, the great and mighty Oz!"

Consider the profound yet mostly unnoticed effect of *things* on entire communities. Realizing that the physicality of a neighborhood can send out unspoken messages that encourage socially inappropriate behavior, George Kelling started a community movement that is largely credited for reducing felonies in New York City by as much as 75 percent. Few people are aware of how this influence expert manipulated *things* to achieve such impressive results.

Before the arrival of George Kelling, New York subways were a favorite venue for muggers, murderers, and drug dealers. Kelling, a criminologist and originator of the "broken windows theory" of crime, argued that disordered surroundings send out an unspoken but powerful message that encourages antisocial behavior. "A broken window left in disrepair," Kelling explained, "suggests that no one is in charge and no one cares." This relatively minor condition promotes more disorderly behavior, including violence.

Committed to lessening the effect *things* were having on the community, Kelling advised the New York Transit Authority to implement a strategy that others before him had simply ridiculed. He told community leaders that they needed to start sweating the small stuff. He pointed out small environmental cues that provided a fertile environment for criminal behavior.

Kelling's crew began a systematic attack against the silent force, attacking things like graffiti, litter, and vandalism. Officials organized crews in the train yard that rolled paint over newly applied graffiti the instant a car came in for service. Over time, a combination of cleanup and prosecution for minor offenses began to make a difference. Surroundings improved, community pride increased, and petty crimes declined. So did violent crime. Kelling taught people to sweat the small, silent, physical world, and they reaped great rewards.

All this talk about the powerful but often undetected influence of *things* is good news. It offers hope. If you can influence behavior by eliminating graffiti, shifting a wall, changing a reporting structure, putting in a new system, posting numbers, or otherwise working with *things*, the job of leader, parent, or change agent doesn't seem like such a daunting task. After all, these are inanimate objects. *Things* lie there quietly. *Things* never resist change, and they stay put once you change them.

There are two reasons that we don't make good use of *things* as much as we should. The first is the problem we've been discussing. More often than not, powerful elements from our environment remain invisible to us. Work procedures, job layouts, reporting structures, and so forth don't exactly walk up and shout in our ear. The effect of distance is something we suffer but rarely see. The environment affects much of what we do, yet we often fail to notice its profound impact.

Second, even when we do think about the impact the environment is having on us, we rarely know what to do about it. It's not as if we're carrying around a head full of sociophysical theories. If someone were to tell us that we need to worry about Festinger, Schachter, and Lewin's theory of propinquity (the impact of space on relationships), we'd think he or she was pulling our leg. Propinquity? Who's ever heard of propinquity?

So this is our final test. To complete our influence repertoire, we must step up to the challenge and become environmentally competent. To the extent that we (1) remember to think about things and (2) are able to come up with theories of how changing *things* will change behavior, we'll have access to one more powerful set of influence tools.

## LEARN TO NOTICE

If it's true that we rarely notice the impact of the physical environment that surrounds us because we simply don't think to look at it, it's time we change. The more we watch for silent forces in the space around us, the better prepared we'll be to deal with them. Equally important, the more we note how we fall prey to simple, silent things that surround us, the more likely it is that we'll extend our vigilance to other domains of our life.

To understand this concept more fully, let's start by sampling just one domain: our personal life. More specifically, our eating habits. How might understanding the power that things hold over us help here? What might we do to warn our friend Henry, who continues to struggle with his weight loss problem?

To answer this, consider the work of the clever and mischievous social scientist Brian Wansink, who manipulates *things* to see how a small change in physical features affects a large change in human behavior. For instance, he once invited a crowd of people who had just finished lunch to watch a movie. As subjects filed into the theater, Wansink's assistants handed them either a small, medium, or bigger-than-your-head bucket of very stale popcorn. The treat was so stale that it squeaked when eaten. One moviegoer described it as akin to eating Styrofoam packing peanuts.

Despite the facts that the popcorn tasted terrible and the crowd was still full from lunch, when Wansink's crew gathered up the variously sized buckets at the end of the movie, it turned out almost everybody had mindlessly gobbled the chewy material. Even more interesting, the size of the container, not the size of the person or his or her appetite, predicted how much of the food had been consumed. Patrons with big buckets ate 53 percent more than those given the smaller portions. The distraction of the movie, the size of the bucket, and the sound of others eating around them all subtly influenced people to eat something they would otherwise have rejected.

Wansink has even more to teach Henry. For example, it turns out—contrary to what you and I might believe—that we don't tend to stop eating when we're *full*. We eat until small things from our environment make us *think* we're full. Wansink demonstrated this by constructing a magic soup bowl. The bowl could be refilled from the bottom without diners catching on to the trick. While people eating from a normal bowl ate on average 9 ounces and then reported being full, those with the bottomless bowls ate 15 ounces. Some ate more than a quart before reporting they'd had enough. Imagine, the two groups were equally satisfied, and yet one group ate 73 percent more than the other because the diners were unconsciously waiting for their bowls to look more empty to cue them that they were full.

Wansink suggests that people make over 200 eating decisions every day without realizing it. This mindless eating adds hundreds of calories to our diets without adding at all to our satisfaction. If half of what Wansink suggests is true, we can profoundly influence our own eating behavior by simply finding ways to become more mindful of these "mindless" choices.

A mere glance at family, company, and community circumstances would reveal the same phenomenon. Much of what we do, for better or for worse, is influenced by dozens of silent environmental forces that drive our decisions and actions in ways that we rarely notice. So, to make the best use of your last source of influence, take your laserlike attention off people and take a closer look at their physical world. Step up to your persistent problem, identify vital behaviors, and then search for subtle features from the environment that are silently driving you and others to misbehave.

## MAKE THE INVISIBLE VISIBLE

Once you've identified environmental elements that are subtly driving your or others' behavior, it's time to take steps to make the elements more obvious. That is, you should make the invisible visible. Provide actual cues in the space around you to remind people of the behaviors you're trying to influence. For example, consider another Wansink experiment in which he gave cans of stacked potato chips to various subjects. Control subjects were given normal cans with uniform chips piled one on top of the other and were allowed to snack casually as they engaged in various activities. Experimental subjects were given cans in which every tenth chip was an odd color. The next nine chips would be normal and were followed by another odd-colored chip. Again, subjects were allowed to engage in other activities while snacking on their chips. Experimental subjects consumed 37 percent fewer chips than control subjects who were given no indication of how many chips they'd eaten.

What was going on here? By coloring every tenth chip, Wansink helped make the invisible visible. Nobody said anything about the chips or the colors. Nobody encouraged people to control their eating. Nevertheless, instructed by the visual cue, suddenly eaters were conscious of the volume of chips they were eating, and that awareness alone helped them make a decision rather than follow an impulse.

Business leaders have long understood the importance of making the invisible visible. For example, Emery Air Freight pioneered the use of containerized shipping in the 1960s. The company came up with the idea of using sturdy, reusable, and uniformly sized containers—and the whole world changed. Uniform containers were so much more efficient than previous methods that international shipping prices plummeted. Along with the unprecedented drop in price, industries that had previously been protected from global competition because of high transportation costs (for example, steel and automobiles) suddenly found themselves competing with anyone, anywhere.

And yet, early on, Edward Feeney, the vice president of systems performance at the time, was frustrated because he couldn't get the workforce to use the new containers to their capacity. Containers were being sealed and shipped without being properly filled. An audit team found they were being properly filled only 45 percent of the time. The workers were extensively trained and constantly reminded of the importance of completely filling the containers, but they were still forgetting to do it more than half of the time. After exhausting these attempts to motivate the workforce, Feeney stumbled on a method that made the invisible visible. He drew conscious attention to the objective by having a "fill to here" line drawn on the inside of every container. Immediately, the rate of completely filled containers went from 45 percent to 95 percent. The problem went away the moment Feeney made the invisible visible.

Hospitals have been making similar improvements by restructuring their physical world. Savvy administrators help people understand the financial implications of their nearly unconscious choices by making invisible costs much more visible. In one hospital, leaders encouraged clinicians to pay attention to even small products that eventually cost a great deal of money. For example, a type of powderless latex gloves cost over 10 times more than a pair of regular, less-comfortable disposable gloves. Yet in spite of regular pleas from senior management to reduce costs, almost everyone in the facility continued to use the pricey gloves for even short tasks. The powderless latex was more comfortable than the cheaper gloves, and besides, what were a few pennies here and there?

Then one day someone placed a "25¢" sign on the box of inexpensive gloves and a "$3.00" sign on the box of pricier latex gloves. Problem solved. Now that the information was obvious at the moment people were making choices, the use of the expensive gloves dropped dramatically.

And speaking of hands in a hospital, we referred earlier to the appalling state of hand hygiene in U.S. hospitals. Remember Dr. Leon Bender and how he used Starbucks gift cards as an incentive to encourage doctors to use hand antiseptic? This influence method alone increased compliance from 65 to 80 percent. This wasn't enough for the tenacious Dr. Bender. He wanted more. But what could he do next? After trying several other methods to motivate people to wash more thoroughly, he figured the hospital efforts had topped out until he too realized that he needed to make the invisible visible.

And what could be more invisible than the nasty little microorganisms that cause disease?

This particular problem of invisibility called for some minor theatrics. At a routine meeting of senior physicians, Rekha Murthy, the hospital's epidemiologist, handed each physician a Petri dish coated with a spongy layer of agar. "I would love to culture your hand," Murthy told them while inviting each to press his or her palm onto the squishy medium. Murthy then collected the dishes and sent them to the lab for culturing and photographing.

When the photos came back from the lab, the images were frightfully effective. Doctors who had thought their hands were pristine when they submitted to the agar test were provided photographic evidence of the horrific number of bacteria they routinely transported to their patients. Some of the more color-ful photos of the bacterial colonies the lab had grown became popular screen savers in the hospital.

When it came to changing physicians' behavior, photos created poignant vicarious experiences and visual cues that reminded them of the need to properly wash their hands. Doc-tors didn't see their germs causing diseases, but they saw the next best thing. They saw whole colonies of the ugly micro-natives they were hosting in their own fingerprints. After a few more opinion leaders were brought "face to colony" with the effects of their own inadequate hand hygiene, the hospital moved to nearly 100 percent compliance—and it stuck.

## ACT LIKE AN INFLUENCER

In the mid-1990s Bogotá, Colombia, faced a terrible water shortage. Mayor Antanas Mockus—a true influencer—rallied various sources of influence to reduce water use by 40 percent in a matter of months. After airing public service announcements in which he taught water-saving vital behaviors, he used the country's overloaded phone system cleverly to cue people to practice the vital behaviors. Every time they got a busy signal, rather than hearing a tedious, rhythmic beep, they got Mockus's affable voice saying, "Sorry. The line is busy at the moment. But remember to conserve water!"

## MIND THE DATA STREAM

The influencers we just cited had one strategy in common: they affected how information found its way from the dark nooks and crannies of the unknown into the light of day. By providing small cues in the environment, they drew attention to critical data points, and they changed how people thought and eventually how they behaved. In these cases, individuals weren't resisting the ideas of washing thoroughly or wearing cheaper gloves or filling containers to the top, but they were not thinking of the behaviors in the moment. So, merely putting the data in front of them was sufficient to change behavior.

The point here is the same one Bandura helped make for us earlier. Information affects behavior. People make choices based on cognitive maps that explain which behavior leads to which outcomes. The problem we're now exploring deals with our own lack of awareness of where we're getting our data, as well as how the data are affecting our behavior. Despite the fact that we're often exposed to incomplete or inaccurate data, if information is fed to us frequently and routinely enough, we begin to act on it as if it were an accurate sample of the greater reality, even when it often isn't.

For example, try this experiment. As quickly as you can, name every place in the world where armed conflict is currently taking place. If you're like most people, you can name an average of two to four places. Now ask yourself why you named these particular locales. Is it because these are the only places? Perhaps they're locations where there is the most bloodshed? Or is it because these are the places of most political significance?

It's probably because these are the sites that have received sustained media coverage. At any one time there are as many as two dozen armed conflicts taking place throughout the world, and it's not uncommon that some of the most horrific battles go largely unnoticed by the international audience. What's shocking about this is *not* that our mental agenda is so heavily influenced by a handful of news producers but that we are typically unaware that this is happening to us.

We frequently make this mental error because of a convenient heuristic we carry around in our head. It's known by cognitive psychologists as the "representative heuristic." To see how it works, take another quiz. What is the greater cause of deaths in the world each year? Suicide or homicide? Fire or drowning? Most people select homicides and fires because these are the catastrophes they see more often in the news.

Suicides are generally kept quiet for reasons of privacy, so we don't learn of them as often; and fires make for dramatic live coverage. The evening news team can hardly wait to show a reporter standing in front of a fiery blaze. And since we see homicides and fires on the news more often than we see suicides and drownings, we assume that this sample represents the underlying whole, when in fact it grossly distorts it. Death by drowning and suicide are more common, but we apply a simple mental heuristic and fall victim to an inaccurate data stream, and rarely do we know that it's happening.

Influencers understand the importance of an accurate data stream and do their best to ensure that their strategies focus on vital behaviors by serving up visible, timely, and accurate information that supports their goals. Instead of falling victim to data, they manage data religiously. For example, imagine what Dr. Donald Hopkins was up against when he kicked off the global campaign to eradicate Guinea worm disease. To get the campaign started, his biggest challenge was to move the parasite to the top of the agenda of developing-world leaders who typically worried a heck of a lot more about bloody coups, economic disasters, and corrupt politicians than they worried about parasites.

If competing priorities weren't enough to keep the worm problem out of the spotlight, the fact that most leaders had grown up in urban areas and were completely unaware of the pervasive effects of the Guinea worm in their own country didn't help. For example, Jimmy Carter, former U.S. president and founder of the Carter Center, told us that the first challenge leaders faced when attacking the Guinea worm disease in Pakistan was that the president of Pakistan had never even heard of the parasite. In addition to the worm's invisibility, even leaders who knew the plague was widespread paid little attention to the villages that were plagued because the leaders drew their political support from urban areas.

Consequently, Hopkins's first challenge was to escalate the importance of the Guinea worm disease plight in the eyes of the ruling forces by changing their data stream. That's why to this day the very first step any Guinea worm eradication team takes is to gather data.

"Data are extremely important in the campaign against Guinea worm disease," reports Hopkins. "We start by getting baseline information about nationwide infections." Actually, they're looking for counterintuitive, eye-popping statistics to catch people's attention. For instance, in Nigeria national leaders assumed that there were only a few thousand cases nationwide. In 1989, after village coordinators from around the country reported the number of infections in their region, leaders were horrified to discover that there were well over 650,000 cases. They had been off by as much as 3,000 percent! This made Nigeria the most endemic country in the world. With that new piece of information alone, support for eradicating the disease skyrocketed.

Since managing the data stream relies on numbers to change people's cognitive maps (as opposed to personal experience), the data have to be fresh, consistent, and relevant if they're going to have much of an impact. Hopkins is quick to point out that with such a small team working at the Carter Center, much of their influence comes from providing leaders with powerful information. Working closely with Dr. Hopkins is Dr. Ernesto Ruiz-Tiben, the technical director of the Guinea Worm Eradication Program. He oversees the Carter Center's efforts and has been key in tracking and communicating the status of the global campaign. Dr. Ruiz-Tiben makes Guinea worm eradication data available through publications such as the *Guinea Worm Wrap Up*, which is published every month by the Carter Center and the Centers for Disease Control and Prevention. This report summarizes the progress and setbacks in each country.

And here's where Hopkins grins a bit. "We publish lots of graphs, charts, and tables. But none has been more influential than the Guinea worm race. We harness the natural competitive instincts of people by preparing a racetrack with the names of each country (or even the faces of the campaign leaders) on each runner. It's amazing to see how people respond not just to how many infections they have but to how many more or less they have than a neighboring country."

Do these data influence behavior?

"I was talking with the president of Burkina Faso," Hopkins reports, "and sharing some concerns about the campaign. I had all kinds of graphs and charts, but the one he wanted to look at the most was the Guinea worm race. They can't stand to be at the bottom. It gets their attention."

At the corporate level, it's easy to see how the flow of information affects behavior. The fact that different groups of employees are exposed to wildly different data streams helps explain why people often have such different priorities and passions. Different groups, departments, and levels of employees worry about very different aspects of the company's success—not because they hold different values but because they're exposed to different data. For example, the frontline employees who interface with complaining customers usually become the customer advocates. The top-level executives who are constantly poring over financial statements become the shareholder advocates. And sure enough, the folks who routinely take quality measures become the quality advocates. No surprise there.

The problem with passion for a single stakeholder group isn't that employees care greatly about someone or something; it's just that it's hard to expect people to act in balanced ways when they have access to only one data stream. For instance, members of a group of senior executives we (the authors) worked with were positively driven by their production numbers, which they reviewed weekly. When issues of morale came up (usually with the issuance of a grievance), they'd become rightfully concerned about "people problems" but generally only after it was too late. The same was true for customer satisfaction. This was also listed as a high priority, but nobody ever actually talked about customers or did anything to improve customer relationships until the company lost a major client to a competitor.

To change the executives' narrow focus, we changed the data stream. Alongside weekly production numbers, executives now enthusiastically pore over customer and employee data. If you watch their current behavior, you'll note that they spread their attention across more stakeholders than ever before. We also provided employees who had long shown passion for customer satisfaction with weekly cost and profit data, and they too broadened their interests. For instance, when faced with a dissatisfied customer, instead of simply throwing money at the problem (often the easiest solution), employees began to seek other, more cost-effective fixes. Before the intervention started, leaders and employees alike had talked about the importance of all their stakeholders, but nothing changed their parochial behavior until their data stream expanded.

One warning about data. When it comes to data, there is such a thing as "too much of a good thing." Corporate leaders often undermine the influence of the data they so carefully gather by overdoing it. The incessant flow of reports, printouts, and e-mails—one heaped upon the other—transforms into numbing and incoherent background noise. Influencers never make this mistake. They're focused and deliberate about the data they share. They understand that the only reason for gathering or publishing any data is to reinforce vital behaviors.

## ACT LIKE AN INFLUENCER

The leaders of a condo association were frustrated with the money they were spending maintaining trees. Every year 50 or more trees died and were replaced at about $500 per tree. As far as the property management was concerned, the process was automatic. After all, a tree is a tree is a tree—right? Then an owner decided to number and tag each tree and to maintain a database. He tagged about 400 trees and added the species of the tree and the problems it faced.

The association quickly discovered that not all trees are alike and that not every tree was suited for every part of their property. In fact, there was one area, a swampy one, where none of the trees they'd planted had survived. And yet they'd faithfully replanted there every year. Creating this simple database influenced people's actions in ways that saved trees, money, and labor.

## SPACE: THE FINAL FRONTIER

As difficult as it can be to notice the effects of data on our behavior, it's much more difficult to notice the effects of physical space. Architects create space, and then we live with its effects for years on end, mostly unnoticed. When social psychologist Leon Festinger and others first started examining the effects of space (and its two-dimensional cousin, distance) on relationships, they had no idea that they had stumbled onto one of the most profound social-psychological phenomena of all time—propinquity. Simply put, *propinquity* is physical proximity, and Festinger and others spent a good amount of time studying how it affects our behaviors and relationships.

For instance, look at who marries whom and how they meet. Look at who collaborates on spontaneous group efforts at work. Examine who has the most friends and acquaintances in an apartment complex. Explore which employees are satisfied with their relationship with their supervisor. Surely most of these complicated interpersonal scenarios are largely a function of personal interests and interpersonal chemistry. Right?

Not really. Festinger discovered that the frequency and quality of human interaction is largely a function of physical distance. Apartment dwellers who are located near stairwells are acquainted with more people than individuals who have fewer people walking by their front doors. People who live across from the mailboxes are acquainted with more of their neighbors than anyone else in the building. At the corporate level, bosses who interact the most frequently with their subordinates generally have the best relationships. And who interacts most often? Bosses who are located closest to their direct reports.

But the opposite isn't necessarily true. That is, too much distance doesn't merely lead to inconvenience and loss of friendship. At the corporate level, when employees don't meet and chat (getting to know one another and jointly working on problems), bad things happen. Silos form and infighting reigns. Employees start labeling others with ugly terms such as "them" and "they"—meaning the bad people "out there" whom they rarely see and who are surely the cause of most of the problems they experience. If you want to predict who doesn't trust or get along with whom in a company, take out a tape measure.

But not everyone suffers from the negative effects of space and distance. Some people use it as a powerful influence lever. And when it comes to exploiting the use of space as a means of fostering vital behaviors, Delancey Street once again sets the standard. Dr. Mimi Silbert's goal, remember, is to foster two vital behaviors. She wants residents to be responsible for others rather than just themselves, and she wants to ensure that everyone confronts everyone with whom they have concerns. But how? These are people who are just as likely to punch each other out as anything else.

The first thing Silbert does is to stack previously mortal enemies on top of one another. She takes three guys—one new resident who's a card-carrying member of the Mexican Mafia, another who six months earlier was a Crip, and another who just a year ago was a leader in the Aryan Brotherhood—and makes them roommates. Nine such diverse folks will share a dorm. Someone from another background will be the crew boss. Perhaps a member of yet another race will be the minyan leader. It's like international spaghetti with every possible politically incorrect grouping tossed into the mix, and then they're asked to help and confront each other—in healthy ways.

We (the authors) watched the effects of placing former enemies in close proximity while eating in Delancey's restaurant. A fairly new employee named Kurt—a white man embroidered with tattoos from neck to fingertips—dropped a plate that smashed to pieces. Kurt had been at Delancey for just a couple of months and had been given the simple assignment of busing tables. Apparently he hadn't mastered the job yet.

And why should he? Kurt had come from a high-crime, largely black area of Richmond, California, where he had been schooled since age six in the hateful propaganda of the white-gang culture, not the restaurant business. He had been homeless for five years before joining Delancey, and for the first 60 days after entering the program he thought he'd die as his body adjusted to a life without drugs. He was hardly in any shape to be impressing customers.

When Kurt's plate shattered on the floor, he ducked his head in shame. A few dozen customers reflexively lifted their heads from their meals to look toward the source of the noise, only adding to his humiliation. Kurt was torn between wanting to curse at the onlookers and wanting to disappear entirely. What happened next was compelling evidence of the power of propinquity. The black maître d'—a former gang rival from Richmond and now a roommate—hurried over to where Kurt was kneeling over the broken plate and put his hand on Kurt's back in a gesture of support. He then knelt down and helped Kurt pick up the broken plate. He smiled at him and shrugged his shoulders, offering a look that said, "It happens." And with that, Kurt shook it off and returned to his duties.

While there's a lot going on at Delancey to influence change, you can't help but notice how propinquity is used to foster relationships. When you assign people interdependent roles and then put them in close proximity, you increase the chance that relationships that had once been the bane of their existence are now a big part of their personal transformation.

Families are also affected by how they make use of their space. For example, a recent study showed that the family dining table is vanishing from homes at a rapid rate. A parallel rise in family dysfunction and discontent suggests that familial unity is declining at a similar rate. Could there be a correlation here? The idea is not that a drop in furniture sales will harm family solidarity. It's that the dining room table is a significant facilitator of family togetherness. Do away with the table, and family members lose a fairly large portion of their time together.

But why would families stop buying and using dining room tables? Behold the microwave. There was a time when the preparation of the evening meal was such a significant undertaking that everyone, of necessity, ate at the same time and in the same place. The microwave changed all that by making it easy to prepare single portions for whomever whenever. Suddenly there was no need to prepare one big meal at one time.

Dining tables disappeared, and so did a regular ritual that brought people into face-to-face communication. Nowadays teenagers are as likely to have dinner alone or with their pals as they are to eat with their parents. Couple this trend with the creation of massive homes and separate TV rooms, and you'll see how space (the final frontier) has contributed to the average parent's loss of influence.

Within corporations, where friendships are less important than collaboration, propinquity also plays an important role in daily effectiveness. Distance keeps people from routinely interacting, and as we've suggested, it often leads to animosity and loss of influence. But it also leads to a loss of informal contact.

Most people don't lament this loss, but they should. When people casually bump into each other at work, they ask questions, share ideas, and surprisingly often come up with solutions to problems. The storied social scientist Bill Ouchi found that one practice at Hewlett-Packard (HP) greatly increased informal contact and collaboration. HP leaders demanded that employees keep, of all things, a messy desk. The goal wasn't to attract roaches; it was to attract humans. By leaving work visible and accessible, they found that it was much more likely that others wandering by would see, take an interest, and get involved in the work of a colleague.

As people bump into one another, take in the contents of a messy desk, and share ideas, they're also much more likely to work together on a formal project. Employees extend what starts out as a casual conversation into a shared task. In an area in which multiple heads are required to solve most problems, this can be a real benefit. And once again, distance kills the chance that people will run into each other and then work together on a shared project. In fact, in a study conducted at Bell Labs, researchers tested for factors that determine whether two scientists might collaborate. The best predictor was, you guessed it, *the distance between their offices.* Scientists who worked next to one another were three times more likely to discuss technical topics that led to collaboration than scientists who sat 30 feet from one another. Put them 90 feet apart, and they are as likely to collaborate as those who work several miles away! The probability of collaboration sharply decreases in a matter of a few feet.

Given the overwhelming impact of proximity on informal contact and eventual collaboration, savvy leaders rely on the use of physical space as a means of enhancing interaction. Instead of simply telling people to collaborate, they move employees next to one another or provide them a shared common area or eating facility. At Hewlett-Packard, executives take it a step further by mandating a daily break where everyone leaves his or her desk, retires to a common area, and drinks fruit juices while chatting with fellow employees about what's happening at work.

Over the years, this forced elbow-bumping has cost the company tens of thousands of dollars in food and drink, but many will argue that the benefits that come from informally chatting, collaborating, and eventually synergizing are well worth the investment. When it comes to corporate effectiveness, you can have propinquity work against you, or, as in HP's case, make it your ally.

Community leaders can benefit as well. For example, Muhammad Yunus discovered the importance of propinquity when working with poverty-stricken women in rural villages of Bangladesh. For generations women had been kept from venturing very far outside their own homes. When Dr. Yunus decided to give Bangladeshi women a hand-up by extending them microloans—in groups of five so they could support one another—he quickly learned that he would have to bring them together under the same roof, and frequently, or his plan would never work. Dr. Yunus wasn't merely changing his customers' financial circumstances when he started his banking business; he was turning the entire social community on end, and this had to be done in small, safe, social groups or not at all.

When we (the authors) were visiting a village called Gazipur in Bangladesh, here's what we learned about what Dr. Yunus had done to enlist the power of propinquity to create a new social order. In addition to promoting economic well-being, Grameen Bank was asking that each borrower commit to "16 Decisions." As we stood in the back of a small building containing a 30-member borrowing unit, we watched attentively as all 30 borrowers stood in unison and recited the 16 Decisions—one of which was: "I will neither give nor receive dowry."

This particular commitment is of grave importance to the group's economic well-being. The dowry—which parents are required to pay a man to marry their daughter—can cause both social strife and economic disaster. Families are brought to penury as they try to scrape together enough money to induce a man to take their daughter in wedlock. Daughters are routinely berated by fathers who lament the fact that they fathered a girl who would later cost them so much money. Now, here stood 30 women at attention, loudly proclaiming their commitment to abolish the "curse of the dowry."

Later, as we chatted with the 30 women, we asked, "How many of you have had a son or daughter marry in the past year?" Five women proudly raised their hands. And then we sprung the follow-up question. "How many of you either gave or received dowry?" Three hands went sheepishly into the air. But two—Dipali and Shirina—didn't raise theirs. Here was evidence that this millennium-old practice was giving way. So we asked the two women to tell us how they had resisted the practice. They smiled broadly, looked at each other, and then Dipali said, "I had my son marry her daughter." With that the 30 women broke into spontaneous applause.

No longer did these women hide behind their own front door and simply take what fate had handed them. Now they met, talked, formed businesses, supported each other, signed for each other's loans, and became a genuine community, all within the confines of their own building where they met weekly.

Several forces are at play every time these intrepid entrepreneurs meet and fight their way out of poverty. Surely the social supports they provide one another help them make it through tough times, and they have plenty of tough times. The fact that they sign for each other's loans goes a long way toward ensuring that the businesses they create are well thought through. By forming 30-person units, they now offer as a group enough potential profit to command a bank's attention—something they never commanded individually.

And now we add one more feature. Yunus and his team had the good sense to design a simple space where this all happens. It wasn't easy. To come up with a building that was inexpensive enough to fit the budget of 30 poverty-stricken women called for a lot of work and careful planning. But they eventually did it, and the design ended up winning several international design awards.

So let's hear it for the architects out there who provide them (and us) with space. Now let's just hope we have the good sense to understand its effects.

## ACT LIKE AN INFLUENCER

The senior leaders of a healthcare system were very proud of their new facility, built by a famous architect. Unfortunately, clinical managers were disappointed with their poor hand-hygiene numbers. One of the solutions they considered was adding hand sanitizers inside and outside every door. It was a good idea, but the architect said it would "interrupt the visual flow" of the hallways.

After some discussion, the senior team decided that "bacteria flow is more important than visual flow." Their decision was the right one. Altering this aspect of their physical space was an important ingredient in bringing their hand-hygiene numbers above 90 percent.

## MAKE IT EASY

For years there was a running debate concerning whether humans are the only animals that use tools. When scientists watched chimpanzees sit next to an anthill and place a stick in the entrance hole as a way of gathering ants—without having to dig—they decided that these creatures, with whom we share almost 95 percent of our DNA, were also using tools. So we now have our answer. Smart creatures, including Homo sapiens, use tools. Why? Because smart creatures do their best to find a way to make hard tasks easier.

Around a century ago, Frederick Taylor, the father of scientific management, decided that it was time that we tool users start using tools more wisely. After noticing that employees at Bethlehem Steel used only one shovel size for every task, he determined that the most effective load was 21.5 pounds, and he set about designing and purchasing shovels of different sizes to ensure that no matter the medium, the weight employees hefted would always be the same. Never again would employees shovel slag and snow with the same instrument.

Nowadays you can't throw a rock without hitting someone who does similar time-study work. These folks don't merely study best practices; they study common practices and then through careful analysis make them better. Unfortunately, the principles of this discipline haven't always found their way into complex human problems such as safety, productivity, time to market, crime rates, and so forth. Dr. Whyte (the innovator behind the restaurant spindle) brought an engineering solution to a social issue, but most people don't naturally think of industrial engineering as a resource for overcoming human challenges.

Influencers don't make this mistake. They apply efficiency principles at the very highest level. Rather than constantly finding ways to motivate people to continue with their boring, painful, dangerous, or otherwise loathsome activities, they find a way to change *things*. Like an ape fashioning a stick to its needs, the influencer changes *things* in order to make the right behaviors easier to enact. And depending on whether the glass is half empty or half full, influencers also use *things* to make the wrong behaviors more difficult to enact.

For example, one of the main reasons the Guinea worm disease was eradicated so effectively across the sprawling subcontinent of India was that influencers took steps to make it far easier to drink good water than to drink bad water. Here's the strategy they implemented.

In developing-world villages, women often spend several hours each day traveling to and from the local water source. Hours that could have been spent in more fruitful or even enjoyable activities are expended walking back and forth to a pool while hauling a heavy pot. If this isn't bad enough, the pools these dedicated women hike to and from are often teeming with water fleas that are, in turn, filled with Guinea worm larvae.

Change agents from the Carter Center had learned that villagers who filtered the water through their skirts had diminished the Guinea worm disease problem. Let's add some more detail to that project. In order to make it easier to filter the water effectively (many skirts didn't filter the water very well), the Carter Center set out on a campaign to develop an affordable and long-lasting cloth filter. People at the center knew that if they could find a way to get an effective, efficient, and durable filter into the hands of everyone who drew water, the parasite could be eliminated.

Former U.S. President Jimmy Carter, in his work with the center, explained how this all-important filter came about:

> *I went to see Edgar Bronfman, whose family owned about 20 percent of E.I. DuPont Company. I asked Edgar if he would donate $250,000 over a five-year period, which in those days was a lot of money. He asked me, "What are you going to use the money for?" And I answered: "The best way to do away with the Guinea worm is to pour water through a very fine filter cloth." And he said, "Like this napkin on the table?" And I said, "Yes." "Then why don't you use napkins?" he asked. I explained, "Well, because if you take this napkin and wet and dry it 8 or 10 times a day, in the tropics it'll rot in a couple of weeks." And he responded, "Well, maybe we could help."*

Bronfman took the case to the DuPont board of directors, which knew of a company in Switzerland that produced a nylon fiber that would likely serve this purpose—a fiber that wouldn't rot in the tropics. DuPont provided these fibers to a company that does precision weaving, and that company created the material for the filters. DuPont then donated 2 million square yards of this cloth to the Carter Center.

"This was the main resource we used to get rid of the Guinea worm," President Carter concluded.

Once the specialized cloth had been produced, the task of getting people to filter their water was made a great deal easier, and with the help of that simple invention, the parasite began disappearing in hundreds of villages.

In India, there was an even more elegant engineering solution available than simply making it easy to filter the water effectively. Unlike sub-Saharan Africa, in India clear, clean water runs close to the surface of the earth. So engineers drilled and capped bore-hole wells in hundreds of villages across the country. This simple one-time strategy made safe water far more accessible and bad water much harder to get to. Guinea worm in India, robbed of its hosts, died off rapidly.

Much of Delancey's success also depends on making the right behavior easier while making the wrong behavior more difficult. This is particularly true when it comes to drug abuse. Imagine the challenge of ensuring that new residents succeed during their first few drug-free weeks. Withdrawing from heroin is described as one of the most excruciatingly painful trials you can experience. Addicts who come to loathe the drug, and who experience little benefit from the high after years of abuse, continue to use the drug just to avoid the pain of withdrawing.

Yet almost every heroin addict who comes to Delancey makes it through this agonizing period. Why? In part because they've changed their zip code. Minutes before walking through the front gate, new residents' environments had been filled with people who used, supplied, or supported their addictive behavior. Now they're in a dorm with eight other people who don't. And outside the dorm are another 50 residents on their floor who don't. And in their building are another 200 who don't. In order to get to drugs, residents would now have to go to much greater lengths and distances than ever before. And all of this happens because Dr. Silbert understands the importance of making the wrong behavior hard, and the right behavior easy—or at least easier.

If you're not a drug addict and don't have worms, what can this simple principle do for you? Or maybe for our friend Henry? Here's some more good news on the diet front. Brian

## ACT LIKE AN INFLUENCER

A volunteer group that was working to reduce graffiti in an inner-city neighborhood identified a vital behavior: paint over all new graffiti within 24 hours. Making the tags disappear worked to discourage the taggers. But it was tough to convince business owners and residents to go to this much trouble.

So, the group made it easier by providing them with free paint that matched the colors on their storefronts and residences. This simple gift of paint made it convenient for people to act on the vital behavior. The paint strategy worked, and the amount of graffiti dropped dramatically.

Wansink has shown that if you make good eating choices a little easier and bad ones a little harder, you can make a substantial dent in your waistline.

For example, Brian Wansink found that plate size affects the amount of food a person will eat during a meal before deciding that he or she is satisfied. Smaller plates left people satisfied with smaller portions. If you want to eat fewer calories, change the dishes sitting in your cupboard. He also learned that the positioning of snacks and whether packaging is clear or opaque can increase or decrease consumption by 50 percent or more. A candy jar placed on a desk rather than a few feet away on a bookshelf can double the amount of candy consumed—once again, propinquity at work. Ice cream with a clear top in the freezer is much more likely to be eaten than the same treat in a cardboard box.

And when it comes to using your exercise equipment, you can bet that distance also takes its toll. Move your exercise bike from your TV room to your basement, and you've just dramatically cut your chances of using it. Travel to a gym for your routine cardiovascular exercise (as opposed to using a piece of home equipment), and this too will lessen your chances substantially.

So, if you're one who struggles to maintain a healthy lifestyle, do a quick inventory of things that affect your behavior. Take a count of how many bad food choices are within your reach at each hour of a typical day. Then take a count of how many good choices are within the same distance. Look at how difficult it is for you to exercise. Do you have to walk to a distant and socially isolated room to get to your equipment? Do you have to unpack something from a closet before you can get started?

Discover how many items in your home you can simply *move* to make the right behavior easier and the wrong behavior more difficult. Sure, you can always hunker down, gut it out, and suffer as a way of ensuring that you eat right and exercise regularly. You can always plug in a motivational tape to keep your spirits high in order to climb that mountain. Or you can just make the right things easier to do and the wrong things more difficult to do. It's your call.

Healthcare institutions have also learned the importance of making the correct behavior easier. Consider what many institutions are doing to reduce medication errors. In the past, pills came in only a reddish-brown bottle that offered no information about its content and looked just like the reddish-brown bottle next to it. Oops. Couple this challenge with the fact that many people who fill medical orders do so after pulling back-to-back shifts while squinting to read that poor handwriting that passes as a prescription, and it's easy to see why medication errors cause tens of thousands of deaths annually.

Nowadays progressive pharmaceutical companies and hospitals are teaming up to make the right choices obvious. By deft use of colored bottles and better labels, many hospitals have significantly reduced medication errors and subsequently needless deaths. It seems odd that something as important as *not killing patients* could be affected as recently as a few years ago with an intervention as simple as, well, making the right behavior simple. But, then again, when it comes to changing human behavior, most people would rather motivate the guilty—for instance, suing the blighters who spoon out the wrong drugs—than help them change the behavior. And when it comes to enabling others, we often turn to training before we look for ways to make the task easier to perform.

At the corporate level, companies are becoming more attuned to the concept of making the right behavior, such as buying their product, easier. For instance, consumer guru Paco Underhill helped increase the sales of doggie treats by making it just a little easier to take them off a shelf. Underhill found that young and middle-aged adults were more likely to buy animal treats than were the elderly and children. This piqued his curiosity. He videotaped customers on the pet aisle and quickly discovered what was keeping treat sales low among certain age groups. Typically the staple items like pet food were on the eye- and waist-level shelves, while treats were placed on higher shelves.

It turns out that the young and old find it significantly more difficult to reach items on a higher shelf. One video clip showed an elderly woman attempting to use a carton of aluminum foil to knock down a package of treats. Another revealed a child dangerously climbing shelves to try to reach the package. Moving the treats down one shelf made the behavior just easy enough to boost sales immediately.

But not everyone is listening. In fact, Bill Friedman, one of the biggest gurus on the effects of the environment on human behavior, is being systematically ignored. He studies gambling casinos. By watching thousands of hours of video of people gambling, he has discovered an interesting fact. The features that make a hotel attractive make gamblers miserable.

Las Vegas hotels compete on the basis of their size and splendor. The higher the ceilings and the longer the vistas, the more valued the hotel. Gamblers, in contrast, seek small, intimate places. When you think about it, sitting in front of a one-armed bandit and pulling a lever is actually quite boring. You'd have to pay production-line workers good money to do such things. What people find interesting at a casino is not the task of gambling but the interactions they have with other people. The job of gambling is made more fun (a surrogate for easy) when other people are around. Consequently, when Friedman helps owners transform large unfriendly venues into cozy ones, profits soar.

But big Vegas hotels nowadays are competing as big *hotels*, so they ignore Friedman's advice and make massive, unfriendly casinos. Consequently, many modern hotels barely break even on their gambling (blasphemous in years past) and rely on entertainment, room costs, and restaurants to make money. Nevertheless, the principle is still the same. If you follow the guru's advice and make gambling more pleasant (that is, easy) by making it cozy and friendly, you'll make money hand over fist. But then again, maybe that's just too easy.

## MAKE IT UNAVOIDABLE

Making use of *things* to enable behavior works best when you can alter the physical world in a way that eliminates human choice entirely. You don't merely make good behavior desirable. You make it inevitable. This is where structure, process, and procedures come into play, and once again, the corporate world leads the way. Engineers, tiring of reminding employees not to stick their fingers in certain machines, build in mechanical features that prevent people from putting their hands at risk. Pilots follow lockstep procedures and rigid checklists that require them to double and triple check their takeoff and landing procedures.

When it comes to the fast-food industry, we've hardwired those tasks that used to call for talent and that often used to put customer satisfaction and profits at risk. For example, when it comes to taking an order, employees can simply push picture buttons, and of course, nobody has to know how to make change because the register does it automatically. It's all been routinized. When it comes to taking an order and making change, it's not only easy to do the right thing. It's now almost impossible to do the wrong thing.

However, when it comes to the profound and complex social problems we've been addressing, we're not as good at hardwiring successes through the manipulation of the physical environment. Fortunately, this is fairly easy to change. Often all that's required to make good behavior inevitable is to structure it into your daily routine. If we've learned only one thing about today's overscheduled world, it's that structure drives out lack of structure. Meetings happen. On the other hand, "I'll get back to you sometime later"—maybe that won't happen. So, if you want to guarantee a positive behavior, build it into a special meeting or hardwire it into an existing meeting agenda.

For example, the CEO of a large defense contracting company the authors worked with saw a massive increase in innovative breakthroughs when he and his senior leadership team scheduled and met regularly with groups of employees to solicit ideas. This calendared practice created a forum that encouraged and enabled new behaviors, thereby making the right behavior inevitable. At Delancey, Silbert makes use of calendared events by taking them one step further and transforming them into *rituals*. These ordered procedures consist of hardwired meetings that are never missed and that are highly symbolic, quite volatile, and enormously effective at making the right behavior inevitable. Consider the Delancey ritual referred to simply as "Games." This particular ritual is not always fun, but it's always done.

Say you're a resident at Delancey. Three times a week you and members of your minyan get together to dump on each other. A disinterested person ensures that nothing gets physical, but beyond that it's pretty unstructured. During the Games people learn the egalitarian approach to feedback that Delancey wants. Anyone can challenge anyone. If you think your crew boss is a jerk, you give him a slip of paper inviting him to a Game. He must show up. And when he's there, you can unload on him to your heart's content. Anyone from Silbert on down can be invited to a Game by anyone else.

Over time, the quality of the Games increases as the volume decreases. Residents become better at sharing feedback. What doesn't change is that this long-standing ritual makes the right behavior inevitable. People don't like to confront others—particularly scary and powerful others. Left to their own proclivities, residents would do what anyone else would do: toggle from silence (holding our complaints inside) to violence (blowing up in a verbal tirade). So Silbert turns feedback into a ritual, calls it "Games," and then lets the Games begin. Three times a week without fail.

## SUMMARY: STRUCTURAL ABILITY

When you first read that sociophysical guru Fred Steele thinks that most of us are environmentally incompetent, it's only natural to become defensive. That's a harsh term. Who died and left him in charge of measuring our competency? But then when you read of the dozens of environment-based strategies influencers routinely employ as a means of bringing about change, you realize that most of us really don't turn to the power of propinquity or the data stream or any other physical factor as a means of supporting our influence efforts.

When it comes to developing an influence strategy, we just don't think about *things* as our first line of influence. Given that things are far easier to change than people and that these things can then have a permanent impact on how people behave, it's high time we pick up on the lead of Whyte, Steele, Wansink, and others and add the power of the space we inhabit to our influence repertoire. And who knows? Someday an everyday person may even be able to say the word *propinquity* in public without drawing snickers.

# 10

# Become an Influencer

*They gave me away as a prize once—a Win Tony Curtis
for a Weekend competition. The woman who won was
disappointed. She'd hoped for second prize—a new stove.*

*—Tony Curtis*

This book started with a bold assertion. We claimed that
if you bundle the right number and type of influences
into a robust influence strategy, you can change virtually *anything*. At first blush, this claim seems ludicrous. Obviously there are thousands of things out there that none of us
will ever change. Take gravity. It's been around for a while and
doesn't appear to be going anywhere anytime soon. From there
we explained that the change we were referring to is in our
inability to alter the *human behaviors* that are key to achieving
many of our most cherished goals.

Notwithstanding the enormous resistance you may often
see, we shared research data and real-life success stories that
clearly demonstrate that you can change almost any human
behavior—and maintain that change for years. That is, you can
if you follow the three keys we've been elucidating.

To breathe life into these three keys, we shared a theory
of influence, originally postulated by Dr. Albert Bandura and

then applied by tenacious influencers such as Dr. Mimi Silbert of Delancey Street—who routinely helps people alter some of the most dreadful and entrenched behaviors imaginable. As a result of Silbert's efforts, thousands of former criminals and drug addicts have transformed into productive citizens. Better still, her success rate hovers above 90 percent in a world where 10 percent is seen as a breakthrough. Mimi is a lifetime student of influence.

We also looked at Dr. Don Berwick and the Institute for Healthcare Improvement (IHI) group. He and his team of dedicated change agents went toe-to-toe with the rather entrenched and resistant medical establishment and found a way to save over 100,000 lives a year—every year. And they did this not through a medical miracle or political power but by applying sound principles of influence. They too figured out how to get people to change.

We also looked at the soon-to-be completed work being done with Guinea worm disease in sub-Saharan Africa. Following a long tradition of outside experts lecturing and tsk-tsk-ing the locals for enacting behaviors that cause them to ingest and harbor Guinea worms, a group consisting of a handful of professionals from the Carter Center, together with the cooperation of hundreds of on-site influencers, has all but eliminated the dreaded disease worldwide. As a result of their efforts, one day soon the very last Guinea worm will have been eliminated from the face of the earth. Forever. And, once again, this heroic accomplishment didn't come through advances in medicine or technology but through the work of influence experts who moved beyond lectures and have found a way to get millions of absolute strangers, spread halfway across the world, to change their behavior.

There's more. With the first release of this book, many of our readers were inspired by the influencers we've spotlighted and decided that they would apply what they learned from these pages to their own goals. Now, scarcely a week passes that we don't hear from individuals who have transformed their relationships, families, work groups, companies, and communities—through the application of these same influence principles.

For example, we will never forget the moving stories of leaders who have reduced costly and tragic industrial accidents to nearly zero. One excited manager called our offices to announce that through the application of sound influence principles, there were 12 families in his company who *hadn't* lost a loved one over the past year. He didn't know who they were, simply that the number of deaths in his company had dropped by a dozen. Other intrepid change agents have stemmed the flow of students leaving school early, reduced hospital-acquired infections, or even helped addicts kick their habit. The list of their impressive achievements only increases as more and more people learn to affect rather than merely be affected by the world around them.

Both these everyday change agents and skilled professionals teach us the same lesson: when it comes to influencing human behavior, the sky's the limit. If you know how to make use of the right influence tools and bring them to bear on a carefully designed effort, you too can change anything.

## WHAT CAN YOU DO?

*We all have ability. The difference is how we use it.*
—*Stevie Wonder*

As you lead out with your own influence challenge, think back to the earlier chapters and remember those three all-important keys to creating change. First, your influence begins when you learn to *focus and measure*. Identify what you really want. Then create measures that rivet your attention on your inspiring goal. Measure frequently. And ensure not just that you measure the right thing, but that your measures are influencing the right behavior.

This step may require more analysis than first meets the eye. For instance, while working with a group of manufacturing executives who were doing their level best to improve the quality of the products they shipped, the company leaders picked their goal. They wanted their quality numbers to improve 30 percent by a certain date. That sounded good.

Then the operating manager pointed out that in the past they had been able to eke out quality improvements, but it felt like squeezing blood from a turnip. It required extraordinary leadership focus and effort. "I don't simply want the quality measure to improve," the manager stated. "I want to create a place filled with employees who care about quality. Just think what it would be like if employees, of their own initiative, were constantly making quality improvements—requiring little or no oversight—because they cared about quality the same as everyone in this room does." That became the leaders' new target of focus and measure.

This challenge of digging until you find what you really want spreads across every potential change project. For instance, when you work with individuals who operate fitness centers, you soon discover that they too have learned to look for what people truly want. Clients routinely explain that they desire to lose a certain number of pounds, but when you peel back the onion's layers, you learn that what they really want is the energy, flexibility, self-esteem, and other benefits associated with healthier living—calling for not merely a change in the foods they consume but in their exercise patterns as well. As the once-popular advertising campaign suggested, people "on a diet" need to focus on what they're going to gain from their change and not solely on what they're trying to lose. With personal health issues, if you don't focus on the complete package of what you really want, you can end up thin but also weak, creaky, cranky, and listless. So, as you start your own change effort, take the time to identify what you *really* want.

Next, *find vital behaviors.* Don't squander your influence efforts by putting a lot of effort on fuzzy definitions of what you want to change. (Not unlike the pilot who comes on the plane's PA system and announces: "I have some bad news and some good news. The bad news is that we're lost; the good news is that we're making good time.") Don't put precious energy into strategies that rapidly propel you in the wrong direction. Instead, identify the two or three behaviors that will drive a disproportionate amount of change and aim your efforts at those.

Where do you find these high-leverage actions? Sometimes they're easy to spot, but tough to get people to do. Other times you can use crucial moments—moments when someone's choices have a disproportionate effect on many things that follow—as a clue to find them. Often there are positive deviants you can study to see what they do differently to produce much better results. And finally, keep your eyes open for behaviors required to bust old cultural norms that are keeping you stuck.

Finally, *engage all six sources of influence.* Like the emphasis in this book, most of your efforts to develop a potent influence strategy should focus on this third key. Figure out which sources of influence are working against you. Then engage all six sources of influence as you create your influence strategy. You probably won't hit upon the best combination of influence tools without personal research, even trial and error. But do it.

Add a source of influence, see how it works, then make adjustments as called for. Here are a few suggestions as you search for the right combination of influence strategies.

## DON'T CONFUSE TINKERING WITH A GENUINE EFFORT

When we first studied corporate leaders who had attempted to create a massive change in their organizations, we asked them how successful they had been in creating widespread and lasting change. Then we asked them to select from an extensive list the actual change methods they had used. The list included everything from speeches to training to the use of opinion leaders. To our astonishment, most of the leaders had used only one or two methods. Not to our astonishment, most of their change efforts had failed.

As we looked for the story behind these startling statistics, we learned that it was common for leaders to enter the serious business of overcoming massive problems with a troubling attitude. It was as if they were saying, "Let's try a couple of things and see what happens." They appeared reluctant to put together a comprehensive effort, for fear that if it failed, they would lose face. Better to merely tinker around; then, if it doesn't work, well, they hadn't tried all that hard, so no big deal. Unfortunately, giving a speech or something equally weak probably isn't going to be sufficient to solve teacher burnout, inner-city crime, project delays, and the like. Nevertheless, many of the leaders we studied felt perfectly comfortable tinkering rather than leading change.

Other would-be influencers we studied appeared to be toying with change because all they really wanted to achieve was the ability to cover themselves. For instance, in one company after an ugly incident in which a group of visiting schoolchildren taking a plant tour walked by a work group only to hear them cursing profusely, the plant manager responded in a curious way. When we asked him about the swearing incident, his response was rapid and angry: "They know better than to curse. I recently wrote a memo!" From there he did nothing to resolve the problem in the future. He had written his memo. He was now covered.

Perhaps the most common form of tinkering with influence is less a function of self-deception and more one of economy. Leaders earnestly apply an element or two from a change program they've recently examined—but only an element or two. They may realize that their entire culture calls for an overhaul, but they choose to implement only a few elements because they're looking to create change "on the cheap."

Dr. Mimi Silbert told us that over the past three decades, she has invested a great deal of time with people who have traveled halfway around the world to learn what she's done to help criminals and drug addicts become productive citizens. Silbert tells those who visit Delancey Street the *whole* story—emphasizing each of the elements required to make the venture succeed. She clarifies the exact vital behaviors the organization tries to encourage. Then she goes to great pains to ensure that the influence strategy makes good use of all six sources of influence.

More often than not, the travelers leave Delancey Street filled with hope. Then they go home and create change "on the cheap" by selecting one idea to add to their existing ineffective effort. Of course, this single element rarely adds enough horsepower to create change, so their "new and improved" strategy fails, and the earnest change agents wonder why their effort didn't work—often suggesting (incorrectly) that Mimi's results are idiosyncratic and can't be scaled.

Would-be influencers are continually relying on this cafeteria-style method of tinkering in which they select only a few elements from a broader change menu. For example, if you look at the diffusion of the North Carolina "Second-Chance" strategy we described in Chapter 8, you'll find that it follows a predictable and lamentable path. Remember the clever crime reduction strategy where soon-to-be-arrested drug dealers were brought into a room filled with pictures of them committing crimes? At one point the local district attorney shows a video montage made up of criminal scenes taken of each of the subjects in action and then asks the subjects to raise their hand when they see themselves committing a felony. And they do.

This method for creating a sense of impending doom is coupled with family support, job training, and several other essential ingredients that have yielded encouraging results. In fact, the designers of second-chance programs go to great pains to ensure that all six sources of influence are incorporated into their efforts.

The impressive results of the comprehensive effort have since been reported in the press. Police leaders enthusiastically read about the strategy and select a few of the elements they think their city council will approve, or they choose a couple for which they can secure funding. Or perhaps they give extra attention to a strategy they are already implementing but can now call a "second-chance program." And sure enough, after they employ only one or two elements from the overall intervention, the change effort fails. In the end, eager would-be influencers search for another change plan that they then choose from selectively and implement poorly—thus failing all over again.

Whatever the rationale for tinkering, the cost of putting forth a tepid effort can be extraordinary. In addition to the fact that addressing profound problems with trivial solutions *doesn't* create the changes you desire, you *do* create a reputation for not being able to create change. At the personal level, repeated failures can lead to a loss of self-confidence. Eventually you stop attempting to make the world a better place and work on honing your coping techniques instead. At the community level, repeated failures can harm your reputation. Soon your latest change ideas are tagged "program-of-the-month" or "another one of Mom's crazy ideas!" When you slip to this state, as you invent new notions, others ridicule your plans, offer no help in implementing them, and wait for them to fail. Which they do.

Think about the challenge in the following fashion. If you were facing six hulking behemoths pulling on one side of a rope, what hope would you have of pulling them in a new direction by sending a fourth-grade child to the other side? Your only hope would be to remove the forces pulling against you and add forces pulling for you or—even better—doing both. In short, you become an effective influencer when, and only when, you learn to *overdetermine change* by amassing sufficient sources of influence to make change inevitable.

## DIAGNOSE BEFORE YOU PRESCRIBE

Be warned, just being aware of the six-source model doesn't guarantee that you'll apply it correctly. If you're facing a daunting influence challenge, you would do well to follow the lead of savvy influencers. Diagnose before you prescribe. Anything else is malpractice. Figure out which sources of influence are behind the behavior you're trying to change before you come up with corresponding influence tactics. Most leaders fail to take this essential step and simply throw together an influence strategy they believe should work under any circumstances. More often than not, they apply the latest and hottest technique they've just heard or read about—often from a friend or relative who knows less about the topic than they do.

Skilled influencers avoid this hasty and costly mistake. For example, consider Dr. Warren Warwick of Fairview University Children's Hospital. He realized that his recommended treatment regimes were no better than his influence strategy. He could recommend various treatments, but if his patients didn't implement them, what good was he? Would he end up acting like the executive who curtly responded: "But I wrote them a memo!"? In one rather intriguing case, an 18-year-old cystic fibrosis patient he was treating wasn't conforming to her treatment plan. Rather than launch into a lecture about how she would suffocate in a few years if she continued to slack off, Dr. Warwick stopped and diagnosed the underlying cause. Rather than asking "What the heck is wrong with her?," Dr. Warwick tried to understand why she would fail to do something that would save her life. As he listened, he learned that there were several reasons behind the lapse.

The patient had a new boyfriend with whom she was staying half the time. Her mother had typically administered the treatments, but now the patient was often not at home at the prescribed times. She had started a job and was working nights. The school she attended changed policies and now required a nurse to administer her medicine. Deciding that this was a pain, she stopped taking the medicine. Worst of all, in spite of losing 20 percent of her lung capacity in the previous two months, she felt fine and concluded that fewer treatments were okay. The more Dr. Warwick listened to the patient, the more he realized that she was failing to follow standard procedure for several different reasons. When he understood the sources of influence he was up against, he and the patient then were able to develop a tailored plan that literally saved her life.

## TRY ADDING A SOURCE

> *At the core of every true talent there is an awareness of the difficulties inherent in any achievement, and the confidence that by persistence and patience, something worthwhile will be realized.*
>
> —Eric Hoffer

As you look at your existing circumstance (including the current problem and the efforts you're taking to resolve it), it's important to realize that even though big influence challenges call for big solutions, you may already be most of the way there. Sometimes all it takes to create change is to add one more source of influence to your existing efforts. Perhaps several sources already support your vital behaviors—and the threshold for change is just one source away. What a shame it would be to have traveled 99 miles of a 100-mile journey only to quit at the very edge of success.

For example, you may have realized that if you simply build deliberate practice into your attempt to help your children learn to love reading, you could make enormous strides. You may have been struck with the insanity of sending people off to corporate training programs and then dropping them back into a social climate where no one reinforces the concepts they were taught. So you've added social and structural reinforcement into your change plan. Perhaps you've carted your treadmill from the basement up to your bedroom where you don't have to fight the deadly power of propinquity.

In any case, don't be intimidated at the prospect of coming up with six new sources. You probably have several of them currently working in your favor. Then, as you do add new ones, consider it an experiment. You can't and don't want to use every possible source of influence, so pick the ones you think are best suited to your circumstances, are the most powerful, and are the easiest to implement, and go from there. Then, don't expect that you can put together the perfect combination of influence methods the very first time. Instead, prepare for "trial and learn." Put a method into play, observe the impact, learn from the effort, make changes, and repeat until perfected.

## JOIN THE COMMUNITY

Influencers not only overdetermine their results. They also rarely work alone. More often than not, big challenges require a community of influencers working in concert. As an increasing number of people apply the works of Bandura, Silbert, Swai, Hopkins, Berwick, and other influence experts to problems of every kind, new and vibrant influence communities are springing up each day.

Join one. Work alongside friends, colleagues, and experts. By collaborating with others to bring every influence tool imaginable to bear on your problems, you'll see how the combined power of your group's influence methods is far greater than the sum of the individual parts. Start by visiting *influencerbook.com*, where we provide a worksheet to help you prepare for and organize your next influence project. On this website you'll also be able to view short segments of interviews with a few of the influencers you've already met in this book.

Finally, if you'd like to take a measure of your existing influence skills, the website offers a self-assessment that not only gives you a view into your existing influence repertoire but can also help you develop the next steps for becoming an effective influencer. Enjoy!

So it's time to get started. Identify what you really want and how you're going to measure it. Discover the handful of high-leverage behaviors that will help you reach this objective. Then identify and get working in your favor not just one or two but all six sources of influence. As you apply each source, carefully study the results; learn what is working and what isn't, and then make changes. As you learn how to keep the right focus, adopt the right actions, and master the six sources, you too will become an influencer.

# Works Cited

## Chapter 1. Leadership Is Influence

P. 3. Danny Meyer: Personal interview with the authors, 2011. Any reference to Danny Meyer or his restaurants is drawn from this interview unless otherwise cited.

P. 7. Rich Sheridan: Personal interview with the authors, 2011. Any reference to Rich Sheridan or Menlo Innovations is drawn from this interview unless otherwise cited.

P. 9. Personal change: Change Anything Labs, Influencing Behavior Change survey (October 2007).

P. 9. Recidivism: Patrick Langan and David Levin, "Recidivism of Prisoners Released in 1994," *Bureau of Justice Statistics Special Report* (Washington, DC: Department of Justice, Office of Justice Programs, June 2002).

## Chapter 2. The Three Keys to Influence

P. 14. Guinea worm: Donald Hopkins, personal interview with the authors, May 3, 2006. Any reference to Dr. Donald Hopkins, Guinea worm disease eradication, or the Carter Center is drawn from this interview unless otherwise cited.

P. 17. Medical deaths: Don Berwick, personal interview with the authors, 2006. Any reference throughout the book to Don Berwick or his work is taken from this interview unless otherwise cited. Information is taken from a report by the National Academy of Sciences: Linda Kohn et al., *To Err Is Human: Building a Safer Health System* (Washington, DC: National Academies Press, 1999).

P. 19. Fundación Paraguaya: Martin Burt, personal interview with the authors, 2011. Any reference to Martin Burt or Fundación Paraguaya is drawn from this interview unless otherwise cited.

P. 23. Soviet Union: Marshall Goldman, *U.S.S.R. in Crisis: The Failure of an Economic System* (New York: Norton, 1983), p. 32.

P. 24. U.S. Army sexual assault statistics: Lt. General Tom Bostick, personal interview with the authors, 2012. Information is taken from *Fiscal Year 2011 Annual Report on Sexual Assault in the Military* (Washington, DC: Department of Defense, 2012).

P. 26. YMCA pools: Kevin Trapani of Redwoods Insurance Group, personal interview with the authors, October 2006.

P. 29. KIPP Schools: David Levin and Mike Feinberg, personal interview with the authors, 2006. Information is taken from the *KIPP College Completion Report 2011* found at http://www.kipp.org/files/dmfile/ExecutiveSummary.pdf.

## Chapter 3. Find Vital Behaviors

P. 36. King's birthday present: Praphan Phanunphack, interview with authors, 2006. Dr. Phanumphack is the director of the Red Cross AIDS Research Center in Thailand.

P. 37. AIDS statistics: Anupong Chitwarakorn and Jai P. Narain, eds., "HIV/AIDS and Sexually Transmitted Infections in Thailand: Lessons Learned and Future Challenges," *AIDS in Asia: The Challenge Continues* (New Delhi, India: Sage Publications, 2004).

P. 37. Five million cases: Reported by Prime Minister Shinawatra in his opening speech at the 15th International AIDS Conference, Bangkok, Thailand, July 11, 2004.

P. 37. Wiwat Rojanapithayakorn: Personal interview with the authors, 2006. Any reference to Dr. Wiwat or the 100% Condom Campaign in Thailand is drawn from this interview unless otherwise cited.

P. 38. Number of sex workers: K. Archavanitkul, "What Is the Number of Child Prostitutes in Thailand?" *Warasan Prachakon Lae Sangkhom*, 7 (1999): 1–9.

P. 40. Mimi Silbert: Personal interview with the authors, 2005. Any reference to Mimi Silbert or the Delancey Foundation is drawn from this interview unless otherwise cited.

P. 40. Delancey statistics: Ibid. Further discussion can be found at http://www.delanceystreetfoundation.org/accomplish.php.

P. 40. Anonymous attendee of Delancey Street. Personal interview with the authors, 2005.

P. 45. Relationship failure: Howard J. Markman, Scott M. Stanley, and Susan L. Blumberg, *Fighting for Your Marriage* (San Francisco: Jossey-Bass, 2001), p. 18.

P. 45. Divorce prediction: Howard Markman, personal interview with the authors, 2006. Any reference throughout the book to Howard Markman and his work is drawn from this interview unless otherwise cited.

P. 47. Relaxation training with alcoholics: Albert Bandura, personal interview with the authors, 2006. Any reference throughout the book to Albert Bandura and his work is drawn from this interview unless otherwise cited.

P. 48. Success during first year in college: University's personal interview with the authors, 2010.

P. 57. Spectrum Health Grand Rapids statistics: These results can be found in the VitalSmarts case study documenting the research conducted by Spectrum Health. The case study can be found here: http://www.vitalsmarts.com/casestudies/spectrum-health/.

P. 60. Ethna Reid: Personal interview with the authors, 2006. Any reference throughout the book to Ethna Reid or her work is taken from this interview unless otherwise cited.

## Chapter 4. Help Them Love What They Hate: Personal Motivation

P. 79. Terri: Mimi Silbert, personal interview with the authors. Dr. Silbert told many stories of individuals who go through experiences similar to that of the fictionalized story of Terri.

P. 83. Fundamental attribution error: Lee Ross, "The Intuitive Psychologist and His Shortcomings: Distortions in the Attribution Process," *Advances in Experimental Social Psychology Education* (New York: Leonard Berkowitz Academic Press, 1977).

P. 86. Therapy length: William R. Miller and Stephen Rollnick, *Motivational Interviewing* (New York: Guilford Press, 2002), p. 5.

P. 86. Therapy type: Ibid., pp. 6, 7.

P. 87. Motivational interviewing results: Ibid., pp. 220, 226.

P. 88. Ralph Heath: Personal interview with the authors.

P. 89. Ginger L. Graham, "If You Want Honesty, Break Some Rules," *Harvard Business Review*, April 2002, pp. 42–47.

P. 94. Daniel Gilbert, *Stumbling on Happiness* (New York: Knopf, 2006).

P. 98. Snake phobics: Taken from interview previously referenced. For further information, see Albert Bandura, N. Adams, and J. Beyer, "Cognitive Process Mediating Behavioral Change," *Cognitive Therapy and Research*, 1 (1977): 287–310.

P. 101. To learn more about Josie's story, see www.josieking.org.

P. 103. *Twende na Wakati* (story of Mkwaju): Arvind Singhal, personal interview with the authors, 2006. Any reference throughout the book to Arvind Singhal or his work is taken from this interview unless otherwise cited.

P. 105. Results of *Twende na Wakati*: Arvind Singhal and Everett M. Rogers, *Entertainment Education: A Communication Strategy for Social Change* (Mahwah, New Jersey: Lawrence Erlbaum, 1999), pp. 152–171, 131–134.

P. 106. "Maude's Dilemma": Ibid., pp. 16, 17.

P. 109. Mihaly Csikszentmihalyi, *Flow: The Psychology of Optimal Experience* (New York: Harper & Row, 1990), p. 51.

## Chapter 5. Help Them Do What They Can't: Personal Ability

P. 114. Lack of training transfer: Mary Broad and John Newstrom, *The Transfer of Training: Action-Packed Strategies to Ensure High Payoff from Training Investments* (Reading, Massachusetts: Addison-Wesley, 1992), p. 7.

P. 116. Mindset: Carol S. Dweck, *Mindset: The New Psychology of Success* (New York: Random House, 2006).

P. 118. Marshmallow studies: W. Mischel, Y. Shoda, and P. Peake, "The Nature of Adolescent Competencies Predicted by Preschool Delay of Gratification," *Journal of Personality and Social Psychology*, 54 (1988): 687–696. See also Y. Shoda, W. Mischel, and P. Peake, "Predicting Adolescent Cognitive and Self-Regulatory Competencies from Preschool Delay of Gratification: Identifying Diagnostic Conditions," *Developmental Psychology*, 26 (1990): 978–986.

P. 118. SAT scores: Daniel Goleman, *Emotional Intelligence: Why It Can Matter More than IQ* (New York: Bantam, 1995), p. 82.

P. 119. S. S. Feldman and D. A. Weinberger, "Self-Restraint as a Mediator of Family Influences on Boys' Delinquent Behavior: A Longitudinal Study," *Child Development*, 65 (1994): 195–211.

P. 119. Mischel and Bandura: A. Bandura and W. Mischel, "Modification of Self-Imposed Delay of Reward Through Exposure to Live and

Symbolic Models," *Journal of Personality and Social Psychology*, 2 (1965): 698–705.

P. 121. Deliberate practice: K. A. Ericsson, R. Th. Krampe, and C. Tesch-Römer, "The Role of Deliberate Practice in the Acquisition of Expert Performance," *Psychological Review*, 100 (1993): 363–406.

P. 124. Thailand condom use: W. Rojanapithayakorn and R. Hanenberg, "The 100% Condom Programme in Thailand," *AIDS*, 10 (1996): 1–7.

P. 126. Skill development: K. A. Ericsson and A. C. Lehmann, "Expert and Exceptional Performance: Evidence on Maximal Adaptations on Task Constraints," *Annual Review of Psychology*, 47 (1996): 273–305.

P. 127. Ten years: Benjamin Bloom, ed., *Developing Talent in Young People* (New York: Ballantine, 1985).

P. 127. Correlation between time and skill level: Karl Anders Ericsson et al., eds., *The Cambridge Handbook of Expertise and Expert Performance* (New York: Cambridge University Press, 2006).

P. 127. Roger Bacon: In Ericsson et al., eds., *The Cambridge Handbook*.

P. 127. Olympic swimming: We compared Johnny Weissmuller's Olympic record times to times of current high school swimming champions.

P. 127. Deliberate practice techniques: Ericsson et al., eds., *The Cambridge Handbook*, p. 699.

P. 128. Deliberate practice and feedback: Ibid., p. 532.

P. 128. Natalie Coughlin: M. Grudowski, "The Girl Next Door Is Hungry," *Men's Journal*, 12 (2003): 72–73.

P. 130. Pills: Albert Bandura, personal interview with the authors, September 7, 2005.

P. 131. Free throws: T. J. Cleary and B. J. Zimmerman, "Self-Regulation Differences During Athletic Practice by Experts, Non-Experts, and Novices," *Journal of Applied Sport Psychology*, 13 (2001): 185–206.

P. 132. Dating skills: S. L. Foster et al., "Teaching Social Skills to Shy Single Men," *The Family Journal*, 5 (1997): 37–48.

P. 136. Hot and cool systems: J. Metcalf and W. Mischel, "A Hot/Cool System Analysis of Delay of Gratification," *Psychological Review*, 106 (1999): 3–19.

P. 139. W. Mischel, "Toward an Integrative Model for CBT: Encompassing Behavior, Cognition, Affect, and Process," *Behavior Therapy*, 35 (2004): 185–203.

P. 140. Children and delay of gratification: H. Mischel and W. Mischel, "The Development of Children's Knowledge of Self-Control Strategies," *Child Development*, 54 (1983): 603–619.

P. 140. Expectation and delay of gratification: W. Mischel and E. Staub, "Effects of Expectancy on Working and Waiting for Larger Rewards," *Journal of Personality and Social Psychology*, 2 (1965): 625–633.

P. 140. Distraction and delay of gratification: W. Mischel and E. Ebbesen, "Attention in Delay of Gratification," *Journal of Personality and Social Psychology*, 16 (1970): 329–337.

P. 140. Teaching skill of delay of gratification: A. Bandura and W. Mischel, "Modification of Self-Imposed Delay of Reward Through Exposure to Live and Symbolic Models," *Journal of Personality and Social Psychology*, 2 (1965): 698–705.

P. 140. Focus and delay of gratification: Mischel and Ebbesen, "Attention in Delay of Gratification."

P. 140. Willpower and delay of gratification: P. Peake, M. Hebl, and W. Mischel, "Strategic Attention Deployment in Waiting and Working Situations," *Developmental Psychology*, 38 (2002): 313–326.

P. 141. Cognitive reappraisal: J. J. Gross, "Emotion Regulation in Adulthood: Timing Is Everything," *Current Directions in Psychological Science*, 10 (2001): 214–219.

P. 142. Handwashing: Jeffrey Schwartz, *Brainlock* (New York: HarperCollins, 1996), p. 212.

## Chapter 6. Provide Encouragement: Social Motivation

P. 146. Milgram obedience studies: Stanley Milgram, "Behavioral Study of Obedience," *Journal of Abnormal and Social Psychology*, 67 (1963): 371–378.

P. 147. Phil Zimbardo discusses Milgram's experiments on the website http://thesituationist.wordpress.com/2007/02/16/when-good-people-do-evil-%E2%80%93-part-i/.

P. 151. Obedience study with confederate: Stanley Milgram, *Obedience to Authority: An Experimental View* (New York: Harper & Row, 1974).

P. 163. Everett Rogers and diffusion of innovations: Everett Rogers, *Diffusion of Innovations*, 3rd ed. (New York: Free Press, 1983), pp. 15, 32–34, 54–56, 247, 258, 266, 271. The story about the "Guy in the Bermudas" was told by Rogers in a lecture at Stanford University in the fall of 1982.

P. 166. Limey story: Don Berwick, "Disseminating Innovations in Health Care," *JAMA* (2003): 1969–1975.

P. 168. *Tinka, Tinka Suhk*: Arvind Singhal and Everett M. Rogers, *Entertainment Education: A Communication Strategy for Social Change* (Mahwah, New Jersey: Lawrence Erlbaum Associates, 1999), pp. 1, 58, 137, 176.

P. 169. Barefoot doctors: Rogers, *Diffusion of Innovations*, pp. 326–328.

P. 175. Silence Fails study: For more information, see VitalSmarts/Concourse Group, http://silencefails.com.

P. 175. *Tinka, Tinka Sukh*: Arvind Singhal, personal interview with the authors, 2006.

## Chapter 7. Provide Assistance: Social Ability

P. 186. Tanika's story: A story told to one of the authors as a microcredit industry leader.

P. 190. Muhammad Yunus and the Grameen Bank: Muhammad Yunus, *Banker to the Poor* (Dhaka, Bangladesh: University Press, 1998), p. 12.

P. 190. Borrower stats: Grameen Bank at a Glance: http://www.grameen-foundation.org/what-we-do/microfinance-basics.

P. 191. Statement of Professor Muhammad Yunus at the ITU World Information Society Award Ceremony, May 17, 2006. Accessible at http://www.itu.int/wisd/ 2006/award/statements/yunus.html.

P. 193. Friends: John Lennon and Paul McCartney, "With a Little Help from My Friends," *Sgt. Pepper's Lonely Hearts Club Band*, 1967.

P. 193. Weight of ox: James Surowiecki, *The Wisdom of Crowds* (New York: Doubleday, 2004), p. xiii.

P. 197. Soul City: Garth Japhet, personal interview with the authors, 2006.

P. 207. Network quotient: Don Cohen and Laurence Prusak, *In Good Company: How Social Capital Makes Organizations Work* (Boston, Massachusetts: Harvard Business School Press, 2001).

P. 209. Physicians: Atul Gawanda, *Complications: A Surgeon's Notes on an Imperfect Science* (New York: Picador, 2002), pp. 11–24.

P. 210. Tragedy of the commons: William Forester Lloyd, *Two Lectures on the Checks to Population* (Oxford, England: Oxford University Press, 1833).

P. 212. HIV/AIDS in Thailand: Wiwat Rojanapithayakorn, "100% Condom Use Programme," manuscript presented in Provo, Utah, 2006.

P. 213. Five million saved: As reported in the Centers for Disease Control and Prevention's Thailand fact sheet: www.cdc.gov/globalhealth/FETP/pdf/Thailand_factsheet.pdf.

## Chapter 8. Change Their Economy: Structural Motivation

P. 219. Rewarding children: M. R. Lepper, D. Greene, and R. E. Nisbett, "Undermining Children's Intrinsic Motivation with Extrinsic Reward: A Test of the 'Over-Justification' Hypothesis," *Journal of Personality and Social Psychology*, 28 (1973): 129–137.

P. 221. Soviet Union: Marshall Goldman, *U.S.S.R. in Crisis: The Failure of an Economic System* (New York: Norton, 1983), p. 32.

P. 223. Privileges and alcohol: Stanton Peele, *7 Tools to Beat Addiction* (New York: Three Rivers Press, 2004), p. 95.

P. 224. Cocaine and vouchers: Ibid., p. 96.

P. 225. Frequent-flier mileage: "Frequent Flyer Miles: In Terminal Decline?" *Economist*, January 6, 2006.

P. 225. Teen suicide: Karen M. Simon, personal communication with the authors, 1976.

P. 227. Colored stars as rewards: http://www.grameen-info.org/index.php?option=com_content&task=view&id=26&Itemid=175.

P. 229. Hand hygiene: Stephen Dubnar and Steven Levitt, "Selling Soap," *New York Times*, September 24, 2006.

P. 231. Employee polls: Employee poll taken from 20 years of polling done at VitalSmarts.

P. 234. Tea leaf consumption: Masaaki Imai, *Kaizen* (New York: McGraw-Hill, 1986), p. 20.

P. 236. Soldiers in Vietnam: Steven Kerr, "On the Folly of Rewarding A, While Hoping for B," *Academy of Management Executive*, 9 (1995): 7–14.

P. 238. Learned helplessness: Martin Seligman, Christopher Peterson, and Steven Maier, *Learned Helplessness: A Theory for the Age of Personal Control* (New York: Oxford University Press, 1993).

P. 239. Crime prevention program: Mark Shoofs, "Novel Police Tactic Puts Drug Markets Out of Business," *Wall Street Journal*, September 27, 2006.

P. 242. Russian oil: Jerome Dumetz, personal communication with the authors, 2006. Jerome is a consultant to many Russian oil firms.

P. 242. Ethiopia: Negussie Teffera, personal interview with the authors, 2006.

## Chapter 9. Change Their Space: Structural Ability

P. 248. Order spindle: W. F. Whyte, *Human Relations in the Restaurant Industry* (New York: McGraw-Hill, 1948).

P. 250. Environmentally incompetent: Fred Steele, *Physical Settings and Organization Development* (Reading, Massachusettts: Addison-Wesley, 1973), pp. 11, 113.

P. 252. Hitler's hallway: Albert Speer, *Inside the Third Reich* (New York: Macmillan, 1970).

P. 252. Broken windows: George Kelling and Catherine Coles, *Fixing Broken Windows: Restoring Order and Reducing Crime in Our Communities* (New York: Simon & Schuster, 1996), p. 152.

P. 254. Food studies: Brian Wansink, *Mindless Eating: Why We Eat More Than We Think* (New York: Bantam Books, 2006).

P. 257. Fill-to-here line: Fred Luthans, *Organizational Behavior* (New York: McGraw-Hill, 1981.)

P. 258. A. M. Dickinson, "The Historical Roots of Organizational Behavior Management in the Private Sector: The 1950s–1980s," *Journal of Organizational Behavior Management*, 20 (2000): 9–58.

P. 258. Latex gloves: Occurred on a consulting project of the authors.

P. 258. Starbucks cards and screen saver: Stephen J. Dubner and Steven Levitt, "Selling Soap," *New York Times*, September 24, 2006.

P. 261. Representative heuristic: For reading on the topic, see A. Tversky and D. Kahneman, "Judgment Under Uncertainty: Heuristics and Biases," *Science*, 185 (1974): 1124–1130.

P. 262. Jimmy Carter, personal interview with the authors, 2007.

P. 267. Effects of space and propinquity: L. Festinger, S. Schachter, and K. Back, *Social Pressure in Informal Groups* (Stanford, California: Stanford University Press, 1950), Chapter 4.

P. 270. Dining room table: This phenomenon is discussed in "Dining Room Table Losing Central Status in Families," *USA Today*, December 18, 2005.

P. 270. Desk proximity: Robert Kraut and Carmen Egido, and Jolene Galegher, *Patterns of Contact and Communication in Scientific Research Collaboration* (New York: ACM Press, 1988).

P. 271. Hewlett-Packard daily break: Personal communication with Ray Price, 1980.

P. 275. Frederick Taylor: Robert Kanigel, *The One Best Way: Frederick Winslow Taylor and the Enigma of Efficiency* (New York: Viking, 1997).

P. 279. Food container: Wansink, *Mindless Eating*.

P. 280. Medication bottles: Adrienne Berman, "Reducing Medication Errors Through Naming, Labeling, and Packaging," *Journal of Medical Systems*, 28 (2004): 9–29.

P. 281. Dog food: Paco Underhill, *Why We Buy: The Science of Shopping* (New York: Simon & Schuster, 1999), Chapter 1.

P. 282. Casinos: Bill Friedman, *Designing Casinos to Dominate the Competition: The Friedman International Standards of Casino Design* (Reno, Nevada: Institute for the Study of Gambling and Commercial Gaming College of Business Administration, 2000).

## Chapter 10. Become an Influencer

P. 296. Cystic fibrosis: Atul Gawande, "The Bell Curve," *New Yorker*, December 6, 2004.

# Index

# About the Authors

This award-winning team of authors has produced four *New York Times* bestsellers—*Crucial Conversations: Tools for Talking when Stakes are High* (2002), *Crucial Accountability: Tools for Resolving Violated Expectations, Broken Commitments,* and *Bad Behavior* (2005), *Influencer: The New Science of Leading Change* (2008), and *Change Anything: The New Science of Personal Success* (2011). They are also cofounders of VitalSmarts, an innovator in corporate training and organizational performance.

 **Joseph Grenny** is an acclaimed keynote speaker and consultant who has implemented major corporate change initiatives for the past thirty years. He is also a cofounder of Unitus Labs, a not-for-profit organization that helps the world's poor achieve economic self-reliance.

 **Kerry Patterson** has authored award-winning training programs and led multiple long-term change efforts. In 2004, he received the BYU Marriott School of Management Dyer Award for outstanding contribution in organizational behavior. He completed doctoral work at Stanford University.

 **David Maxfield** is a leading researcher, consultant, and speaker. He has led research studies on the role of human behavior in medical errors, safety hazards, and project execution. He completed doctoral work in psychology at Stanford University.

 **Ron McMillan** is a sought-after speaker and consultant. He cofounded the Covey Leadership Center, where he served as vice president of research and development. He has worked with leaders ranging from first-level managers to executives from the Fortune 500.

 **Al Switzler** is a renowned consultant and speaker who has directed training and management initiatives with leaders from dozens of Fortune 500 companies worldwide. He also served on the faculty of the Executive Development Center at the University of Michigan.

# Want to get better?
# Attend a **Vital**Smarts Training Course

### PERSONAL
**Self-directed change**
Successfully solve any individual behavior challenge—
at work or at home.

### INTERPERSONAL
**Open dialogue**
Foster open dialogue around high-stakes,
emotional, or risky topics.

### TEAM
**Universal accountability**
Enhance accountability, improve performance, and
ensure execution.

### ORGANIZATIONAL
**Influential leadership**
Drive rapid and sustainable behavior change for teams
and even entire organizations.

To receive more information on learning these skills or
becoming a trainer for your organization, call 1-800-449-5989,
or go online to **www.vitalsmarts.com.**

# About **Vital**Smarts

An innovator in corporate training and leadership development, VitalSmarts combines three decades of original research with 50 years of the best social science thinking to help organizations achieve new levels of performance. Specifically, we focus on human behavior—the underlying written and un-written rules that shape what employees do every day and create the cultural operating system upon which an organization functions.

VitalSmarts' work within the halls of some of the world's top organizations has led us to identify four skill sets present in successful companies. When used in combination, these high-leverage skills create healthy corporate cultures that spur flawless execution and consistent innovation. These skill sets are taught in our award-winning training programs and *New York Times* bestselling books of the same titles: *Crucial Conversations*, *Crucial Accountability*, *Influencer*, and *Change Anything*.

VitalSmarts has trained more than one million people worldwide and helped more than 300 of the Fortune 500 realize significant results using this proven method for driving rapid, sustainable and measurable change in behaviors. VitalSmarts has been ranked by *Inc.* magazine as one of the fastest-growing companies in America for eight consecutive years.

# SPECIAL VALUE FOR BOOK READERS

Authors Joseph Grenny, Kerry Patterson, Al Switzler, Ron McMillan, and David Maxfield are offering book readers the following **FREE resources (a $275 value).** All you have to do is go online to get them. Read on.

### Access Influencer Video Case Studies

See first-hand how the Influencer model has nearly eradicated a deadly disease without the use of vaccines or medicines. Or, listen to the authors share insights for changing your own or others' behavior.

### Authors' Discussion Questions

Use these relevant discussion questions to guide your next book club or reading group. You'll strengthen your skills by learning with others.

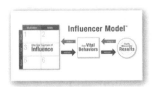

### Cue Yourself with the Influencer Model

Download and display this visual reminder of the Influencer Model.

### Join the *Crucial Skills Newsletter* Community

Subscribe to our weekly e-newsletter and ask the authors for advice in solving pressing Influencer challenges. The authors answer a reader's question each week, providing powerful insights into the tough, real-world challenges you face.

To access these resources, visit **www.vitalsmarts.com/bookresources**.

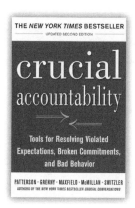